FV

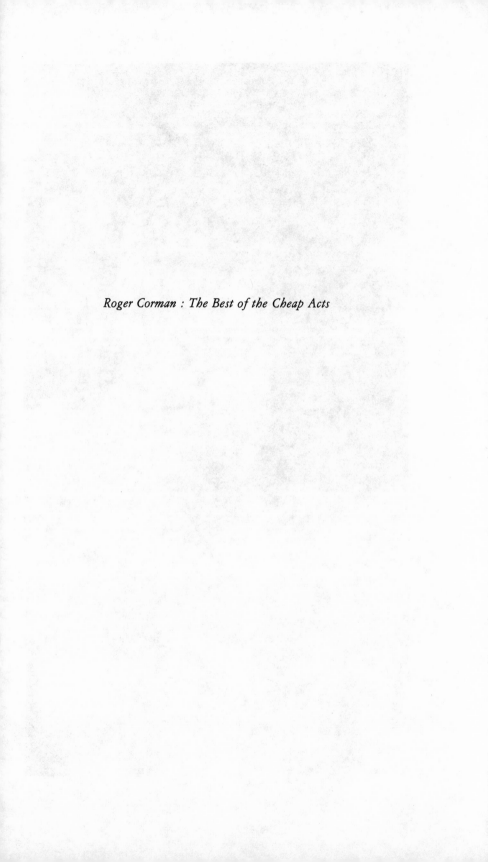

Roger Corman : The Best of the Cheap Acts

Roger Corman
The Best of the Cheap Acts

by
Mark Thomas McGee

McFARLAND & COMPANY, INC., PUBLISHERS
Jefferson, North Carolina, and London

Frontispiece: Roger Corman in 1965.

Library of Congress Cataloguing-in-Publication Data

McGee, Mark Thomas, 1947–
Roger Corman, the best of the cheap acts.

Filmography: p. 87.
Includes index.
1. Corman, Roger, 1926– . 2. Motion picture
producers and directors—United States—Biography.
I. Title.
PN1998.3.C68M34   1988   791.43′0233′0924   [B]   87-46389

ISBN 0-89950-330-6 (50# acid-free natural paper)

Manufactured in the United States of America.

McFarland & Company, Inc., Publishers
Box 611, Jefferson, North Carolina 28640

To
Wendy Wright, Nick Seldon, and Jim Stewart,
who will read this because I wrote it,
and to
Steve, Barbara and Chris McGee,
who'll now feel guilty if they don't

Acknowledgments

When you think about it, it's asking a lot of someone to intrude on their time to share old memories with someone they don't even know. So thank you Roger Corman and Gene Corman for your help with this endeavor. And thank you John Ashley, Ed Byrnes, Beverly Garland, Leo Gordon, Jonathan Haze, David Kramarsky, Jacques Marquette, Dick Miller, Wyott Ordung, Talia Shire, Ronald Stein, Yvette Vickers, and Mel Welles.

Special thanks to Samuel Z. Arkoff for a pleasant afternoon and lunch and to Charles Griffith for getting me stoned.

As for Beach Dickerson, while I greatly appreciated your allowing me into your home, I must confess that the sight of you in your jockey shorts was slightly unnerving.

To my friends Forrest Ackerman, Bob Burns, Miller Drake, Mark Frank, Alex Gordon, Don Glut, Marty Kearns, Bob Villard, Bill Warren, Tom Weaver, and Jim Wynorski, I also want to say thanks.

And the same to the late Paul Blaisdell and the late Barry Brown.

Several people wished to remain anonymous. You know who you are. Thanks to you, too.

Table of Contents

Foreword

Movies have always been magic to me, as I suspect they have been for a lot of people. As a child I looked upon movie theaters as holy places. The garish posters behind glass frames were my stained glass windows. Naively, I believed that all of the people who made movies loved them as much as I did. It never occurred to me, in spite of the box office out front where I stopped to pay my quarter, that movies were a business. I sort of ignored that part of the movie-going experience the way I suspect people in church politely overlook the collection plate. It was a necessary evil, like watermelon seeds. But as Jim and Tammy Bakker reminded us, religion *is* a business and so, I finally had to admit, were movies. Yet movies are also an art form, the art form of this century in fact, and thus perpetuate a war between the artist and the guy who keeps the books. Sometimes, these two people are one and the same, as is the case with Roger Corman.

For over three decades, Roger Corman has been somewhat of a maverick in the film business. He's been a producer, a director, and now and then an actor. He knows the business inside and out and like all good businessmen, he's had to keep his eye on the dollar. Steven Spielberg and Stanley Kubrick have to keep their eyes on the dollar too, and if you don't believe it you're still ignoring the box office. You can't make movies if your movies don't make money. Unless you're Dino De Laurentiis.

But if money was Roger Corman's only concern I suspect he could have made a great deal more of it in real estate. The fact that his films were consistently superior to his competition suggests that he enjoys making movies.

On its level, and you must take into account that we're discussing low budget, exploitation pictures here, Corman's *Teenage Doll* was as accurate in its depiction of teenagers in the 1950s as the bigger budgeted *Blackboard Jungle*, and in some respects hit closer to home. *A Bucket of Blood*, which Corman made in five days, was and still is Hollywood's only legitimate representation of the beatnik phenomenon. And while other low budget filmmakers were happily following genre formulas, Corman continued to produce offbeat things like *Gunslinger*, *Not of This Earth*, *The Undead*, *Sorority Girl*, and *Machine Gun Kelly*. These were not, however, the pictures that established his reputation as a filmmaker. That came later when the budgets got a little larger and he was able to make things like *The Pit and the Pendulum*, *The Wild Angels*, and *The Trip*.

Corman became the youngest director to have retrospectives of his work at the National Film Theater in London and the Museum of Modern Art in New York. He became (as one critic described) the Orson Welles of Grade Z Cinema. He's been the subject of dozens of magazine articles over the years and has become a cult figure. A number of books have been written about him, the first one published over 15 years ago, shortly after Corman formed his own film company, New World Pictures. The authors of that first book postulated the theory that Corman had a millennic vision. I read that book, or tried to, and I confess that I couldn't understand it. I couldn't even find the word *millennic* in the dictionary, though I know it's derived from the word millennium which refers to a thousand year period of righteousness and happiness. What exactly that has to do with *Viking Women and the Sea Serpent* or *Stripped to Kill* is over my head. But in fairness to the authors of that book, trying to find a central theme in a body of work as large and diverse as Corman's is like trying to find a straight line in Ronald Reagan's responses to the press.

Actress Talia Shire once said that you could understand what Roger was all about by running all of his movies back to back (which is often the way he made them). Roger agreed: "If you look at all of my films, you'll see I work on two levels—the text and the subtext. The text, or surface of the film, is generally an exploitation subject that can be advertised and sold to the public. Beneath the surface I'm saying something that is important to me; my feelings about the world or my political convictions. Or both. Somewhere there is a vision of hope, a statement that things have been, or will be better."

And that, insofar as this book is concerned, is that. There will be no further delving into the deeper meanings of Roger's films. If I did that, this wouldn't be a book about him, it would be a book about me.

The reactions of film critics to Corman's work are absent from this book. Generally speaking, most of his films (with some exceptions, of course) were well received. But since film criticism is nothing but an intellectual attempt to justify an emotional response it has little value as far as I'm concerned. Certainly the record shows that the majority critical viewpoint, pro or con, is often contrary to the public's taste. An opinion in print is no more valid than the opinion of the guy next door. But since this is my book, and for the record, I would like to say that my favorite Corman films are *The Day the World Ended, It Conquered the World, Attack of the Crab Monsters, Not of This Earth, Teenage Doll, A Bucket of Blood, The Little Shop of Horrors, The Pit and the Pendulum, The Raven,* and *The Haunted Palace.* Each of these films, and many others, will be covered in depth but for now I'd like to single out *The Intruder,* a film that one New York paper de-

Wearing painful contact lenses, Paul Birch hopes this scene from *Not of This Earth* (Allied Artists, 1957), produced and directed by Roger Corman, won't take too long to shoot.

scribed as a credit to the entire film industry. *The Intruder* was probably Corman's proudest moment even though it was the first time one of his films lost money.

"We all worked very hard on that film because we believed in it," Corman said. It was a film about racial segregation in the United States with William Shatner in the lead. "When we finished that film we had a great feeling of elation. I coach my son's basketball team and when we beat good teams we have a better feeling than when we beat easy teams. It was the same with *The Intruder*. The problems we faced, in making and distributing that picture, were tremendous. Yet, we felt we had beaten those problems. And we knew we'd made a good film. I wasn't that upset about losing money, because I was proud. The public just didn't want to see it."

It may well be that Corman's greatest strength as a filmmaker lies in his enjoyment of solving problems. Why else would he impose a five-day shooting schedule on himself. Or two days for that matter. And one of the ways he's been able to succeed is through his uncanny ability to spot talent. Corman has been responsible for launching the careers of many of the industry's top filmmakers. Peter Bogdanovich, Francis Ford Coppola, Joe Dante, Ron Howard, Gary Kurtz, Martin Scorsese, and Robert Towne all started with Corman. The list of performers is just as long: Burt Convy, Robert De Niro, Dick Miller, Ed Nelson, Jack Nicholson, Talia Shire, Sylvester Stallone, Robert Vaughn. But make no mistake about it, all of these people had to earn their keep. There's no room for slackers on a Corman film because everyone's constantly working against the clock.

Up front you should know this is not a biography. Good biographies are always written after their subjects are dead. The very best stories are always saved for when it's safe. What this book is about is the business of making movies, low budget, exploitation movies to be exact. So if you like sex and violence, as I obviously do, then read on and enter the world of the exploitation filmmaker, a world furthest from the mythology of Hollywood and closest to its heart.

Mark McGee
Duarte, California

Salad Days 1

Walking toward the edit bay, the feeling that things were happening faster than he could keep up with them kept nagging at him. It wasn't like the old days when you could make an exploitation movie for children and practically be guaranteed a profit. Millions of dollars were being poured into children's pictures now.

Speaking of children, he wondered if he shouldn't be home with his own children. He had four of them now: Catherine, Roger Martin, Brian, and Mary. Just one more stop and then he'd go.

He could hear voices coming from the edit bay. But they weren't voices from the track of his wife Julie's new picture. At least, he didn't think so. They were familiar somehow, but he couldn't place them.

Maybe the video tape market was the answer. People were willing to spend a buck or two bucks for a movie that they wouldn't've spent five or six for. Video might prove to be the new home of low budget movies. He'd have to give it some thought. But not now. Right now he had to check on the progress of Julie's picture and then get home. He stepped into the edit bay.

There on the moviola, like a ghost come back to haunt him, was the climax to one of his old black and white pictures: three people running around the beach on a cold December's day, chased by a thoroughly unconvincing and decidedly ludicrous twenty-five foot Styrofoam crab. He watched it for a few wistful moments then shook his head. "Those were the days," he said, more to himself than the young man sitting in front of the moviola. "I'd spend a hundred thousand and make a million. Now I spend a million and make a hundred thousand."

Yeah. Those were the days.

It was a modest brick building at the east end of Sunset, near Hoover. Once it had been the home of Monogram but now it was called Allied Artists because the folks in charge were trying to attract better talent and over the years Monogram hadn't exactly earned itself the finest of reputations. The way the industry more or less felt about the studio was best summed up by an actress working on one of their movies a few years back. For reasons best left unexplained it became necessary for her and her four costars to climb through a hole in one of the sound stage floors. Waiting for the director to call for action the woman sadly took stock of their situation and sighed: "Well, here we are, in the cellar at Monogram. Jesus Christ! How low can you sink?"

And it was to this studio, which was in the process of trying to upgrade its image, that Roger Corman came to peddle his script, "The House in the Sea," which had been inspired by his visit to the Salton Sea, a large saltwater lake near Palm Springs. Roger had seen a lot of turn-of-the-century homes buried in water there and he thought a chase through one of those homes would be pretty exciting. In his mind he visualized weird light patterns dancing across the walls from flashlights reflected off the water as people raced along the upper floor and plunged into the water below. It never occurred to him that his "exciting" climax would be filmed in two inches of water on the Allied Artists backlot. Not that it would have made a difference in his decision to sell them the script. Not with that all-important screen credit at stake. Without it, he couldn't work "in the business," which is to say in motion pictures.

Everyone who works in the motion picture industry simply refers to it as "the business" as if it were the only business, the same way people in

Southern California refer to the San Fernando Valley as "the Valley" in spite of the fact that there are four other valleys in the neighborhood. And if you want to work in "the business" you have to have a screen credit and you can't get a screen credit unless someone gives you the work. So far the best Roger'd been able to wrangle was a reader's job at 20th Century–Fox at a depressing $65.00 a week. Before that he'd been a gofer and before that a stagehand at KLAC-TV. That's why selling the script was more important than what sort of a picture was made from it. Because in addition to a writer's credit, Roger wanted an executive producer's credit. That would give him some credibility when he went to raise money for a project of his own. He knew that by peddling his own material he was violating one of the rules of the theatrical agency he was working for and that he would be fired for it, but the screen credit was more important than the job.

He grew up in Detroit, born on April 5, 1926, to William and Ann Corman. In 1940 William retired and moved his family to California, Beverly Hills in fact. It was at Beverly Hills High that Roger and his younger brother Gene developed an interest in "the business." Roger took part in school plays but in spite of his interest he went to Stanford during World War II to study engineering, following in his father's footsteps. School was easy for him. He'd always been good at math and he liked building things. While at Stanford Roger joined the Navy as a member of the Officers Training Program.

"In wood shop, in high school, I can still remember I completed all the things I was supposed to do for the entire term in the first three weeks," Roger said. "The teacher let me build anything I wanted for the rest of the term. So I had a great time. In retrospect, I think that ability and desire was a manifestation of the creative impulses which later led me into motion pictures, not a sign that I was mechanically oriented as such."

He returned to Stanford after the war and earned a degree in engineering, but even as it was being handed to him he knew he didn't want to be one. He'd known it for over a year. He'd been dabbling in writing. Sold a few articles too. It seemed to him that writing was a lot more enjoyable than engineering but by the time he was willing to admit that to himself he'd gone too far in his studies to turn back. It would have been a waste not to go ahead and get the degree. Besides, it might come in handy one day. As it turned out, it came in handy sooner than he thought.

Roger's decision to try his hand at show business met with no resistance at home. His parents encouraged him to pursue whatever sort of career he thought would make him happy. The reception he received in the world at large was quite another matter. In 1947 he knocked around Hollywood trying to find work and, finally, out of desperation, took a job with U.S.

Director Wyott Ordung playing a scene with Anne Kimbell in *Monster from the Ocean Floor* (Lippert, 1954), Roger Corman's debut as a producer.

Electric Motors, which bored him to death. He didn't last a week. Next was work at Fox, a reader's job that paid $65 a week. So he went to England to study literature at Oxford on the G.I. Bill. When he got back to Hollywood he worked at KLAC, and then took a job with the Dick Irving Hyland Agency as a literary agent and used the position to peddle his own script to Allied Artists.

Meanwhile, Gene Corman had become an agent himself. During his own days at Stanford, Gene had read some short stories by Arthur Coburn who wrote about Hollywood through the eyes of an agent. And the agent made all his contacts during tennis games at the Beverly Hills Tennis Club. Since Gene had always been a passionate tennis player, he thought the job seemed like a natural for him. He found out that Coburn wasn't too far off the mark.

It was Gene who helped orchestrate a deal for Roger's first picture, *The Monster from the Ocean Floor* (1954). Roger had to raise the money to make it but it was Gene who arranged the distribution deal with Robert Lippert.

Lippert once owned sixty theaters in Southern Oregon and California before he went into production in 1946 with a fellow named John J. Jones. Together they formed Screen Guild, the embryo of Lippert Pictures, Incorporated. Lippert never owned his own studio, preferring to rent space. Eventually, he got out of distribution altogether and went into production under the Regalscope banner, making low budget films for 20th Century–Fox to release. In his later years he would look back at the list of films his company released (over 130 features between 1948 and 1955) and point with pride at some of those pictures.* *The Monster from the Ocean Floor* was not one of them.

The idea for the picture came from a magazine article that Roger read about a one-man submarine manufactured by the Aerojet-General company. "I called Aerojet," Roger said, "and told them that if they would let me use it in the picture, it would give them a lot of free publicity. They said yes. I then talked the writer into writing the script, raised six thousand dollars, and we made the picture for a total of twelve thousand, and six thousand deferred, as I recall."

The picture was originally to be sold to Lippert for $110,000 until Lippert got wind that the thing was made for considerably less than Gene had led him to believe. Ten thousand was shaved off the deal, which still left a pretty hefty profit. But not enough to suit Roger. At the rate he was going he'd be lucky to make a film a year.

With some of the money from the Lippert deal Roger produced a low budget crime drama — *The Fast and the Furious* (1954). Both Columbia and Republic offered to buy it but Roger wanted the kind of money that would allow him to make pictures at a faster rate.

Over at a little outfit called Realart, the sales manager, Jim Nicholson, was itching to start his own distribution outfit. Through Wyott Ordung, the director of *Ocean Floor,* Nicholson learned that Roger had a film for sale.

There were only seven films that Lippert felt held their own: The Baron of Arizona, Hell Gate, I Shot Jesse James, Little Big Horn, Rocketship X-M, Sins of Jezebel, *and* Steel Helmet.

Jonathan Haze is about to get a surprise in *Five Guns West* (American Releasing Corp., 1955).

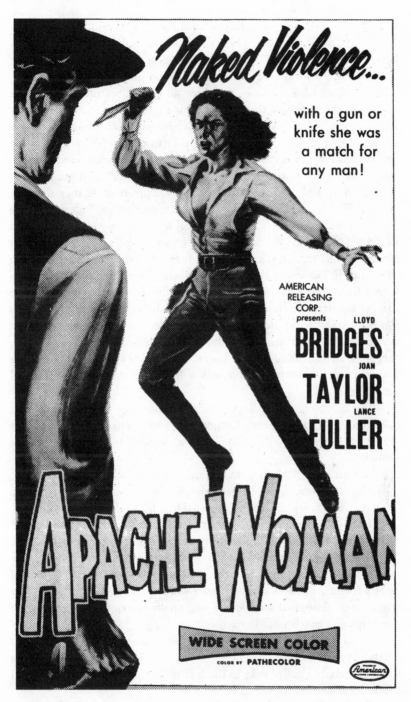

Newspaper advertisement for *Apache Woman* (American Releasing Corp., 1956).

Nicholson wanted to use it to help close a deal with exhibitors across the country. His plan was to sell Roger's picture on the condition that the exhibitors advanced the money for three additional features. Roger gave Nicholson thirty days to try to put his plan into operation. The two flew across the country with $3,000 Nicholson borrowed from a friend. This was the beginning of American International Pictures. Jim Nicholson was the president, a lawyer named Sam Arkoff was the vice president, and for fourteen years Roger Corman was the company's unofficial third musketeer.

"He was American International's only supplier when they started," said Mel Welles, an actor in several Corman films. "So he made ten, twelve pictures a year for them. The deal was that upon delivery of the picture he would get fifty thousand dollars negative pick-up plus a fifteen thousand advance on the foreign sales. So he made every picture for under sixty-five thousand. In fact, every third picture he would send out and get it bootlegged for twenty-eight thousand or thirty thousand and deliver that one and get the sixty-five thousand. Not that he didn't share in further profits but Sam Arkoff was a pretty clever guy too, so you really never saw much later other than what you got up front." ("In defense of Sam and of AIP, they were an honest company," Corman said. "They always paid off their participations. Sometimes there was a little foot-dragging but no real problems.")

The first picture that Roger made for American International, then called the American Releasing Corporation, was a western: *Five Guns West* (1955). And it was at this time that he decided to direct the picture himself.

"He sat with his eyes glued to the script the whole time," recalled Jonathan Haze, one of the actors in the film. Haze had been working in a gas station when Wyott Ordung recruited him for a role in Roger's first picture. Haze drove one of the race cars in *The Fast and the Furious* and would ultimately prove to be one of the most valuable members of Corman's team, doubling as an actor and a stunt coordinator, in addition to bringing new talent to Roger's attention. In fact, *Five Guns West* was written by one of Haze's friends, Bobby Campbell, who wrote a meaty part for Haze as a return favor. Campbell was the one who finally had to tell Roger to forget the script and watch what the actors were doing.

"I was sick to my stomach the whole time," Roger confessed. "I was so nervous I couldn't eat. It rained the first day. I was on my way to the location when it started. I pulled over to the side of the road and threw up. But I think it was natural for me to be nervous."

In spite of his petrified state, Roger managed to bring the film in on schedule but not quite on budget. And as he went into production on his next film, *Apache Woman* (1956), he realized that unless he could figure out a way to make the third picture for half price, the difference would be coming out of his pocket. So while he went to work on *Apache Woman,* he gave $28,000 to Lou Place, who'd served as both an actor and a production manager on the previous pictures, and told him to shoot a nonunion picture in the desert. The picture was shot from a science fiction script by Tom Filer called "The Unseen," about an invisible monster from space that takes control of animals and people. Unbeknownst to everyone involved, Jim Nicholson had changed the title of the film and had sold it to the exhibitors as *The Beast with 1,000,000 Eyes* (1956). When the exhibitors actually saw the picture and found out there was no monster in it they were furious, so Roger had to find somebody who could make one cheap. And that's when a young fellow named Paul Blaisdell was called into the project.

"I was working for Bill Crawford as the art editor for *Spaceway* magazine," Blaisdell recalled. "Forrest J Ackerman, who considered himself quite a film critic as well as being America's number one fan (whatever the hell that means) was doing an article for it and I was doing the illustrations for it. Roger Corman contacted Forrest Ackerman, who at the time also thought he was quite a literary agent in terms of science fiction stories and stuff like that, but here was his chance to be a theatrical agent. Forry just looked all around in a wild flap to find somebody that could do a monster for this picture. So I told him okay, I'd give it a whack. Most of the people that Ackerman knew wrote or they could illustrate but that was all in two dimensions. I thought of all the models I'd built when I was a kid, the clay models I'd made and the soap carvings and I figured it couldn't be all that difficult."

For the cost of materials and $200 Blaisdell built a little hand puppet and a miniature spaceship which were quickly photographed and inserted into the movie. The reaction to the film was so terrible that Lou Place asked that his name be removed and the director's credit was given to Place's assistant, David Kramarsky.

Nevertheless, Roger's contractual obligation to ARC had been fulfilled so he went to Louisiana to make *Swamp Women* (1955) for Bernard and Larry Woolner, the owners of a drive-in theater in New Orleans. Roger had met them during his trip with Jim Nicholson. The Woolners were looking to get into production.

Deluxe accommodations were arranged for the cast and crew at an abandoned hotel, a dreary, dilapidated old barn of a place that offered running water as its sole convenience. The first night there one of the actresses was drifting off to sleep when her bed collapsed.

"Roger was always very professional, except when it came to putting

Top: Ad art for AIP's first combination program; bottom: Lori Nelson clutched by atomic-mutated fiancé, played by monster-maker Paul Blaisdell; in Corman's *The Day the World Ended* (American Releasing Corp., 1956).

us up in a good hotel or giving us a decent meal," Beverly Garland remarked. She was one of the five "swamp women," an actress that Roger had seen at a little theater group called The Player's Ring on Santa Monica Boulevard. Miss Garland was a regular in Corman's films. For a short time they dated. Looking back on those days she concluded that they both got pretty much what they wanted out of the deal.

"Roger didn't really have any money to speak of when he made those pictures so you can't really fault him for trying to save wherever he could," she said. "I mean, you knew up front what to expect so nobody really had any business complaining because you had to do your own stunts or your own makeup or because your dressing room was the nearest bush. Roger never forced anybody to work for him. It was a choice. And some of the people he hired didn't always turn out to be very professional and sometimes the only way to get the work done was to crack the whip."

Roger's next film was again made for American Releasing, a science fiction yarn titled *The Day the World Ended* (1956). It was an important picture for the company in that it was part of an experiment to worm a percentage deal out of the exhibitors. So far, all of ARC's pictures were mostly booked as second features which meant that the company received a flat rental rate: $100, $200, $300. Regardless of what the theaters took in, ARC got a low ball figure and to stay in business they needed a percentage. So Nicholson and Arkoff decided to stick two pictures together and sell them as a package for the same money the exhibitors were paying the major studios for a single feature. Roger's film was hooked with another sf entry, *The Phantom from 10,000 Leagues* (1956).

At first, the exhibitors wanted to split the pictures up and book them at a flat rate but Nicholson and Arkoff held firm. Finally, during the first week in December, they got a booking in Detroit. That week there was a blizzard and a newspaper strike that threatened to keep the theater empty so Nicholson and Arkoff went through the streets with a "horror caravan"; people dressed in monster costumes. The stunt paid off and the experiment was a success.

The target audience for these combination programs was young people between twelve and twenty-five, so naturally the best business was done at children's matinees and drive-in theaters. Teenagers went to drive-ins mainly looking for a place to neck, which is why the theaters came to be known affectionately as passion pits. It didn't matter too much what was on the screen as long as it moved and for that reason Roger and Gene spent as much time nurturing and solidifying relationships with the theater owners as they did making the pictures. They found a friend in Bert Pirosh, the head of the Pacific Drive-In Theater chain in California.

Top: Corman shooting outdoors; bottom: Corman between scenes, *The Day the World Ended*.

Jock Feindel (left) and Corman (standing) shooting indoors, *The Day the World Ended*.

"If you couldn't play his drive-ins, you weren't playing Los Angeles," Gene stated. "That's where all the money was. There were certain givens, of course. One, that you understood where the market was in terms of subject matter and, two, what audience you were aiming for. If you brought them together and you were spending in the area of fifty thousand, it was almost impossible not to make some money."

But raising that $50,000 could be a problem. Some of it came from the franchise holders as we have already mentioned. Another chunk might come from foreign sales, the film lab, and the rest might be deferred. Using this formula, Roger Corman made sixteen feature films by the close of 1957, mostly for American International but he had deals with Howco International and Allied Artists as well. He developed what came to be known as "The Corman Crew."

Roger told Todd McCarthy and Charles Flynn, in their marvelous book *Kings of the Bs,* that when he began he found that a large percentage of the people he hired were not (as Beverly Garland suggested) particularly competent at their jobs. "So when I did my second feature, I simply hired back the ones I thought were good, dropped the ones I thought were bad. I repeated that process on the third and fourth pictures.

So by the time I had made four or five pictures, I had assembled a crew who were the best men I could find. And I worked with that crew for many years. It got to the point where they worked together much like an athletic team. One man knew in advance how another man would function, and they knew how I would function. They were so good they began to be hired by other producers as a unit."[1]

Academy Award winner Floyd Crosby, who photographed Roger's first feature, became Roger's number one cinematographer. Daniel Haller was the art director and Ronald Sinclair was the editor. Marjorie Corso was in charge of costumes, Dick Rubin and Karl Brainard took care of the props, and Jack Bohrer was Roger's assistant director. And, as stated before, Jonathan Haze was in charge of choreographing the fights.

"I've heard so many people from those days say nasty things about Roger," Haze told Sharon Williams in *Filmfax* magazine. "But damnit, here was a guy who gave us a chance to do what we wanted to do. Sure he was cheap, but that was fine. His act was to be cheap. But look at all the people he gave opportunities to. If you said you could do something, he'd give you a shot at it. He wouldn't pay you right but that doesn't matter. Nobody else was giving anyone a chance."[2]

"I have to admit that Roger Corman, one of the most talented producers of any kind of films, is successful mostly because he lets people do what they could do best, and very often, fortunately for him, the chemistry worked," said Ronald Stein, who composed scores for over a dozen Corman films. Stein told Randall Larson in his article for *CinemaScore* that when he first thought of leaving St. Louis to come to Hollywood he wrote 22 letters to the various studios and the only response came from Lionel Newman at 20th Century–Fox who told Stein to stay home. He came anyway.

"One stop that I made was in the office of Roger Corman...," Stein told Larson. "I stopped in and left a record of my music and about a week or so later I received a phone call from him saying that they'd take a chance on me. 'We don't have much money, but we'll give you a full credit with your name on it by itself.' I suppose, to break into the field, I would have been willing to do it for nothing with no credits, but I didn't say that! They gave me a percentage of the net profits of the picture [*Apache Woman*], something which is probably unheard of in this country to anyone like a film composer, and that amounted to thousands of dollars later on, when they bought out all the percentages."[3]

1. *Charles Flynn and Todd McCarthy,* "Roger Corman," Kings of the Bs, *E.P. Dutton, p. 303.*
2. *Sharon Williams, "Jonathan Haze,"* Filmfax, *vol. 1, no. 5, p. 35.*
3. *Randall D. Larson, "The Film Music of Ronald Stein,"* CinemaScore 1984–5, *p. 52.*

Russ Bender (left) tells Jonathan Haze and Dick Miller they're under communist attack in *It Conquered the World* (AIP, 1956).

In addition to *Apache Woman*, Stein composed the scores for *The Day the World Ended*, *The Oklahoma Woman*, *Gunslinger*, *It Conquered the World* (all 1956), *Not of This Earth*, *Attack of the Crab Monsters*, *Naked Paradise*, *The Undead*, *Rock All Night*, *Sorority Girl*, and *She-Gods of Shark Reef* (all 1957), which was every film that Roger made during those two years. Stein may have been the finest composer working in low budget films at the time. His music was always a plus, both memorable and supportive. And if it hadn't been for Roger Corman, we may never have had the opportunity to hear it. And Roger not only gave people chances in the films he made, he extended the effort by backing other people's projects.

"It started in the late 1950s," Roger said. "I was doing fairly well as a young producer-director and I knew people around town who moved in a certain milieu. And I'd made a little bit of money and was looking for some way to invest it. A friend of mine—I think it was Al Kallis*—came to me

---

*Kallis was hired by Roger to design the advertising campaign for *Gunslinger*. *Jim Nicholson liked his work so much that Kallis was in charge of advertising every AIP film for the next fifteen years.*

Ad art for *Attack of the Crab Monsters* (Allied Artists, 1957).

and said he knew Irv Kershner and Andy Fenady who wanted to make a very low budget film. Al wanted to know if I'd back them. They were just out of school, doing TV documentaries for one of the local television stations. I put up the money and they made a little picture called *Stakeout on Dope Street* (1958) which we sold to Warner Brothers and did extremely well. Irv Kershner was laughing as we handed out the checks. He'd heard all of these terrible stories about people suing each other for profits and here we were, laughing and drinking champagne. It was a great evening."

Paul Blaisdell said Roger was "one of the most honest people I ever met in Hollywood. If he said, 'Jeez, Paul, I gotta give you a deferred payment. You can't get any money for six weeks' so help me (and I don't care if Roger was shooting a movie at the North Pole) six weeks later I could go to my mailbox and BINGO! I'd have my money."

Stakeout on Dope Street was photographed by Haskell Wexler whose later credits include *Who's Afraid of Virginia Woolf?* (for which he won an Oscar in 1966), *In the Heat of the Night* (voted Best Picture of 1967), *One Flew Over the Cuckoo's Nest* (which won all five top Oscars in 1975), *Coming Home* (another award winner for 1978), and the exquisitely photographed *Days of Heaven* (for which Wexler won another Oscar in 1978). For *Stakeout* Wexler used the pseudonym Mark Jeffrey (the names of his two children).

Irv Kershner's later directorial credits include *The Luck of Ginger Coffey* (1964), *A Fine Madness* (1966), *The Return of a Man Called Horse* (1976), *Eyes of Laura Mars* (1978), and *The Empire Strikes Back* (1980).

Since he had such good luck with *Stakeout,* Roger continued to act in an executive producer capacity on three other projects in the late fifties, all of them science fiction pictures.

The Brain Eaters (1958) was cooked up as a favor for Ed Nelson, an actor who'd appeared in minor roles in many of Roger's pictures. Nelson wanted to get into production so Roger sponsored a six day, $26,000 picture which Nelson produced and Bruno Ve Sota directed. The story concerned parasites from the center of the earth that attached themselves to humans they wanted to control. With so little money available, Nelson took it upon himself to supply the parasites. The director recalled the evening when Nelson first unveiled them:

"I got a call from Ed. He wanted me to come out to his place in Pomona. He said he had something he wanted to show me. I said, 'Okay,' and he met me outside of his house. It was night and he had a flashlight in his hand. 'Bru,' he said, 'I want you to look at this. See what you think.' I had no idea what he was up to. We went into his garage. The place was pitch black. He left my side for a couple of seconds and when he came back

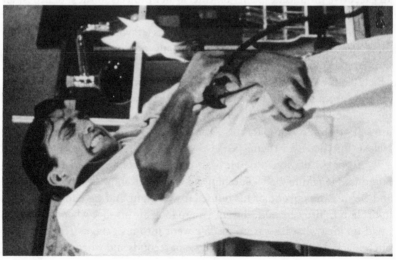

I heard this buzzing noise. Then he flicked on the light and pointed the beam at something on the floor. I looked down and saw this furry little thing coming toward me across the cement. It looked like it was breathing. It had little antennae moving back and forth. I tell you it looked terrific. 'What do you think?' he asked and I told him it was great. What he'd done was buy this orange toy ladybug that you could buy in stores at the time, a wind-up thing, and he'd covered it with fur from an old coat he'd bought at a thrift shop or something. The antennae were nothing but pipecleaners. As I said, it looked terrific that night in his garage. But when we put them on the grass, outside in the daylight, they looked terrible."

But good enough ... for a $26,000 movie that is. At least everyone must have thought so because Nelson's furry little critters were in the movie. And as one might expect, it did little to advance Nelson's career as a producer or an actor. And shortly after the film's release, noted science fiction author Robert Heinlein leveled a $150,000 lawsuit against it, charging its makers with copying, imitating, and appropriating his serial, "The Puppet Masters," which had appeared some years earlier in *Galaxy* magazine.

"They stole it," Roger frankly admits. "No question whatsoever. Bruno brought that script to me and I said I'd back it. It was a pretty nice little script. Then I got this letter from Heinlein's lawyer. I called Bruno and asked what it was all about. He said it was absolute nonsense. So I told my secretary to get me a copy of *The Puppet Masters*. I read it. Now Heinlein was (and is) one of the most respected science fiction writers in the world and they were denying they stole his story. They changed a few things so it wasn't exactly the same but it was really obvious that they took it. So I had a meeting with Heinlein and his lawyer, and I explained what had happened. I told them I could probably go to court and fight them, claiming enough had been changed to make it a murky issue, but I knew it was stolen because there were too many points of similarity. We settled for a $5,000 amount because it was such a low budget picture. Heinlein was a good man. As a matter of fact we even talked about doing a film together. He had a novel I was interested in but it was ultimately too expensive for me."

Nelson was back in a leading role in *Night of the Blood Beast* (1958), again with Roger acting as executive producer, with Gene Corman producing. The bulk of the picture was shot at the overly familiar Bronson Canyon and at a little radio station in the Hollywood Hills, just above the

Left: Ed(win) Nelson is distressed that one of *The Brain Eaters* is on his arm (AIP, 1958). Right: Nelson (right) with Angela Greene and John Baer, preparing for another frantic *Night of the Blood Beast* (AIP, 1958).

Hollywood sign. There was a lot of day-for-night shooting in the picture so the crew kept trying to block the sun.

"That was one of the most *mobile* units I ever worked with," Gene said. "Usually everyone chases the sun; we were chasing the shadows."

When the film was previewed, the writer was overheard in the lobby of the theater telling a friend that he wished he had enough money to buy the negative so he could burn it. *Variety* thought better of it: "Although the screenplay does fall into expected pitfalls, it is strong enough to sustain interest all the way." *Boxoffice* was equally favorable: "The screenplay by Martin Varno is no more imaginative and unbelievable than others of its ilk. While the cast boasts no names that will overweight the marquee, under the play-it-for-spine-tingling direction of Bernard L. Kowalski, performances are sincere and enthusiastic with a mite of special credit due the trio of topliners."

"It was a tremendous learning ground," director Kowalski told Tom Weaver in *Fangoria*. "I found that the Corman brothers were the type of producers who would make very tough deals with people in the sense of protecting *their* dollar investment. But I found them to be full of integrity and honesty. I know that no one worked harder than either Roger or Gene on whatever the project they were involved with. Their input was tremendous, and they were very tasteful gentlemen."[1]

Bernard Kowalski was in show business since he was five, playing extra parts in films at Warner Brothers. He learned a lot from his father who was an assistant director and a production manager. Kowalski was already directing television episodes when Gene hired him for *Hot Car Girl* (1958), which also featured Ed Nelson in a supporting role. Kowalski's ability to bring the picture in on time and budget earned him a place in the Corman ensemble. After *The Blood Beast* he went to work on *Attack of the Giant Leeches* (1959), which had an eight day shooting schedule and a $70,000 budget. Ed Nelson was supposed to make the leeches but he was called away on another project and the job went to UCLA basketball player Guy Buccola and to Ross Sturlin, who'd played the blood beast. Because of their size the two were hired to play the leeches but to get the job they had to make the costumes too, which they did, out of old raincoats.

The exteriors were shot across the street from the Santa Anita Racetrack in Arcadia at a place called the Arboretum which provided the outdoor setting for television's *Fantasy Island* and many a Tarzan epic. The Arboretum's lake doubled for the Florida swamp called for in the script. Yvette Vickers, the film's leading lady, said it was quite a hectic and harrowing experience.

---

1. *Tom Weaver and John Brunas, "Kowalsssssssski," Fangoria, vol. 3, no. 41, p. 58.*

Top: John Brinkley (left), Dick Bakalyan and June Kenney in one of the few happy moments of *Hot Car Girl* (Allied Artists, 1958). Bottom: Michael Emmet and Yvette Vickers (top row) after the *Attack of the Giant Leeches* (AIP, 1959).

"There were some real incidents there, shooting at night with flashlights. We always seemed to be going late and they didn't have enough light. They literally *did* come out with flashlights besides the movie lights. Gene Corman was on line all of the time. I adore him. He was like a mother hen. I'm afraid of the water; I don't swim. So they were constantly watching over me during those scenes where I was falling into the water. And when we came out they'd put these Army blankets around us and give us some Brandy to warm us up. Gene was the one who ended up with pneumonia. Serious. He was in the hospital."

Gene's hospitalization was more or less the result of his desire to save a couple of bucks. As Miss Vickers indicated, many scenes in the picture were filmed around and in the water, which meant that the camera often had to be mounted on a raft and in order to move it, somebody had to get into the water, for which the union demands extra money for its people; a water rate. And Gene didn't want to pay it. Bernie Kowalski pushed the raft around the first day and that was plenty for him. He begged Gene to pay the extra money. The next day Gene stripped down, jumped in the water and did it himself.

The film's most memorable moment is when the audience is shown the leeches' underwater lair where victims are kept like six-packs of Coke, a sequence filmed at the old Chaplin studio, just below Sunset on La Brea. It turned out to be a memorable moment for the actors as well as for Yvette Vickers as they all nearly lost their lives! "We were in a tank, on the set," Vickers explained, "and they had this plastic barrier, an enclosure, to contain the water. And we were doing our final death scene, rolling around with the leeches sucking our blood. I had these awful sores all over my face. And all of a sudden, out of nowhere, the thing broke. It looked like a typhoon. You never realized the tank held *that* much water. I saw the cameraman being spun around in his chair. It was really something. Some electrician fortunately had the presence of mind to pull the plugs or we could have all been electrocuted."

After *The Leeches* Bernard Kowalski returned to television where he enjoyed quite a success as the executive producer of *Baretta* and co-owner of *Mission: Impossible.* He's done several television movies — *Terror in the Sky, Black Noon* (both 1971), *Flight to Holocaust* (1977) — and was in the late 1980s directing episodes of *Airwolf* and *Knightrider.* His theatrical non–Corman credits include *Stiletto, Krakatoa, East of Java* (both 1969), *Macho Callahan* (1970), and the creepy *Sssssss* (1973).

Ed Nelson continued to appear in films *(Elmer Gantry,* 1960, *Judgement at Nuremberg,* 1961, *Soldier in the Rain,* 1963, *Airport 1975)* but was more active in television, best known for his role in *Peyton Place.*

Jack Nicholson's debut was as *The Cry Baby Killer* (Allied Artists, 1958), here with Carolyn Mitchell.

Of all the people Robert Corman discovered in this early period, the most surprising was a young man he met in Jeff Corey's acting class who seemed to show little promise as an actor, to everyone but Roger that is. Roger gave him the title role in *The Cry Baby Killer* (1958) which was written by another actor, Leo Gordon, who gave himself the film's best line: "Teenagers! We never had 'em when I was a kid."

"I went to Roger with the Goddamn story," Gordon said. "It was probably something I saw in a newspaper article or some damn something." His scenario concerned a teenager who believes he has accidentally murdered someone and in a panic adds to his troubles by taking hostages, which attracts the attention of the police, television cameras, vendors and gawkers. "It was a Roman circus, for crissakes!" Gordon added. "The travesty of commercialism when human life is involved. Everything's for sale."

When the picture came out, its lead was certain it would make him a star but *Cry Baby* came and went with little notice and for the next ten years Roger kept that young man busy until *Easy Rider* (1969) made him commercial and *One Flew Over the Cuckoo's Nest* made him a star. The young man's name, of course, was Jack Nicholson. When asked if he'd ever appear in another Corman film, Nicholson replied, "Of course. As long as I don't have to watch it."

By 1959, with over two dozen features to his credit, Roger Corman began looking for new avenues of the film business to explore. He'd been a producer, a director, an executive producer, and even an actor. (Roger played small roles in *The Cry Baby Killer* and *War of the Satellites.*) And, for the most part, he was calling all the shots.

But not quite all.

Against the Odds 2

Using American International's blueprint for success, a plan already proving to be outdated, Roger Corman opened his own distribution company, The Filmgroup. Although the market for low budget double features wasn't as lucrative as it had been when he first entered the business, Roger was convinced there was still a profit to be made if the cost of the films could be kept at $50,000 or below.

John Ashley (center) in *High School Caesar* (Filmgroup, 1960).

"I wasn't trying to be my own AIP," Roger said, "but I felt that I was making these films that *they* were distributing and *they* not only had certain controls over what I was doing but *they* were getting a disproportionate share of the proceeds. And I had a little bit of money to invest so I thought I could continue to produce and direct while I ran my own company."

It seemed unlikely that, given the budget limitations, Filmgroup would produce anything noteworthy. Yet, during the brief period that the company was in operation, Roger Corman not only made his most famous motion picture, he also attempted his first multimillion dollar spectacle, risked his life to make a film about segregation, and launched the career of one of Hollywood's most respected filmmakers.

Things began inauspiciously with a series of low budget, juvenile delinquency melodramas, one of which was made by a high school teacher and his students. Actor John Ashley recalled his participation in Filmgroup's *High School Caesar* (1960). "I remember that Dale Ireland, the director, thought one scene that he did was really *cinema,*" Ashley said with a grin. "I was home in my room, talking to my father on the phone, hoping that he'd come home. When I hung up I started to cry. Dale panned from me to a pair of copper baby shoes. He felt we were really saying something but I think what we said was that we all got paid."

The first picture that Roger personally directed for his new company was *The Wasp Woman* (1959) which, in all probability, was an attempt to capture some of the audience that had made *The Fly* (1958) such a success for 20th Century–Fox. The title character was played by the late Susan Cabot, who described the picture as "great fun"; as difficult as it may be to believe, *The Wasp Woman* was probably Miss Cabot's most challenging role. She had to play a forty-year-old character who, through a scientific experiment, becomes twenty again. And she did it convincingly. She also, of course, turned into a wasp now and then.

"One thing I remember in particular was that, as I attacked each character, I was supposed to bite their necks and draw blood," Miss Cabot told Tom Weaver in *Fangoria.* "As I pierced the neck, to get the drama of the moment, Roger wanted to *see* blood. And so when I attacked everybody, I had Hershey's Chocolate Syrup in my mouth—which I proceeded to blurp, right on their necks! What we did for Roger Corman."[1]

The best thing about the picture was the poster it inspired: the artwork had a man in the clutches of a wasp the size of a bus. Of course there was nothing to even suggest such a moment in the film but then the folks that handled the advertising for the Filmgroup pictures were generally a little reckless with the truth. For instance, the poster for *The Devil's Partner* (1960) was a highly provocative illustration of a naked woman riding a centaur, a far cry from the runaway horse that was actually featured in the film.* One critic was shocked to discover that Filmgroup's *Battle of Blood Island* (1960) seemed to be missing a battle.

The companion feature for *The Wasp Woman* was *Beast from Haunted Cave* (1959), which was shot back-to-back with *Ski Troop Attack*

---

1. Tom Weaver and John Brunas, "Wasps! Vikings! Sea Serpents!" Fangoria, vol. 4, no. 52, p. 60.
*Special effects expert Jim Danforth was planning to do a centaur movie at the time and naively went to Partner to see if he could get some pointers.

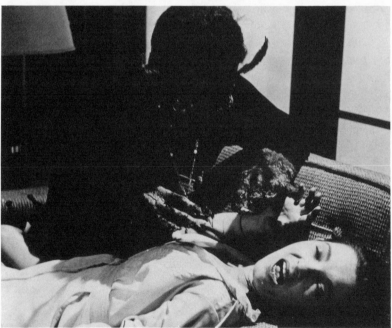

Top: Fred (who changed his name to Anthony) Eisley and Barboura Morris; bottom: as *The Wasp Woman* (Filmgroup, 1959), Susan Cabot kills Lani Mars.

(1960) on location in Deadwood, South Dakota, to escape the cost of shooting union pictures. Deadwood is best known for its Black Hills gold and for being the resting spot of Wild Bill Hickok and Calamity Jane. *Beast* was directed by Monte Hellman, a UCLA film school graduate, and the latter film was directed by Roger. Both pictures were scripted by Chuck Griffith and were pretty standard low budget stuff. Who could have guessed that Griffith's next script would become Roger Corman's most profitable and best known film?

There are a couple of stories about how *The Little Shop of Horrors* (1960) came about. According to Griffith it was conceived during the making of *A Bucket of Blood,* the film it is obviously patterned after. When actor Julian Burton finished the zany poetry that opened *Bucket* there was applause on the set. It was the first time anybody expressed that sort of approval and it sort of fired Roger up. He pulled Griffith to one side and told him that he wanted to make another comedy right away. Not a sequel but a variation on the same story. Roger's account is slightly different: "There was applause and I told Chuck that I thought it was really great and that we ought to do another one. And I let it go at that. I had no thoughts of really doing another one until I found another standing set."

One afternoon, while dining with a friend, the friend mentioned that he knew where there was a standing set if Roger had any use for it. Roger didn't have a particular project in mind but made a bet with his friend that he could not only come up with something before they tore down the set but that he'd make said project in two days.

Griffith's original title for *Little Shop* was *The Passionate People Eater* and it was written with Dick Miller in mind for the lead. Miller had been the star of *A Bucket of Blood.*

"It was the same part," Miller said. "I'd already done it and I didn't see any point in doing it again. So I told Roger to give it to Jonathan [Haze] and that I'd be glad to do one of the other parts. I was Fouch, the guy that eats flowers. And Jonathan got the lead."

Jonathan Haze played Seymour Krelboined, the nebbish who inadvertently cultivates a people-eating plant. Haze said he played the character like the dumb gangster he played several years before in a play called *Brooklyn U.S.A.* but his characterization seemed a little reminiscent of Jerry Lewis. Of course, to Haze it was just another job in an ultracheap Corman film and not likely to do his sagging career any good. He was correct, it didn't, but it is his best known performance.

"It just happened. I don't know how," Haze remarked. "When we were doing it nobody thought it was going to be this thing that everybody thought was so great. And you can't point to any one thing and say that's

A Bucket of Blood (AIP, 1959): top, Barboura Morris as beatnik artist Carla and, bottom, Dick Miller is the center of attention at the Yellow Door.

Jonathan Haze, Mel Welles and Jackie Joseph admire Audrey Jr., in *The Little Shop of Horrors* (Filmgroup, 1960), filmed in less than a week.

why it was successful. I mean, you can't say it was successful because of Roger's wonderful direction or because the script was so great or because my acting or anybody else's acting was so great because it isn't any of that. It just all *happened* somehow. If there's any one factor you can point to I think it's that the picture is so sleazy. If it had been made by a big studio I don't think it would have been the same."

The movie was photographed like an old *I Love Lucy* episode with two cameras grinding away simultaneously, most of the action taking place in that standing set that became Mushnik's Flower Shop. Principal photography took two days and a night. Chuck Griffith played four parts: a thief, a shadow on a wall, a guy who runs out of a dentist's office with his ear bitten, and the voice of Audrey, Jr., the plant. Griffith sat off-camera and read the plant's lines to give Jonathan Haze something to react to; another actor was supposed to dub in another voice later. But everybody thought Griffith was funny so Roger decided to leave it the way it was.

The actors had an incredible amount of dialogue to do and according to Griffith a lot of it was ad-libbed. But Mel Welles, who portrayed the chintzy owner of the skid-row florist shop, Gravis Mushnik, said otherwise.

"He doesn't remember," Welles said. "He wrote every word. The brilliant thing that Chuck did was that he wrote that part *for* me. We were best friends. And when I used to do my Jewish accent around him I used to have certain expressions. And he knew them all because they broke him up all the time. He incorporated them into the script. I didn't have to make up one word."

After Roger finished the interiors Jonathan Haze, Chuck Griffith and Mel Welles took a cameraman down to skid row and shot all of the exteriors in four days for $1,100. They hired bums for ten cents a shot to act in the picture. The whole picture came in for $27,000.

At first no one wanted to book it. Because of the Jewish references the exhibitors thought the picture was antisemitic. Roger withdrew the picture from general release and attempted to book it in art theaters but he had no better luck. Then American International needed a second feature for their Italian import, *Black Sunday* (1960), a stylish horror film about witches and vampires. And that's how *The Little Shop of Horrors* finally got its exposure. Critics were amused by it and the word of mouth spread until the picture developed its own little following.

There were only two United States films showing competitively at the Cannes Film Festival that year—*A Raisin in the Sun* and *The Hoodlum Priest*. Two films were "unofficially" screened: *Exodus* and *The Little Shop of Horrors.*

With the release of *Hercules* (1959), an Italian muscle-man picture with Steve Reeves, a new genre began in the United States. Joe Levine was the man responsible. He bought the picture for practically nothing, dubbed it into English, then spent a fortune to promote it. Levine's marketing technique paid off handsomely and in no time at all other producers were rushing off to Italy in the hope of finding their own bargains. Hercules became a household name and was the subject of a rash of films: *Hercules Unchained, Hercules Against Rome* (both 1960), *Hercules in the Haunted World, Hercules in the Vale of Woe* (both 1961), *Hercules Against the Sons of the Sun, Hercules and the Captive Women* (both 1963), *Hercules Against the Moon Men, Hercules and the Tyrants of Babylon, Hercules, Prisoner of Evil,* and *Hercules vs. the Giant Warriors* (all 1964).

And if you got tired of Hercules, you could always see what Goliath, Samson, or Ulysses was up to.

Instead of buying one of these gladiator pictures to import, Roger Corman decided to make one of his own. He planned to shoot it in the jungles of Puerto Rico. Then he made a deal with Vion Papamichalis, a Greek producer, who agreed to put up the majority of the money if Roger supplied the principal actors, the writer, and his own expertise as director. The picture they planned to make was *Atlas* (1960) and to use Ed Sullivan's old expression, it was going to be a "really big shew," Roger's first million dollar movie. But during a tearful lunch, Papamichalis confessed that he'd been unable to raise the cash. By that time Roger had already sunk about twenty thousand of his own money into the project and rather than lose that money he decided to scale the story down to something he could shoot for the usual Filmgroup budget. He paid Chuck Griffith two hundred to rewrite the script and fifty dollars a week to be the associate producer, production manager, and action director.

"We had a Greek cameraman and a Greek crew," Griffith said. "It was hysterical. Nobody knew left from right and nobody could march. The guys playing the guards wanted their relatives to recognize them so they tore the nose guards off their papier-maché helmets so you had all this paper hanging from their helmets. The tips of the spiers were made at a tire shop and they all drooped. We had to shoot in public buildings, of course, because there was no money. We had permits to shoot, but not with actors, so we were constantly being thrown out."

Griffith wanted to call the picture *Atlas, the Guided Muscle* but after everything that had happened, Roger was in no mood for comedy.

Roger returned to the United States to make his most ambitious film, *The Intruder* (1961). For the first (and last) time in his career, he wanted to take a stand and make his feelings known about something that he felt needed correcting in the United States. That the whole thing should end in disaster is sad and ironic but hardly surprising considering the subject Roger chose to tackle: bigotry.

"I think the idea to do a film like this one came to me during the Little Rock crisis," Roger said. "I was down in Brazil at the time, scouting locations for a jungle adventure film and I was appalled by the bad reputation Little Rock gave us among the South Americans."

Roger was referring to Governor Orval E. Faubus's open defiance of the Supreme Court ruling that said separate educational facilities were unequal and created a feeling of inferiority in Negro students and were therefore outlawed. Faubus ordered the state militia to prevent the enrollment of nine black students at Central High School and federal troops had to be sent to the state to restore order. Firm in his resolve to keep his schools lily white, Faubus closed all of the schools in his state for a year, presumably in the belief that it was better to have students ignorant than integrated.

Charles Beaumont had written a novel in 1958 that fictionalized an incident that occurred in Clinton, Tennessee, where a militant segregationist

Scene from *Atlas* (Filmgroup, 1961).

did everything he could to thwart the Supreme Court ruling. Beaumont's novel caught the interest of Ray Stark and Elliot Hayman at 7-Arts but nothing was ever done with it and a few years later the option they'd taken was allowed to lapse. When Roger got a hold of it, he thought he'd be making the film version for producer Edward Small who at that time was working through United Artists. Tony Randall was chosen for the lead. But when Small realized what the project was about he backed out and Roger soon discovered that everyone else in town pretty much felt the same way: *The Intruder* was too controversial.

Conveniently, Pathé film lab, the company that did all of American International's lab work, wanted to get into production and distribution, so Roger made them a deal. He'd recently made two very successful movies for AIP based on the works of Edgar Allan Poe (see Chapter 3). Roger promised to make a Poe picture for Pathé if Pathé agreed to help finance and distribute *The Intruder.*

But Pathé was willing to bear only a small portion of the cost so most of the money came out of Roger's and Gene's pockets. They didn't have enough to hire a name actor like Tony Randall so they chose the lesser known William Shatner for the lead. Shatner had done some repertory work in Canada and had appeared in a few low budget features.

"We had no idea what we were getting ourselves into," Gene Corman remarked. "As we got further and further into the thing, it became a major scene in which, I believe, the FBI was floating around in the background of the thing. I think there was a lot more going on behind all of it than any of us knew at that particular time."

Since there was no money to build sets, and because it was imperative that the film have an authentic feel, Roger insisted that they shoot on location in the South.

"The black ghetto area in Charleston was called 'The Badlands,'" Gene recalled. "It was important for us to film there so we had to have all the support of the black community. Now here's a white fellow wandering in from the North, talking about *The Intruder* and all of this. I mean, nobody knew what I was talking about. I met a white teacher from the high school who introduced me to a black pastor in the Badlands who became my conduit for the whole scene. And he thought I was a communist. He gave me a lot of help. He was able to marshall the black community. I had no idea. You know, people were getting killed every night, stabbed to death in drunken brawls.* Here I was wandering around there. I mean, the whites in the community didn't go there during the day let alone at night.

"I'm wandering around this place, meeting people, you know, what you do to set up a film—locations, deal making, casting. I met Charles Barnes [Barnes played Joey Green in *The Intruder*]. He had never acted before. He was, as I look back, braver than anybody. He was an honor student and an athlete. He'd just graduated high school and was looking to go to college. He'd been working with a road construction team. We had a couple of meetings and I gave him the script to read. This was the first time anybody had read the script by the way.

"I asked him to please respect what I was doing. He knew who Louis

*According to Roger, "Gene's exaggerating a little here. People were getting killed but the town only had a couple of thousand people. One a night would mean 365 murders a year."

De Rochmont* was and I said we were trying to give that immediacy to the film. I said we were going to bring in actors but that it would be wonderful if he would be in the picture. It was an important role and he was wonderful in the film. Terrific. And he read it and he was in awe of what he read. 'I think it's wonderful,' he said, 'but do you realize how dangerous it is to make this film?' I said, 'Charles, this is America. Nothing's going to happen.' Then he said, 'I'm going to have to show this to my mother.' I said, 'Fine. Please ask her not to discuss it.' And she didn't want him to play the role. There were a couple of rough days back and forth but at the end of it his mother agreed that he could do the film. And I still didn't believe anybody was going to get serious."

But the people in America *were* getting serious. Fed up with the continued denial of their rights, blacks all over the South were staging protests, much to the displeasure of some angry people who forgot what America was supposed to be all about.

As early (or as late) as 1946, the United States Supreme Court outlawed segregation on interstate buses, trains, and terminals, yet Southern stations chose to ignore the law so an integrated group of students who called themselves the Freedom Riders boarded two buses in Washington, D.C., and planned to test all the terminals to New Orleans. The first bus was torched. Fortunately, the passengers managed to escape before it exploded. When the second bus stopped at Birmingham, the riders were brutally attacked by members of the Ku Klux Klan, an action that was sanctioned by the local authorities.

More Freedom Riders were beaten with pipes and clubs at a Montgomery station. When civil rights leader Martin Luther King flew to Montgomery to support the students, an angry white mob cornered King and the Freedom Riders in a church. Had a frantic call to Robert Kennedy not produced the federal marshals, King and his cohorts would very likely have been burned alive.

The people in America were getting serious, all right. Roger and Gene were in danger of finding themselves at the bottom of the Mississippi.

Making *The Intruder* proved to be "a trial from beginning to end," according to Roger. "In the first town where we tried to work—Charleston—

De Rochemont was a cameraman turned producer, a pioneer in the trend toward realism, a maker of newsreels and semidocumentaries.

Top: Robert Emhardt (left) leads the mob that wants to lynch Charles Barnes for a crime he didn't commit; bottom: Corman (lower left) directs William Shatner; from *The Intruder* (Pathé/Filmgroup, 1961).

we told the people, just roughly, what the movie was about, and they agreed to let us go ahead. Then some of the townspeople sent to St. Louis for a copy of Charles Beaumont's novel on which the picture is based, and out we went. After that, we moved quickly to other towns. Sikeston and East Prairie, just one step ahead of our reputation."

By necessity, since the police kept dogging their heels, the climax of the film, which takes place in a schoolyard, was filmed in three separate locations. The first location was a school in East Prairie, Missouri, where Roger managed to film about half of what he needed before the cops gave him the shoe. In Charleston he found a public park that didn't exactly match the East Prairie locale but he had no choice but to use it. He'd barely gotten started when the cops showed up. Gene, in his most diplomatic fashion, ran interference.

"What seems to be the trouble, officers?" Gene asked most politely, keeping his tone respectful.

Of course he knew what the trouble was. The cops didn't want them there. No "troublemakers" in their town.

"Naturally, we want to cooperate with you in any way we can," Gene told them. "Let's step over to the wagon here and get some coffee. You gentlemen could use some coffee, couldn't you? And I think there's some doughnuts left."

Gene stalled them for three hours while Roger filmed at a fever pitch. But Roger knew Gene couldn't last indefinitely so at the lunch break he told his production manager, Jack Bohrer, that they were moving on. The rest of the scenes were shot at an isolated country school. But Roger didn't have a master shot of the school in East Prairie, and he needed it to establish location. So he sneaked back into East Prairie, alone. As soon as he set up the camera he saw the police car at the other end of the town square. Roger got his shot, quickly stuck the camera in the back seat of the car, and drove carefully out of town with the sheriff at his heels.

"The preview is the best part of the story," said Gene. "I phoned Bert Pirosh and I said to him that I wanted to set up a preview. I asked for Baldwin Hills or a place that was on the cusp of the black and white scene. I used to take previews at the Paradise on Sepulveda or Warners in Inglewood or places like that but I told Bert that I wanted to take it to a place that normally didn't have a preview. He asked, 'What's the subject matter?' I said, 'It has to do with schooling and a person striving for self-respect. A very American story.' 'Gee, that's certainly a different picture of you,' he said and I said, 'Maybe that's why I'm cautious where I want to take the preview.' Five minutes into the picture the audience was bristling. We had a black and white audience. Mostly white. You shoulda heard the people in the lobby. I mean, they weren't writing cards, they were ripping them up, throwing them down. 'Trashy Hollywood communists!' I mean, here I am, a dyed-in-the-wool Republican, you know. You have seldom heard what went on. I got a call the next day from Bert. He said, 'Gene, what the hell are you up to?' I said, 'Bert, I think we're on to something.' He said, 'Gene, this is very simple. There's no way we're going to play your film in any of our theaters. The theaters that have this problem don't want this picture and the theaters that *don't* have this problem certainly aren't going to play this picture. You're lucky that they didn't rip the theater apart last night. Who knows what could have happened.'"

Unfortunately, Bert Pirosh, the head of the Pacific Theatre chain, was right. Contrary to what the movies would have us believe, bigotry was not restricted to the Southern states. Martin Luther King met many of his most violent opponents in the streets of Chicago. *Making* the movie had only been half the battle. Now Roger and Gene had to find someone to play it.

Then the Motion Picture Association of America threw another obstacle in Roger's and Gene's path. Because of the use of the word "nigger" in the film, *The Intruder* was denied the Seal of Approval. This was shortly after a speech made by MPAA president Eric Johnston in which Johnston declared that it was "time to exercise more courage and more conviction" in motion pictures.

Roger was flabbergasted. He told the press that he and his brother had made over sixty pictures, "all for exploitation purposes. We made money on every picture we made, and we made them solely for that purpose.

"Now, when we want to show some of Johnston's courage and conviction, when we want to release an honest, sincere film about a very real and very important social problem, the office hits us on the head before we start."

Gentlemen's Agreement (1947), *Pinky* (1949), *Home of the Brave* (1949), and *The Defiant Ones* (1958) had all used the word "nigger" and those films had been given the Seal.

"What it boils down to is that a major company gets special privileges from the office," Roger charged. "A smaller production company is discriminated against in this respect."

The MPAA took another look at the film in March of 1962 and this time passed it on the grounds that the "employment of the words was essential to the authenticity of the story." In other words, Roger had backed them into a well-earned corner and the only way out of that corner was for the MPAA to do what was right.

There was no hesitation over the use of the word outside of the University of Mississippi in Oxford a few months later when James Meredith tried to register there. Meredith was a young Air Force veteran. He was also black. A riot broke out and in the battle that followed two people were killed and 375 people were injured.

With racial tension high, Roger and Gene were informed that in spite of what they'd been told, *The Intruder* would not be shown at the Cannes Film Festival. It was not "in the best interest of Hollywood" to have it "represent the current motion picture scene."

Then came the final blow: the loss of their distributor. As mentioned before, Pathé agreed to distribute *The Intruder* in exchange for one of Roger's Edgar Allan Poe adaptations. Keeping his end of the bargain, Roger went to work on *The Premature Burial* (1962), but when Jim Nicholson and Sam Arkoff heard what Roger was up to they put pressure on Pathé to sell their interest in the film or face reprisal. Pathé decided to drop out of the distribution business altogether and stick to what they knew. And although it hadn't been their intention, Nicholson's and Arkoff's desire to corner the market on Edgar Allan Poe pictures had left *The Intruder* without a distributor. AIP certainly didn't want anything to do with it. So this very important and personal picture, one that Roger and Gene had been courageous enough to risk their lives to make, was left to fend for itself.

Most of the reviews applauded the film's noble intent but even the most supportive of the critics had reservations. And perhaps the picture wasn't as good as its intentions but it was good enough, if only because it was addressing an issue that was in desperate need of examination. Whether or not it would have attracted enough of an audience to pay for itself will never be known. Few people were given the opportunity to see it. It was later given the title *I Hate Your Guts* in the hope that it would attract a less cerebral audience but the new title didn't help. The picture lost money and the lesson that Roger learned was to keep his opinions to himself.

Between running Filmgroup and making Edgar Allan Poe movies for AIP, 1962 was a busy year for Roger. But as summer approached he found himself with a block of time he didn't know what to do with. So he convinced AIP that for around $180,000 he could make a movie about Grand Prix racing. It was just an excuse to spend a few months in Europe. And since the races were held every two weeks or so, there'd be the time in between to actually relax for a change. Naturally, there was no shortage of volunteers. Bobby Campbell offered to write it as long as he could play a part in it. He revamped an old bullfighting script he'd been unable to peddle. Chuck Griffith signed on as an assistant director. And a young man named Francis Ford Coppola said he'd be happy to be the soundman.

Coppola had been working for Roger for several months. One of his first assignments had been to write new dialog for a Russian science fiction picture that Roger had primarily bought for its special effects. At Roger's insistence, Coppola removed the politics from the story and added a couple of monsters. Coppola was told to make the monsters phallic, which is precisely what he did. He had a couple of his fellow students from UCLA build two monsters, one that looked like a vagina with teeth and one that looked like a penis with eyes. Roger's jaw hit the carpet when he first saw it but Coppola assured him that they'd be able to get away with it. Roger was impressed with the young man's energy and eagerness to please. There were many mornings when Roger found him slumped over the moviola, bleary eyed and disheveled from working all night. Roger suspected that Coppola didn't know anything about sound recording but figured he'd learn it quick enough.

Normally, Roger would have made plans to shoot two movies while he was in Europe but he'd already signed with AIP to make another Poe picture. Yet, as production on *The Young Racers* drew to a close, the temptation to make a second movie proved to be too great. He told Coppola that if he could come up with a *Psycho*-type of premise, he'd let him direct a feature. There wasn't time for Coppola to devise a plot but he was able to come up with an opening sequence that intrigued Roger. So Roger gave him $22,000 and told him to go to Ireland to shoot what was to become *Dementia 13* (1963). Coppola raised an additional $20,000 by selling the European release rights to a producer named Raymond Stross. And when he started running short on cash, he pried another couple of thousand out of Roger by selling him an idea for another project, *Red Is the Color of My True Love's Blood,* a variation on the title of a then-popular song by folk singer Donovan. The money Roger advanced Coppola was done with the understanding that if Roger decided not to make it, the money would be deducted from Coppola's share of the profits on *Dementia 13.*

During production, Coppola kept in touch with Roger by mail, assuring him that the picture was loaded with sex and violence, so much so that it bordered on being sick.

"He left me alone during the shooting," Coppola told writer Digby Diehl in his article "Roger Corman: The Simenon of Cinema." Afterwards, however, during the editing, the two men had a number of major disagreements. "He insisted on dubbing the picture the way he wanted it, adding voiceovers to simplify some of the scenes. Worse, he wanted some extra violence added, another ax murder at least, which he finally had shot by another director named Jack Hill. But I must say I like Roger (who doesn't?), and I am grateful for the chance he gave me."[1]

1. *Digby Diehl, "Roger Corman: Simenon of Cinema," Show, vol. 1, no. 5, p. 86.*

Luana Anders in Francis Ford Coppola's first feature, *Dementia 13*
(AIP/Filmgroup, 1963).

According to Jack Hill, another UCLA film school graduate, when
Coppola first screened the picture for Roger and Sam Arkoff, Roger broke
several pencils in two and stormed out of the room. Hill added a poacher
who gets his head chopped off.

To help promote the picture, Roger hired Dr. William J. Bryan to provide a test which would, supposedly, weed out viewers who might be
adversely affected by the film. If you answered more than three of the ques-
tions incorrectly you were in bad shape.

So now . . . if you dare . . . take Dr. Bryan's D-13 test! Ready?

> 1. *Have you ever spoken aloud to yourself in a mirror?* (The answer
> is YES. Everyone has experienced this behavior. To be able to admit
> your behavior as it is, is a sign of emotional stability.)
> 2. *Do you always think carefully before you speak?* (The answer is
> NO. Excessive caution like excessive recklessness may indicate your
> mind is preoccupied with fear of becoming involved in a situation
> dangerous to your security.)
> 3. *Have you ever raised your hand in anger to a close relative?* (The

answer is YES. Almost everyone has "lost control" once in a while. It is the teakettle that is **prevented** from letting off steam that is in danger of exploding.)

4. *Do you believe yourself to be sincere although others may not be?* (The answer is YES. Everyone believes himself to be "sincere." It is always the other fellow who is insincere. A normal method of transferring guilt feelings is to project them onto others.)

5. *Were you ever involved in what passed for an accident but which you really purposely caused?* (The answer is NO. Unresolved guilt feelings seek expression in self-punishment which may result in anti-social or other unacceptable behavior.)

6. *Have you ever been seriously depressed to the point of considering suicide?* (The answer is YES. Everyone has been depressed and everyone has considered suicide at sometime or another. Failure to appreciate these feelings in yourself may be a danger.)

7. *Do you feel that as a child you were rejected by one or both of your parents?* (The answer is YES. All children are occasionally rejected by their parents. Persons unable to appreciate their parents as human beings with virtues and vices not dissimilar to their own have not fully matured. Continuance of a relationship in which unrealistic virtues are heaped on parents may result in mental illness evidenced by departures from reality.)

8. *Did you ever do anything seriously wrong for which you felt little or no guilt?* (The answer is NO. It is normal to feel guilty when you do something you feel is seriously wrong. A complete absence of a conscience may be an indication of a psychopathic personality.)

9. *Has your general state of mental health deteriorated over the years?* (The answer is NO. One's mental defenses and ability to deal successfully with problems should improve with knowledge and experience. If your evaluation of yourself is progressively deteriorating, you need to see your doctor.)

10. *Death by drowning in a pond is best described by the word "exciting."* (The answer is NO. Actions described as "exciting" frequently indicate the person may be drawn toward the activity by a subconscious desire.)

11. *Have you ever actually attempted suicide or purposely tried to injure a friend?* (The answer is NO. Even an actual suicide attempt during an emotional crisis is not necessarily an indication of mental illness. It may mean subconscious unresolved violence.)

12. *The most effective way of settling a dispute is with one quick stroke of the axe to your adversary's head?* (The answer is NO. While effective, one who prefers an antisocial act of such violence may be nursing subconscious homicidal tendencies.)

13. *Have you ever been hospitalized in a locked mental ward, sanitarium, rest home, or other facility for the treatment of mental illness?* (The answer is NO. Persons who have recovered from mental

Corman wanted something "phallic" but was taken aback when Francis Ford Coppola delivered these two monsters, in *Battle Beyond the Sun* (Filmgroup, 1963).

       illness should be especially careful to avoid possible harmful suggestions.

    Michael Linden, the director of the Advertising Code Administration, was not amused. To him the test seemed to be endorsing the idea that motion pictures *could* in fact cause someone to commit a crime, the fuel the censors needed for their ever-ready fire. Linden also felt the emphasis on the axe murder in the trailer was equally ill-advised.

    After *Dementia 13*, Coppola went to work on *The Terror* (1963), one of Roger Corman's most notorious pictures.

    The legend behind *The Terror* is that it was shot in three days, on sets left over from one of Roger's Poe pictures. That's only partly true. The scenes with Boris Karloff were shot in three (or two) days which was all the time that Roger had before the sets were torn down. Then, for the next eight months, several directors, including Coppola, contributed additional sequences to the patchwork until there was finally enough footage to call it a movie. There was never a story. All the scenes shot were totally unrelated.

Both *The Terror* and *Dementia 13* were distributed by American International along with a number of the other Filmgroup pictures.

"The Filmgroup made money every year," Roger said, "but we never made much money. I finally just let it drift away because I realized I could not produce, direct and run a distribution company at the same time. It was too many things. My feelings at the time were that I wanted to produce and direct. So I let Filmgroup fade and went out of distribution knowing however that I'd been slightly successful at it."

In Search of a Script 3

Writer Robert Towne once said that one of Roger Corman's greatest strengths was his lack of patience. Yet, in regards to the making of his most acclaimed Edgar Allan Poe adaptation, *The Masque of the Red Death* (1964), Roger exercised a great deal of patience. Four years' worth.

It began in 1959, the same year Roger opened the Filmgroup. Jim Nicholson and Sam Arkoff had decided that unless they upgraded their

Top: Corman (left) in conversation with AIP president Jim Nicholson (center) during production; bottom: Roger directs Barbara Steele and Vincent Price; from *The Pit and the Pendulum* (AIP, 1961).

product, American International was headed for financial ruin. So instead of spending $200,000 for two pictures, they'd spend $300,000 on a single feature and hope they could make it look good enough to demand a percentage of the box office. It was a sink or swim proposition and they put everything they had into *House of Usher* (1960). It was photographed in CinemaScope and color with a third of the budget going to its star, Vincent Price. Richard Matheson, a writer who'd made quite a name for himself in the fantasy field, both as a screenwriter and novelist, adapted the Edgar Allan Poe story. Roger Corman produced and directed it in fifteen days. The picture was put into release and Nicholson and Arkoff held their breaths. And when it grossed over a million dollars in only seven months, Roger decided to make his own Poe picture. After all, AIP had no claim on the author. Poe was in the public domain, which was the reason AIP chose him in the first place. And the Poe story that Roger wanted to make was *The Masque of the Red Death*. He discussed the idea with Charles Beaumont while they were working on *The Intruder*. Then, unbeknownst to Beaumont, Roger started to develop a treatment with John Carter, a writer in Fayetteville, Arkansas. Confident that Carter could handle the material, Roger made a deal with Alfred Wagg Pictures in England. With any luck, Roger hoped to be shooting the picture by fall in Greece.

Meanwhile, Jim Nicholson and Sam Arkoff were anxious for him to make another Poe movie. So, as soon as Roger finished making *Atlas,* he made *The Pit and the Pendulum* (1961) for AIP. Roger sent a copy of the script, which again had been written by Richard Matheson, to John Carter to give him an idea of how to write dialog with an archaic feel without getting lost in archaic speech patterns. Roger wanted a mixture of *Great Expectations, Psycho,* and a heavy dose of Ingmar Bergman's *The Seventh Seal.*

The treatment finally arrived while Roger was in the middle of his third Poe film. He showed it to Charles Beaumont for an opinion. Naturally, since Beaumont was under the impression that he'd be writing the picture, his reaction was harsh. He told Roger to forget about Carter's script. It was scholarly but dull. Beaumont promised to write a script "worthy of Bergman's best." Roger went ahead and sent Carter's script to Wagg. They didn't like it any better than Beaumont had. It seemed to them something better suited for the stage. Roger sent Carter the money he owed, wished him well, and went looking for another writer.

At this point there must have been some concern on Roger's part that the Poe pictures would play themselves out before *Masque* could get off the ground. With time clearly working against him, it's odd that he would give the assignment to Robert Towne.

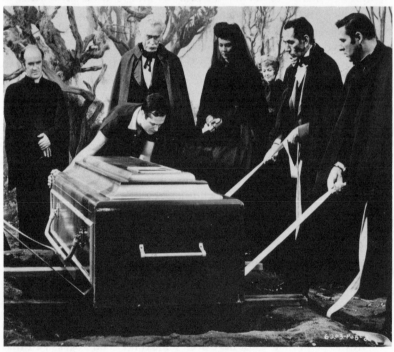

Top: Filming Ray Milland's burial sequence; bottom: Corman inspects the coffin while Brendon Dillon (left), Alan Napier, Hazel Court and extras look on; from *The Premature Burial* (AIP, 1962).

A few years earlier, Robert Towne and Roger had worked together on a treatment that Roger sold to a company in Europe. Roger stayed in Europe, waiting for Towne to turn the treatment into a script—which Towne was never able to do. Before that they'd worked on something called *Fraternity Row* but Towne took over a year to write that script and by that time Roger had lost interest in the project. Towne's script for *The Last Woman on Earth* had to be written as they were shooting because he'd been unable to complete it on schedule. Obviously Roger had faith in Towne's ability if not his speed.

Things started looking bleak for Poe. As if AIP wasn't glutting the market as it was, they changed the title of Corman's *The Haunted Village* to *The Haunted Palace* so they could sell it as an Edgar Allan Poe film, even though it had been based on a story by H.P. Lovecraft. But since most of the pictures had little to do with Poe anyway, and with Vincent Price in the lead, it was assumed that audiences wouldn't know the difference.

And there was a producer over at United Artists named Eddie Small who felt pretty much the same. He figured it was Vincent Price, not Poe, that drew the audience. Now Price was under contract to AIP and promised not to make a Poe picture for any other studio. But there was nothing to say he couldn't star in a similar kind of costume horror drama. So with Gene Corman producing, and Roger directing, Small bankrolled a black and white Poe rip-off based on Shakespeare's *Richard III*, the second film version of *Tower of London* (1962), written by Leo Gordon.

"I'd been to London," said Gordon. "The damn tower. I had a feel for it. I'd have liked to have had Basil Rathbone but Rathbone wasn't to be had, you know."

The picture opened fairly well until the distributors learned it was a black and white picture. After that the bookings dropped off and the picture disappeared.

Small learned his lesson. The next horror film he made with Price was in color, inspired by Roger's *Tales of Terror* (1962), a trio of Poe stories. Small's film was *Twice Told Tales* (1962), based on three stories by Nathaniel Hawthorne.

Edgar Allan Poe's *The Raven* (1962), again produced and directed by Corman for AIP, was a comedy. After four pictures, writer Richard Matheson had had it with all the gloom and decided to spoof it. And his comic tone was enhanced by Peter Lorre who had a penchant for ad-libbing. The film took the critics and the public by surprise and outgrossed all of the previous films in the series. But the picture's success cast some serious doubts about the future of Poe at the box office. *Abbott and Costello Meet Frankenstein* (1948) had been successful too but it was the kiss of death for

Top: Jack Nicholson (left), Olive Sturgess, Hazel Court and Vincent Price enact Corman's comical interpretation of Poe's *The Raven* (AIP, 1962). Bottom: Jane Asher and Vincent Price acting away in *The Masque of the Red Death* (AIP, 1964) as Corman directs.

Frankenstein movies. There wasn't another one made for nearly a decade. The same thing could happen to Poe.

There was simply no time to lose. Roger couldn't wait for Towne. He asked Barboura Morris to write a draft of *The Masque of the Red Death*. And, finally, he asked Charles Beaumont. Beaumont's script was rewritten by Bobby Campbell and on November 19, 1963, principal photography began in England. Roger was given a six-week schedule, his longest yet! And he had access to the sets from *Becket* (1964), a multimillion dollar Paramount picture. He couldn't've anticipated such luck.

Just when everything was looking good, Alex Gordon tried to get an injunction to stop the release of the picture. Several years earlier, in 1959, before anybody was interested in making Edgar Allan Poe movies, Gordon was peddling a script written by Mildred and Gordon based on Poe's *The Masque of the Red Death*. According to Alex Gordon, Vincent Price agreed to star in the picture. The script was shown around at a lot of places before Alex had his agent drop it off at AIP. Now Alex, who had recently parted company with AIP on something less than friendly terms, was accusing them of stealing his script.

Judge Macklin Fleming denied Gordon's petition saying there was only coincidental similarities between his script and the one coauthored by Charles Beaumont and Bobby Campbell. Gordon pursued the matter since he had, in his possession, a copy of the script written by Beaumont that contained sixty-eight points of similarity to the one written by the Gordons. Beaumont died before they could get a deposition out of him and Sam Arkoff decided to settle the matter out of court.

"I don't blame Roger," Alex remarked. "I don't think he ever saw my script."

The Masque of the Red Death was given a lukewarm box-office reception but the critics loved it. Sam Arkoff blamed Roger's arty-farty approach for the lack of ticket sales. And maybe he was right. Then again, maybe the films, as Roger feared would happen, had played themselves out.

American International gave it one more try and much to Sam Arkoff's displeasure, *The Tomb of Ligeia* (1964) strayed even further from the conventional trappings of the series. It was written by Robert Towne as a love story. Towne was unhappy with it, mostly because AIP insisted on casting Vincent Price in a role suited to a much younger performer. Roger had some trouble keeping track of when actress Elizabeth Shepherd was supposed to be possessed by the ghost of Ligeia and when she wasn't. Many people watching the picture were equally confused.

Roger discussed the problem with writer Larry French in *Fangoria* magazine: "So I sat down with the script and I worked out a chart for myself, saying from page so on and so. . . . You know. From page eighty to eighty-two it is Rowena. From page eighty-two to eighty-five it is Ligeia. So I had the chart so I wouldn't become confused myself. I think it was partially in the script and that there were too many transitions. We went back and forth so many times that eventually you got lost. It is actually totally correct. If anyone were interested (and I can't think of why anyone should be) they could stop the film, look at it, and run a chart. They could see it all adds up exactly correct. However, for me to say that does not excuse the fact that the film itself becomes confusing to audiences."[1]

After making ten gothic horror movies—seven Poes, one Lovecraft, and two Poe rip-offs—Roger was relieved when AIP wanted him to make a contemporary film.

1. *Larry French, "The Corman Interview,"* Fangoria, *vol. 2, no. 12, p. 29.*

New World Coming 4

"I think it was *Life* magazine that had a cover on the Wild Angels," said Sam Arkoff and then he remembered that "They weren't called Wild Angels. *Hell's* Angels. At least three or four people came in with that, all of whom take credit—Milt Moritz. Al Kallis. I looked at the cover and said, 'Jesus, this is a natural.' So we called up Roger. I'm sure people from other companies saw that cover too and maybe they didn't think twice about it because it was a tough subject. People didn't really want to tangle assholes with those boys."

The motion picture that resulted from that *Life* cover, *The Wild Angels* (1966), was branded by *Newsweek* as an "ugly piece of trash." In a somewhat lengthy diatribe against the film and the general ill state of AIP the *Newsweek* writer went on to say: "De Sade would have stayed for two shows. Machiavelli would have adored the final, feeble, transparently hypocritical attempt at a moral posture when hero Peter Fonda, whose buddies, including his girl friend (Nancy Sinatra), have just hightailed it out of town, unaccountably decides to wait for the cops. . . ." The *New York Times* dismissed it as "an embarrassment." Exhibitors were afraid to run it.

From the beginning it was a trouble project. There was some question as to whether or not the bikers were entitled to compensation for the use of their name. None of the bikers had property rights but AIP considered offering the Oakland branch a token payment — until they realized if they made a deal with one chapter they'd have to make a deal with all of them. The simplest thing was to eliminate the name. So what began as *Hell's Angels on Wheels* became the *Angry Angels, All the Fallen Angels,* and finally *The Wild Angels.* All references to the lead character having been a Hell's Angel were deleted from the script.

San Jose: United Artists, 1st week	$8,960
Bayshore, 1st week	$13,854

Charles Griffith wrote the screenplay, based on stories told to him and Roger at a place in Venice, California, called the Gunk Shop. Griffith asked a biker friend of his if they could hang around.

"Roger went down there once and he sat with a grin from ear to ear the whole evening," Griffith recalled with a grin of his own. "They were all so funky — putting us on. I recorded a lot of the speech. It was pretty obvious what sort of people they were but it was what they *believed* they were that was interesting."

"The Angels were interesting because they represented the darker side of our society," Roger observed. "Some people don't like to admit these kind of people exist. But of course they do. They're part of a growing group of people who have no place in our technological society. At one time they might have been janitors or something like that but even those jobs are being automated now. Naturally, the Angels claimed that they didn't want to be part of our society but that's because they're not really capable of it. They're frozen out. So it's only natural that they'd drop out. In a way, you can't blame them."

San Francisco: Esquire, 1st week	$15,292
Spruce, 1st week	$10,588
Crown, 1st week	$ 7,657

"I did *The Wild Angels* as a silent movie almost," Chuck Griffith said. "There wasn't more than 120 lines of dialogue. My story constantly paralleled the police motorcycle cop and the scungey bikers, showing they were both motivated by the same impulses." But Roger didn't want a movie about cops and asked Griffith for a rewrite which he didn't like any better. He couldn't make Griffith understand that he didn't want to make a statement of any kind. He'd learned his lesson after *The Intruder.*

In *The Movie World of Roger Corman,* Peter Bogdanovich, the director of *The Last Picture Show* (1971), *Paper Moon* (1972) and *Mask* (1986), told writer J. Philip di Franco how he came to be involved with *The Wild Angels,* which was Bogdanovich's entry into the business: "On a Friday Roger called and said he was starting to shoot a picture that was titled *All the Fallen Angels,* and he asked me if I would like to work on the picture. I said, 'I'm working on this other script for you.' 'Put that aside,' he said. 'Would you like to work on this picture?' I said 'What would I do?' He said, 'Well, just . . . I don't know. Just hang around and help me. Be my assistant. There's no script yet. Chuck Griffith is writing the script, but it's not in yet. We'll have it in a week or so, but I want you to look at some locations.' I said, 'Well, what the hell do I look for?' He said, 'Why don't you take your wife and I'll give you some expense money.' Roger never said, 'Did you look for locations before?' He just said, 'Go look for locations.'"[1]

When Griffith was unable to deliver a suitable script, Roger gave it to Bogdanovich to rewrite. "He turned it into that very cornball prototype of all the motorcycle movies," Griffith remarked.

Oakland: Stadium, 1st week	$16,222
Auto Movies, 1st week	$10,938
Grand Lake, 1st week	$ 6,570
Rancho, 1st week	$11,043

Because he'd been the leader of a gang of toughs in *West Side Story* (1961), AIP wanted George Chakiris for the lead. But after one ride on a chopper Chakiris insisted on a double which meant that any time the lead character was on a bike the camera would have to be far enough away to conceal the fact that it wasn't Chakiris and Roger knew it would not only detract from the excitement but the authenticity that he was trying for. So Chakiris was dropped and Peter Fonda, who'd been hired to play the second lead in the film, was bumped into the number one slot.

Fonda had been in movies for several years playing "square" types in films like *Tammy and the Doctor* (1963) and *The Young Lovers* (1964). His

---

1. *J. Philip di Franco,* The Movie World of Roger Corman, *pp. 46, 47, Chelsea House, New York.*

Behind the scenes on the controversial *The Wild Angels* (AIP, 1966): top, director Corman with Bruce Dern; bottom, Peter Fonda (left), Corman, Nancy
Sinatra (man in hat not identified).

appearance as Heavenly Blues in *The Wild Angels* ultimately led to the production of his own biker film, the critically acclaimed *Easy Rider* (1969) which grossed millions of dollars. For *The Wild Angels,* however, Fonda received $10,000.

Sacramento:	Fox, 1st week	$ 7,202
	Thunderbird, 1st week	$12,222
San Mateo:	Peninsula, 1st week	$ 5,531
Berkeley:	California, 1st week	$ 4,555
Palo Alto:	Sunnyvale, 1st 17 days	$ 7,981

As most of the Hell's Angels had warrants out for their arrest, the police kept a watchful eye on Roger and his crew when they were on location in Mecca, California, a little town near the Salton Sea. Roger's production manager, Jack Bohrer, ran interference, much the way Gene Corman had when Roger was filming *The Intruder.* Bohrer pointed out to the police that for the first (and possibly last) time in their lives, the motorcycle desperadoes were putting in an honest day's work. Why arrest them now?

And so the filming commenced: a scene of the bikers coming into town for a funeral, the calm before the storm, so to speak. More so, in fact, than Roger could have guessed. For no sooner had he called for action than suddenly, from the opposite end of the dusty street, there appeared an impossible convoy of trucks, packed with Nazi soldiers, firing machine guns. There was a mild panic until it was obvious the soldiers were firing blanks. Brother Gene was in the desert a few miles away, filming a war movie, and was in need of a good laugh.

As was Colby Denton, the actor playing the role of Bull Puckey, who left his gas heater on one night without opening a window. He was half dead the following morning and some people expected Roger to stop production that day and were shocked that he didn't. But in show business there's one old cliché that always applies: the show must go on.

Reno:	Crest, 1st week	$5,067
Salinas:	Auto Movies, 1st week	$6,190
Belmont:	Auto Movies, 1st week	$4,769
North Carolina:	Colony, 1st 3 days	$3,163
South Carolina:	Flamingo, Wednesday	$ 779
	Thursday	$ 854

Toward the end of production a rift had developed between Roger and the bikers, who decided to vent their anger on Peter Bogdanovich. During a fight sequence they stopped pulling their punches. After the film went into release, the Angels instigated a lawsuit against Roger and AIP for depicting them as an outlaw motorcycle gang instead of a social organization dedicated to spreading technical information about motorcycles. They claimed that the film had made it virtually impossible for them to appear unharmed in public. They wanted two million dollars in damages and when it looked like they weren't going to get it, they called Roger and threatened to snuff him out. "If you kill me," Roger told Big Otto Friendly, "how do you expect to collect the two million?" It was a question that provided the biker with a moment of consternation.

At first nobody wanted to book the picture. The film was run at a Theater Owners Association convention and before the picture was over there was a mass exodus. Jim Nicholson and Sam Arkoff stood in the lobby counting angry expressions. "We wish you luck," one exhibitor told them, "but it's too strong for my theater." A few months later that exhibitor phoned AIP's general sales manager, Leon Blender, furious that the picture had been given to his competition. Arkoff got on the phone and reminded him what he'd said in the lobby. "You didn't have to take me seriously!" the man countered.

Slowly but steadily the bookings increased and once it did the picture took off. It was shown at the 27th Venice International Film Festival and later at the Cannes festival, much to the outrage of the American film critics. But the European critics loved it. As a result, Roger Corman was sub-poenaed to appear before Thomas Dodd's United States Senate committee investigating the root causes of juvenile delinquency, to see if he could shed some light on the subject. Which is sort of like asking Raymond Burr for legal advice.

Virginia:	Lust, 1st 8 days	$12,950
	Roselle, 1st week	$ 3,550
	Park, 1st week	$ 2,193
	State, 1st week	$ 4,003
	Auto, 1st week	$ 6,082
	Golden Spike, 1st 2 days	$ 1,658
Nebraska:	76 Drive In, 1st day	$ 2,514

It was Charles Griffith's contention that if *The Wild One*, Stanley Kramer's 1954 biker drama with Marlon Brando, had been made in color instead of black and white, with the gang riding choppers instead of Triumphs, it might have kicked off a whole cycle of biker films back in the fifties. But the fact of the matter is, it didn't. And *The Wild Angels* did. Of course AIP was the first to mine the vein they'd struck and Chuck Griffith was asked to write *Devil's Angels* (1967), on which Roger acted as executive producer. He couldn't direct it because he was already preparing for his next contemporary look at the world around him, focusing on the drug scene.

Nashville:	Paramount, 1st week	$13,697
Texas:	Viking, 1st week	$10,423

	Texas, 1st week	$12,982
Georgia:	Hilltop, 1st week	$ 7,337
Alabama:	Airshow, 1st 2 days	$ 1,167
	Bama, 1st day	$ 755
Iowa:	S.E. 14, 1st week	$10,300
	Cedar Rapids, 1st week	$11,286
	Starlite, 1st week	$ 9,545
Michigan:	Starlite, 1st day	$ 1,468
	Douglas, 1st 2 days	$ 2,723
	Lansing, 1st 2 days	$ 5,048
	Auto, 1st 2 days	$ 1,948
	Twilite, 1st 2 days (Saginaw)	$ 4,050
	Twilite, 1st 2 days (Great Falls)	$ 3,258
Illinois:	Waring, 1st week	$ 6,026

While he was still in preproduction on *The Wild Angels,* Roger Corman purchased the American rights to another Russian science fiction film, *Planet of Storms,* with the intention of writing a story around just its special effects. But by the time Roger was finished with it, he'd milked three films out of it.

The first was *Queen of Blood* (1966), originally titled *Flight to a Far Planet* and later showing up on television as *Planet of Blood.* Curtis Harrington, who'd written and directed *Night Tide* (1961) for the Filmgroup, was hired by Roger to fashion a new film out of the Russian footage. Harrington, and producer George Edwards, were given around $65,000 to accomplish this task. A special deal was cut with Basil Rathbone. For $3,000 the actor would work for a day and a half on *Queen of Blood,* and the remainder of the second day would be spent on *Voyage to the Prehistoric Planet* (1965), which AIP intended to make strictly for the television market and which would also make use of *Planet of Storms* footage. Rathbone ended up working overtime and the compensation that the Screen Actors Guild demanded threatened to break the budget. Producer Edwards told the Guild the extra time was the result of Rathbone's lack of preparation. Edwards charged the actor often had to read his lines off idiot cards and, concerning the matter of his meal violation, it had been Rathbone who insisted they skip lunch in order to get the thing done. And if the Guild had any doubts about where the responsibility for the delays rested, Edwards had some outtakes to show them.

A few years later, when AIP was asking for another product for television, Roger handed *Planet of Storms* to Peter Bogdanovich to see what he could do with it. The result was *Voyage to the Planet of Prehistoric Women* (1968), which Bogdanovich wrote and directed using the pseudonym Derek

As the *Queen of Blood* (AIP, 1966), Florence Marlay accepts a drink from Dennis Hopper but it's really not her cup of tea.

Thomas. The film starred Mamie Van Doren as the leader of a group of gillwomen. It could hardly be considered her or Bogdanovich's finest moment.

From 1960 to 1970 the estimated number of Americans who had sampled marijuana jumped from a few hundred thousand to eight million. Dr. Timothy Leary, a Harvard professor, dropped out of university life and spent most of the decade telling people to "Turn on, tune in, and drop out." Leary was convinced that a drug called LSD (lysergic acid diethylamide) was the equivalent of Western yoga. "The aim of all Eastern religion, like the aim of LSD, is basically to get high," Leary said, "that is, to expand your consciousness and find ecstasy and revelation within." Since the majority of Leary's followers ranged from twelve-year-old kids to college seniors, the drug scene was ripe material for an exploitation film. And after the success of *The Wild Angels,* AIP was anxious for Roger to get busy and crank out another winner. Roger told Chuck Griffith he wanted to make *The Trip* (1967), a film about LSD. Griffith thought a little firsthand experience was in order and suggested that Roger drop acid. Roger read Leary's book and learned that a beautiful setting with friends you could trust was the best way to insure a good trip. Roger thought Big Sur was one of the most beautiful places in the world.

"I was the most conservative of a very wild crowd," Roger said. "What started out as a couple of us going up to Big Sur ended up as a caravan when they found out I was going to take LSD. There must have been twenty people or more. We had to draw up the equivalent of a production schedule — who was going to be taking acid at what time."

Chuck Griffith remembered the incident in detail: "We went up to Big Sur — my girlfriend Sandy Kane, and Sharon Compton, a good friend who was nine months pregnant, Max Windies — in my tent trailer. Roger stayed in the motel and we stayed in the tent trailer. On the morning of his trip I was to take a tiny bit and I was to be the link with reality and the beyond. And Sharon was there, pregnant, to be completely real. Roger took acid with some milk and we hung around in the woods. Nothing happened. 'I've been swindled,' he said with a rage about how he'd bought this acid and nothing was happening and it was a rip-off and he'd come all this way out here for nothing. He finally ran down. He was sitting there, sort of staring. 'Excuse me a moment,' he said. He lay down on his face on the ground and was gone. He had the best trip I ever saw anybody have."

(Roger: "I came up with an interesting concept while I was lying on the ground. I believed that simply touching the ground you could create art in your mind and it would be transferred to the mind of anyone who was touching the earth anywhere in the world. You could have an audience larger than a television audience.")

"He would say things like 'I'm humping the earth. The earth is a woman,'" Griffith continued. "Boy scout troops went by. Nuns went by. They would all see him groveling in the dirt and they were all disgusted. I thought it was very funny. He kept saying, 'Where's Sharon?' Sharon had gone off and was climbing a sheer cliff with her belly out. He said, 'She's been gone fifteen minutes.' I said, 'She's been gone fifteen seconds. Your time is off.' He didn't want to leave when they closed down the park at night. I said, 'We have to leave now.' He said, 'You're a jealous guru. I've got enough money. I'll buy the park. It's a good thing I made all my money before this happened. Now I don't care about it.' Which was a bald-faced lie in the depths of his trip."

(Roger: "It was really a wonderful experience. When I was coming down the thought occurred to me that there was no particular reason to go back to Hollywood. No particular reason to exist in the real world at all.")

"He kept trying to analyze himself. He saw Golden Galleons and all kinds of imagery...."

(Roger: "At one point I saw this old clipper ship coming toward me. It turned out to be a woman's body and I knew it loved me.")

"The next day was my turn to 'get on'," said Griffith, "and his turn to take notes. And he sat with a note pad, staring. I couldn't get on. I took one hundred, three hundred, took five hundred micrograms but with him sitting there with the pad it was too ridiculous. I could not go anywhere. So, finally, I took off through the woods, walking as fast as I could go. I had Roger and an entourage stumbling over logs, following me. I would sit down and find an acid bug. (I don't know if you're familiar with any of this world but it seems that you find bugs that don't exist otherwise. They actually do but you never see them; curly, luminescent, marvelous bugs.) I was chased all up and down the hills. Roger asked if I had any insights. I said, 'The entire world can be described as existing on the inner surface of a cone.' Which was just a lie. Bullshit. I don't know what he got out of the trip. But we all watched him for a long time. He would reminisce about it but he would never change his ways. Too ingrained.

"I wrote two full screenplays of *The Trip*. The first one was about three inches thick, 'cause Roger wanted all the social issues of the sixties in it: race, drugs, everything. It was kind of amazing. I put in a lot of time on that. I said it was too much and it can't be done. I said we should concentrate on the drugs and the music. That's it. It should be based on music and about drugs.

"So the second version was an opera. It was all lyrics. That to me was a fascinating script because it was about a character, Sid Cassidy, Jr., who picks up a girl named Pamela and then loses her again and is looking for her all through the picture. He gets involved in alcohol, then pot, hash, then something else. A series of drugs. In each one he undergoes parallel experiences but different. For instance: drunk driving. He's all over the road. The red lights in the rearview mirror are faint. He doesn't pick up on them. They have to siren him down and then he smarts off to the cop, can't walk a straight line and they throw him in jail. His father gets him out, slaps him on the back and says, 'It could happen to anybody.'

"The next time he's inadvertently turned on by this rock group who pick him up wandering around the highway. He gets stoned and rides their minibus. And he flies through the towers of downtown Los Angeles inside the bus, like an airplane. And when the red lights appear this time they bang bang bang bang and almost knock him out. And the kids are slammed against the side of the car and roughed around and his father won't bail him out of jail. It moved constantly and it cut constantly. It was a little like

Susan Strasberg and Peter Fonda about to take *The Trip* **(AIP, 1967).**

Peter Fonda (sitting) gets instructions on how to handle LSD from Dennis Hopper, in *The Trip.*.

A Hard Day's Night in its tempo. Anyway, that one wasn't made either."*

Unable to get the script he wanted from Griffith, Roger turned to Jack Nicholson, who'd not only written a few scripts—*Thunder Island* (1963), *Ride the Whirlwind* (1965), *Flight to Fury* (1966)—but had a working knowledge of the drug. Only his experiment with LSD, unlike Roger's, had been with a psychiatrist. Nicholson was blindfolded for five hours during which time he regressed and re-experienced his own birth. Roger's budget made it impossible to film much of what Nicholson wrote, and a lot of the things that were deleted were things that Nicholson liked best, but still he felt it was the best movie Roger ever made. It won a major award at the Italian National Film Festival. Roger's major regret was AIP's tampering with his ending, which simply had the lead character, played by Peter Fonda, wondering where his life would lead him after his LSD experience.

This reminiscence by Chuck Griffith is from a lengthy interview with the author.

AIP superimposed a shattered glass over Fonda's image to imply that his life had been ruined and then attached a disclaimer before the opening titles.

"Some people tell you they're not interested in commercial success and that all they want to do is good work, and I think for the most part those people are not being honest," Roger said. "Then there are people who tell you they're *only* after commercial success and that they don't care about the quality of their films and I don't think those people are telling the truth either. I think they care very much. They just don't want to admit it."

And so, in an effort to get some control back, Roger Corman signed a contract with Columbia Pictures to make what he thought would be higher calibre pictures. But Columbia wasn't interested in Corman's artistic aspirations. They were after his ability to make short-schedule pictures and the first thing they handed him to make was a medium budget western. After only a few days the studio wanted him off the project. And Roger wanted out of his contract. He signed a deal with 20th Century–Fox to make a low budget gangster film. At least it was low budget for Fox. To Roger a million and a half was a lot of dough.

What Roger had in mind was a blow by blow description of the events leading to *The St. Valentine's Day Massacre* (1967), done in semidocumentary style. He hired an oldtime newspaperman who'd lived through the period to write the script. Then he went looking for someone to play Al Capone. His first choice was Orson Welles but the executives at Fox wanted no part of Welles who was known to be troublesome. Jason Robards was hired instead.

The rest of the cast included a lot of Roger's stock company players: Barboura Morris, Bruce Dern, Jack Nicholson. Nicholson was given what was essentially a bit part with few speaking lines. He'd been offered a meatier role but he wanted the lesser part because the character was in more of the picture, which meant more money.

Working in a major studio gave Roger's picture a much richer look than he was used to but he was troubled by the fact that he couldn't keep control over where the money was going. He learned that a large bureaucracy moved slower and far more expensively than he would have liked. Still, he finished the picture for $400,000 less than was expected and was convinced he could have brought it in for a million less if he'd made it independently.

He still owed AIP one more picture so with no particular project in mind he returned to the company and was handed a stack of scripts and told to pick the one he liked best. None of them sparked much interest so for lack of anything better he chose a fictionalized account of Kate Barker whom

J. Edgar Hoover had called "the most vicious, dangerous, and resourceful criminal brain this country has produced in the past generation." *Bloody Mama* (1969) starred Shelley Winters in the title role. On a television show in 1985 Miss Winters took the time to publicly remind Sam Arkoff that she still hadn't received her share of the film's profits.

American International made a deal with Warner Brothers to shoot the picture on the back lot but Roger had had enough of big studios after his experience at Fox and went on location to the Ozarks instead.

Simultaneously, Roger was involved in the production of another AIP film, *The Dunwich Horror* (1969), based on the novel of the same name by H.P. Lovecraft. A number of actors were considered for the male lead: James Caan, David Carradine, George Chakiris, Tom Courtney, Bruce Dern, Keir Dullea, Fabian Forte, Elliot Gould, George Hamilton, Noel Harrison, Jim Hutton, Chris Jones, John Phillip Law, Gary Lockwood, George Maharis, David McCallum, Jim Mitchum, Tony Perkins, Roy Thinnes, and Rip Torn. The part went to Dean Stockwell.

Likewise, several actresses were considered: Diane Baker, Candice Bergen, Geraldine Chaplin, Yvonne Craig, Sandra Dee, Mimsey Farmer, Rosemary Forsythe, Jill Hayworth, Sue Lyon, Carol Lynley, Ann-Margret, Susan Oliver, Nancy Sinatra, Pamela Tiffin, Deborah Walley, Leslie Ann Warren, and Leigh Taylor-Young. Nancy Sinatra wanted $60,000. Sue Lyon wanted $75,000. And Sandra Dee wanted almost double that. But Sandra Dee was the one *they* wanted and when her agent hinted that she might do it for less, AIP offered her $65,000 and five percent of the profits.

There were script problems from the get-go and Roger sent volumes of notes to the writer in an effort to help him produce something they could shoot. The finished script was forwarded to the Motion Picture Association of America for approval. They cautioned that unless certain scenes were handled properly the picture would most certainly get an X rating. Specifically, the MPAA objected to the amount of nudity indicated in the script and weren't happy about a scene of Sandra Dee's character "undulating sexually."

In view of the difficulty they were having with the MPAA over *The Dunwich Horror*, it's curious that Jim Nicholson would decide to make *De Sade* (1969). Even more curious that Roger would agree to do it. "I got together with Dick Matheson with whom I'd worked a number of times," Roger recalled. "We worked out a rather intricate flashback structure. And

The St. Valentine's Day Massacre (20th Century–Fox, 1967) was a violent and factual account of the infamous slaughter masterminded by Al Capone.

I stayed with it through the first draft. I went to lunch with Jim and told him that I wanted to step off the project. I was supposed to get some development money but I said I would walk away and give him the benefit of the work I'd done. I thought the picture was a trap. If we tried to show what De Sade did, or as Dick Matheson and I did, some of his fantasies, or more specifically what De Sade did in his fantasies, we'd be arrested. And if we *didn't* show it, the audience was going to be cheated. They were going to be cheated because of the title and because of the way I knew American International would sell the picture. So I stepped away and Jim got a first draft from me for nothing. Matheson went on to do a second draft."

The script was given to Gordon Hessler to produce, and Michael Reeves, who'd done a marvelous job on AIP's *The Conqueror Worm* (1968), was going to direct it. But Reeves was undergoing shock therapy and another director, Cy Endfield, was assigned to the project.

"I got a call from Jim on a Thursday," Roger said. "Cy had become ill. He had some sort of nervous problem that prevented him from finishing the picture. And they only had a few days of pick-up shooting left. Every major scene in the film was shot. They needed somebody to go to Berlin for just a few days to finish it and I was the only person who knew the script. Jim wanted to know if I could leave on Friday and, with no credit, finish the film. I said I had to clean up a few things on Friday but that I would go on Saturday. Which I did. I met with Cy Endfield and he was very friendly. I explained to him that I was not there to do anything but carry out what he wanted. So he told me roughly what he had planned for the last few days and I went out and did the shots. It was a pleasant, easy time. An easy type of shooting. We didn't use the term then but it was really second unit directing. I remember one of the shots. There was a young German actress, a very pretty girl (I've forgotten her name) and she played a scene they had already shot where she was talking with one actor on one side of the room and was then talking with John Huston on the other side of the room. It might have been an auditorium. Whatever it was, there was no connecting shot of her walking from point A to point B. So, I was shooting really elementary footage."

Prior to his trip to Berlin, Roger had been asked to go to Paris and New York to help publicize some of AIP's product and at the same time work on something called *The Great Peace Scare*. To his surprise, Roger discovered that AIP planned to deduct the expense money from his salary on *De Sade*. Roger wasn't about to sit still for that. Not only did he want the full amount that he was entitled to, he also wanted to know what had happened to his profit percentage on some of the Poe pictures, four

Roger Corman's final film for American International, the comedy-satire
Gas-s-s-s (1970), heavily cut by AIP before its release.

John Phillip Law as the chivalrous German fighter pilot in *Von Richthofen and Brown* (United Artists, 1970), Corman's last film as a director.

Filmgroup pictures, some of his old Balboa productions, and nine other films that totalled something in the neighborhood of $200,000.

Editing hadn't even begun on *Bloody Mama* when Roger started making plans for what would ultimately be his final film for American International, a satire about the end of the world called *Gas-s-s-s* (1970). It was shot on location in New Mexico and Texas for under $300,000, its cast drawn from the drama departments of the University of Albuquerque and the University of New Mexico. It was written as it was being filmed and Roger never saw the dailies but sent notes to his editor in Los Angeles who prepared the rough cut. When Roger returned from location he went back and forth from the small editing room off the Sunset Strip where George von Voy was cutting *Gas-s-s-s* together to the dubbing room at AIP to mix *Bloody Mama*. Sitting in the room, watching the same sequence for the eighth time, surrounded by twice as many people as he needed, Roger wondered if *Bloody Mama* was any better than the movies he'd made six or seven years earlier for a fraction of the cost. And a fraction of the pressure.

And while he was still wondering, Gene made a deal with United

Artists to make *Von Richthofen and Brown* (1970) in Ireland. Before leaving, Roger discussed the way to market *Gas-s-s-s* with Jim Nicholson. Because of the unusual nature of the picture, Nicholson thought it would be a good idea to open it in a New York art house to build reaction rather than to dump it citywide and hope for the best and Roger agreed. In the middle of his production in Ireland, Roger learned that AIP had removed everything that was controversial from the picture.

It was funny. In the old days, nobody tampered with his pictures. Nobody cared enough to tamper with them. But somewhere along the line that had changed. First it was just a little scene snipped from *The Wild Angels*. Then they altered the ending to *The Trip*. Three minutes were trimmed from *Bloody Mama*. But with *Gas-s-s-s* they'd not only managed to trim scenes, they'd removed one entire character! And the picture flopped.

Roger was still fuming over what AIP had done to him when the bigwigs at United Artists decided that all of the German characters in *Von Richthofen* had to be redubbed. Prior to the actual filming of the picture, Roger had discussed the various ways they could handle the German characters and UA had agreed that they should speak English without accents. But once they saw it, they didn't like it.

Disgusted, Roger left the dubbing job to somebody else. And he hasn't directed a film since. At least, officially.

New Directions 5

With little money and no exploitable trend in sight, Roger Corman went into business as New World Pictures. The company was so successful he was able to sell it and open another, Concorde. As the man in charge, Roger is still very much in control of the pictures he finances and distributes. Not the intimate control that he once enjoyed as a director but then, when he was behind the camera, it was near impossible for him to work on more than one picture at a time.

He's often asked if he ever intends to return to directing again. Actually, when he first went into business for himself he thought he might once he got his company well oiled and found someone to run it. But he's not found anyone yet and it doesn't look as if he ever will.

"As a matter of fact," Roger confided, "I've never been convinced that this is the position I should be in. And I'm not necessarily convinced of it today."

But the truth of the matter is he fills the position very well. If that weren't true, he wouldn't have been in business for as long as he has. It was a struggle at first, of course. With so little money to work with one of the initial problems was finding ways to keep production costs at a minimum. Roger knew he'd have to find a location outside of the United States. The question was where? Actor-producer John Ashley pointed the way.

"I got a call from Fred Roos," Ashley said, taking the story back to its beginning. "He wanted to know if I would like to go to the Philippines. It seemed there was a company in New York called Hemisphere, run by a guy named Kane Lynn, and he was doing a little horror picture called *Brides of Blood* (1968). The original title was something different but that's what it came to be. I said, 'Okay,' because I just wanted to get away.

"Debbie [Walley] and I were about to get a divorce. We were living in Encino but the writing was on the wall. We had a couple of little separation things and finally opted amicably to go ahead and get the divorce. It's a tough thing. It was very hard on me and I'm sure it was hard on Debbie too. I had watched my parents be married for fifty something years and divorce was always something that I never really thought would happen to me. Modesty aside, I've always been damn successful with almost anything I've ever done. It was my first real taste of failure. Debbie and I were really the product of this business and the fan magazines. We were paired together for a fan mag.

"I'm not saying I didn't love her," Ashley continued. "But it was all of a sudden the thing for us to do to get married. And for the first year or so our marriage was great. Then we came to a crisis. Jerry Bresler, the producer of the *Gidget* films, wanted her to do *Gidget Goes Hawaiian* (1961). I told her that if she wanted to go, then go, but I couldn't just go and hang around the set. It wasn't that my ego prohibited it, although maybe that was part of it too, but I was also working and I just couldn't find it in myself to do that. I'm sure that all of today's 'libbers' would say, 'Jesus, what a pig this guy is,' but. . . ."

So when he got the call from Kane Lynn to do *Brides of Blood,* Ashley jumped at the chance. "And I really got caught up with the Philippine people. There's a certain country, I think, that you have a real affinity for. I was going through a period of my life where I wasn't too happy with myself and I went over there and did this film and it was real interesting because it was all done on location. So even though they were able to do it much cheaper because of the labor, it had the look and feel of a kind of a big film. You could have a hundred people in one shot and it cost practically nothing. Anyway, I came back home and got involved in exhibiting. The picture didn't come out for two or three years. Finally, I got a call from a guy named Bev Barnett who owned Mercury Distributors in Kansas City. He had the picture and asked me if I would make some personal appearances around Kansas City. I said, 'Sure.'

Roger Corman, president of New World Pictures, at a Disneyland Hotel lunch.

"One night we had just finished three or four days of P.A.'s, going to drive-ins and signing pictures, and Bev said: 'Why don't we stay and watch the film?' So we stayed. And because of the scope of the thing it had turned out better than I thought it would. Bev said, 'You know, this damn thing isn't bad. It's really got a lot of production value for the money.' He asked if I would go back and make another one if he got some guys together to finance it. I said, 'Sure,' because it gave me a chance to get away from Oklahoma and the theaters.

"So that's how it started. I went back and made a picture called *Mad Doctor of Blood Island* (1969). Then we did a direct sequel, *Beast of Blood* (1970). While we were making *Beast of the Yellow Night* (1971), Roger Corman was forming New World Pictures. He called me in the Philippines and said he'd be interested in handling the distribution on *Beast*. He flew over while we were shooting it and looked at some dailies and said he'd take it and gave us a little advance on it. He told me he was getting ready to do a picture called *Big Doll House* (1971) and was thinking about shooting it in Puerto Rico. Well, the outgrowth of everything, after some conversation, was that Roger shot it in the Philippines."

Jack Hill was the one sent to the Philippines to do the job. He described the experience as "a fun nightmare." Hill told Jeffery Frentzen in *Fangoria* magazine, "The people are wonderful, and I love them, and they try so hard to please you. You ask, 'Can you do this and that?' 'Oh yes, sure, no problem' — they like to see you smile. Then, of course, they can't do any such thing at all. They had stunt men who'd get up to take a fall, and cross themselves and jump. If they want to have a man on fire, they just set a guy on fire who'll try and jump into the water as quick as he can."[1]

Hill's picture was the first in a series of women-in-bondage films. Simultaneously, New World took a look at the prurient possibilities of nursing, teaching, stewardessing, and modeling. The pictures were aimed at a male audience and more or less intended for drive-in theaters. The best thing about these pictures was their trailers which often featured used car salesman Ron Gans reading copy like, "Their overheated passions burst forth in a wild rampage of vengeance and destruction!" with unsurpassed zeal. These early trailers were the handiwork of Joe Dante, more recently the director of *Gremlins* (1984) and *Explorers* (1986).

Dante exhibited a certain genius for making good trailers out of terrible pictures. He learned that what he *didn't* show was often as important as what he *did* show. For instance, if the picture had lousy sound it was better to let Ron Gans carry it. And if the photography was poor there were always other movies to borrow scenes from.

Like the Filmgroup before it and any film company that Roger Corman would likely head, New World and Concorde continue to be training grounds for would-be filmmakers. Sort of an earn-while-you-learn film school that could just as easily be called the Corman College of Motion Picture Arts. Joe Dante graduated with high honors after he made *Piranha* (1978), which outgrossed *Jaws* (1975) in some of the countries it played.

---

1. *Jeffrey Frentzen, "Not Just Another Cog in the Corman Factory," Fangoria, vol. 3, no. 45, p. 64.*

Pam Grier (left) and Margaret Markov in *The Arena* (1973), one of the many women-in-bondage flicks made by Corman's New World Pictures in the early seventies.

Jim Wynorski, another Corman school graduate, recalled some of his early days with the company's publicity department: "Dick Kaye and Harry Rybnick, the men who brought you *Curucu* [*The Beast of the Amazon*, 1956]* bought this picture called *Island of the Fishmen* from some Italian company. Joe Dante and Miller Drake had trimmed about thirty minutes out of it and Miller Drake had filmed new sequences for it. It was basically

---

Kaye and Rybnick were the ones who initially bought Godzilla *(1956) which they sold to Joe Levine.*

a PG monsters-on-the-loose picture and Roger wanted to sell it as a Friday the 13th picture. He wanted a knife in the ad art, eyes from the Humanoids, a girl, and he wanted to show this monster slashing people with a knife. It went out under the title *Something Waits in the Dark,* played a weekend and disappeared. Miller Drake and I were in with Roger. *Scanners* (1981) was out at the time. There was only ten cents left to re-do the advertising campaign and Miller suggested we call it *Screamers* (1981). Roger liked that idea. So Miller went out and got Rob Bottin for free to make a Screamer for the TV spot and the trailer. Roger said, 'You can use footage from *Humanoids from the Deep'* (1980). The *Galaxy of Terror* (1981) sets were still up so we hired a girl to walk through these sets and be hit by a monster."

Wynorski's own film about killer robots loose in a shopping mall underwent a similar campaign change when it was decided to advertise the film like a slasher movie. The title was changed from *Killbots* to *Chopping Mall* (1987), and the film did quite well. But then Roger has always been able to spot the people who can deliver the product.

"Because you're so eager and so thrilled to be working, you'll kill yourself to make [the movie] as good as you can," Ron Howard told *People* magazine, referring to his directorial debut in Corman's *Grand Theft Auto* (1977). "Maybe that's why he hires new people all the time."

It was Gene Corman who actually discovered Paul Bartell but Roger who put him to work as a second unit director on *Big Bad Mama* (1974) and then gave him *Death Race 2000* (1975) to direct. Against Roger's wishes, Bartell turned the picture into a comedy, aided by writer Chuck Griffith.

"There are many times when a Corman picture can only be a comedy," Griffith said. "Roger didn't want it to be a comedy and felt we were in a conspiracy against him. Actually, we were in a conspiracy *for* him."

"This thing about turning it into a comedy against my wishes is wrong," Roger said emphatically. "I told Bob Thom, who'd written *Bloody Mama* for me (which was a serious picture with comedy, insofar as these films can be serious), that what I wanted was something along the lines of *Dr. Strangelove:* a serious comedy about violence. To me, *Death Race* was about gladiator fights in ancient Rome or boxing today—the need the public has to experience vicarious thrills. I wanted to treat it with humor but what Paul Bartell and Chuck Griffith wanted to do was make it a silly comedy. A farce comedy. I wanted it to be a smart comedy.

"I drove one of the cars in that picture. You know, you get really bored just sitting around the office and I figured I could drive as well as any of the stunt drivers. Besides, I like driving fast cars. (I did it in *The Fast and the*

Furious and in *The Young Racers.*) I was with a cameraman and an assistant director. There was somebody else shooting on the street near where we were, only they had a full crew and the police and everything else. I drove by in this insane car, wearing David Carradine's helmet. Of course not having any police assistance, I had to time everything so I didn't run any red lights."

What Roger wanted was an action picture with an emphasis on violence. When he saw what Bartell had done to it he snipped as much of the humor as he could, leaving build-ups with no punch lines, and hired Griffith to film some violent inserts.

"First time I went out I was having everybody get it in the ass," Griffith said. He intentionally exaggerated all of the violence to make it funny. "But Roger caught that and put a stop to it."

Some of the violence had to be cut when the MPAA threatened to slap the picture with an X rating. According to *Variety* it earned $5,250,000 domestically. Since it only cost $500,000 to make, that was a pretty tidy profit. But Roger believed if they had played it straight it would have made even more.

After that experience, Bartell continued to work on New World and New Horizon pictures but as an actor, not a director. He appeared, in fact, in Joe Dante's first film, *Hollywood Boulevard* (1976), which Dante codirected with Alan Arkush. The picture made extensive use of footage from previous New World films and was a satire of the New World operation. Bartell, in the role of a director, tells his leading lady that they're not making a movie about the human condition, they're making a movie about tits 'n' ass!

Roger was skeptical of the project until Dante and Arkush convinced him that they could make it for $60,000. The picture was hardly a rousing success but both Arkush and Dante were given a second chance. Arkush made *Rock 'n' Roll High School* (1979) and Dante made *Piranha*. Dante's film did so well Roger wanted a follow-up but by that time Dante had moved on to Avco Embassy where he made *The Howling* (1981). So once again Roger turned to Chuck Griffith and sent him to the Philippines to make *Up from the Depths* (1979).

"That was the worst picture I've ever been involved with," Griffith said. "It was a bad picture that should have also been a comedy. After all, it was just a rip-off of *Jaws* and *The Deep* (1977), a totally unimaginative repetition of all the things that were in those pictures. So I did this zany version and the Filipinos were crazy about it. Unfortunately, the producers liked it so much that they sent Roger a copy. That was the end of that."

If nothing else, the picture inspired someone in Roger's publicity department to put the following suggestions in the promotional section of the film's pressbook:

> Sneak into your local yacht club and cut giant teeth marks into the boats using a sabre saw. Leave some blood in the area and some shark teeth stuck into the boats . . . the following day go to the club with some friends and begin screaming and pointing at the bites . . . watch your grosses soar. . . . (Sell your boat dealership before you do this one!)

> Invite the local YMCA to stage a charity "Swim for Your Life" contest at the shark tank of the local aquarium. Coat the little boys and girls with bacon grease and throw them into the tank. For every minute that the little buggers survive get sponsors to donate money to the cause. Just in case none of the kiddies swim more than a minute, film the event and sell it to the local television station billed as "The Making of Up from the Depths." . . . Don't forget to consult the local SPCA for approval before you do this one!

> Rent some scuba gear, tie a large plastic fin to your back and terrorize the local beaches. (Watch out for any real live monsters falling in love with your great disguise!) Watch your grosses soar!

This sort of tomfoolery can be found in many of the New World pressbooks, some of it illegal, immoral or ridiculous. The pressbook for *Hollywood Boulevard* suggests that exhibitors stick "Hollywood Boulevard" over existing street signs, promising that any confusion that might result would be good material for "whimsical human interest" stories. Even the ad copy for New World's product was outrageous, often bordering on self-parody, usually in questionable taste, and just as often tempting the wrath of the censors. I have selected some of the better ad lines so that they may be recorded for posterity and for laughs:

> **"A howling hellcat humping a hot steel hog on a roaring rampage of revenge."** *(Bury Me an Angel, 1972.)*

> **"Women are made for men TO HUNT! Set your sights on the Tastiest Game of all."** *(The Woman Hunt, 1972.)*

> **"Only the monster she made could satisfy her strange desires!"** *(Lady Frankenstein, 1972.)*

> **"She sucks the life from the bodies of men."** *(Night of the Cobra Woman, 1973.)*

> **"It's always harder at night."** *(Night Call Nurses, 1972.)*

> **"Soft skin bursting through hard prison walls!"** *(The Big Bust-Out, 1973.)*

"I can't resist the student body!" *(The Student Teachers,* 1973.)

"This airline serves three wild dishes. Take your choice: 'I'm Toby, fly me as far as you want.' 'I'm Sherry, buy a ticket and I come free!' 'I'm Andrea, my foreign lay-overs are very stimulating.'" *(Fly Me,* 1973.)

"They're over-exposed but not under developed!" *(Cover Girl Models* . . . the girls with the centerfold spreads, 1975.)

"Happy harlots: turning tricks before they turn 18!" *(Street Girls, 1975.)*

In its first few years in operation, New World Pictures could never be accused of being highbrow, not with output like *The Student Nurses* (1970), *Private Duty Nurses* (1972), *Night Call Nurses* (1972), *The Young Nurses* (1973), *Candy Stripe Nurses* (1974), *The Big Doll House* (1971), *Women in Cages* (1971), *The Hot Box* (1972), *The Big Bust Out* (1973), *Caged Heat* (1974), *The Student Teachers* (1973), *Summer School Teachers* (1976), and *Bury Me an Angel* (1972).

To balance the potboilers Roger purchased a number of foreign films for distribution, movies by Fellini, Truffaut, and Bergman which paid off both in PR and in profits, much to the surprise of some of the people at New World.

"Roger is neither fool nor saint," observed actress Diane Ladd. "He just always makes money."

Roger said, "During the time that we were distributing foreign films, we won more Best Foreign Film awards than any other company in the business. I did it partially to make money but also because I really wanted to distribute those films. I loved those films and I thought I could do well by them. Major studios weren't geared to properly distribute them and the afficionados hadn't the clout to get good terms. I was able to give them more personal attention. For instance, there was a rose, I think a yellow rose, that was significant to the plot of *Cries and Whispers*. We had a charity screening at one of the art houses in Westwood and two of my assistants, dressed in long gowns, gave a yellow rose to the women who attended the screening. Normally we played off the art houses and that was the end of it, but we put *Cries and Whispers* into the drive-ins. Not many but a few. Everybody said we couldn't do that. Ingmar Bergman thanked me when I met him at the Cannes Film Festival. I'd given him a bigger audience for his films."

Films like Paul Bartell's *Death Race 2000*, Alan Arkush's *Rock and Roll High School,* and Joe Dante's *Piranha* helped to bolster the New World image. To further raise the image of his company, Roger put a little more money into the production of *Avalanche* (1978) so that director Corey Allen

Top: New World's answer to George Lucas—*Battle Beyond the Stars* (1980), a space version of *The Magnificent 7,* itself a western version of *The Seven Samurai*. Bottom: Footage from *Battle* was used to beef up *Forbidden World* (1982), an *Alien* rip-off whose writers, Jim Wynorski and R.J. Robertson, say they actually went to Corman's *Attack of the Crab Monsters* for inspiration.

could afford to hire Rock Hudson and Mia Farrow. And when Peter Bogdanovich's career was suffering from a series of flops, Roger gave him a chunk of change to make *Saint Jack* (1979).

Battle Beyond the Stars (1980), which was New World's attempt to cash in on the phenomenal success of *Star Wars* (1977), supposedly had a budget of five million, which was highly exaggerated. It was probably brought in for under a million. When he first conceived the project, Roger thought he could hire a bunch of enthusiastic youngsters to build his miniatures for a couple of hundred dollars. When that didn't work out, Roger bought an old lumber yard and turned it into a special effects studio and sound stage. To this day the "Hammond Lumber" sign still graces the property, supposedly because Roger doesn't want to pay what it would cost to take it down. I also suspect he doesn't want to call attention to the place since his office building near Westwood is equally obscure.

Like most of Roger's investments, the lumber yard has served him well. He's able to rent the facilities when he's not using them and for a while he considered turning one of the rooms into a sound studio after a bill for dubbing nearly sent him through the roof.

Normally, Roger has his sound work done by Rydar, which bills him in increments. But when Rydar was busy and Roger needed a rush job he went to another company that billed him in one lump sum. For a couple of days Roger had everyone taking measurements for sound equipment until he found out what the equipment would cost.

Roger sold New World in 1983 for a reported $16.9 million to a group of lawyers, a deal that Roger hoped would free him from the bother and overhead of running a distribution company. The new owners were supposed to distribute Roger's films at a very low rate. "Unfortunately," Roger said, "there were some problems in accounting; paying me my share of the money my films had earned."

Harry Evans Sloan, Lawrence Kuppin, and Larry Thompson filed a lawsuit against Roger, claiming he was trying to set up his own distribution company, a violation of the sales agreement. Roger sued simultaneously, charging that the lawyers refused to honor his guaranteed distribution clause. Both suits were dropped the same month and Roger found himself back in distribution.

"My original goal was to make pictures," Roger said, looking back over his career. "To start as a writer and then become a producer and then become a director, always getting closer to the core of making pictures. To be a writer-producer-director is to be as close as you can to an often misused word—an *auteur* in motion pictures. Filmmaking is inevitably a collaborative enterprise. Yet, at the same time, recognizing that, my attempt has been to gain as much control over the project or to immerse myself as totally as I can. I have probably more control over our productions than other people in similar positions, yet at the same time I do not have the control I once had. I think that's only natural."

"People are fond of leaving Roger and doing other things and talking about how Roger loused up their movie by interfering too much," Joe Dante told *Fangoria* magazine. "But then, if you really look back at it, if Roger made your rubber-fish movie a little worse, or your women-in-cages movie a little worse, whatever he did, in the long run it probably was more beneficial than you originally thought at the time, and was certainly worth the experience."

As a sort of "thank you" for giving them a break, many of the filmmakers who started with Roger give him parts in their pictures. Joe Dante was convinced that if everybody that Roger started in the business put him in a picture he'd be on screen more often than Clint Eastwood.

"To a certain extent, movies are more fun to think about than they are to make," Roger said. "In my mind a picture that should have a big budget never becomes a small budget picture. Every actor is brilliant. There are no weather problems. So it's more fun. Yet, at the same time, there's a certain stimulation in actually getting there and dealing with the problem. The frustrations come, and there are frustrations as well as rewards as you see the original concept starting to fade. I don't think anybody who's ever made a film has made a film that in reality was as good as what was in his mind.

"I've gotten a lot of good performances but I don't think I ever got the performance I really wanted. Individually there were some good sequences in my films. And specific actors did good jobs. But I've never been able to look back and say, 'I really did it that time.'"

Filmography

The films covered on the following pages represent all of the films that Roger Corman personally directed. This Filmography does not include all of the pictures that he personally produced or in which he acted in an executive producer capacity.

Abbreviations

C — Color
B&W — Black and White
PRO — Producer
DIR — Director
EXEC PRO — Executive Producer
SP — Screenplay

DP — Director of Photography
ED — Film Editor
ART DIR — Art Director
CHOR — Choreography
SPFX — Special Effects
MUS — Music

Apache Woman. "Call Her Half-breed and All Hell Breaks Loose!" 1955 C 83 min. PRO-DIR Roger Corman, EXEC PRO Alex Gordon, SP Lou Rusoff, DP Floyd Crosby, ED Ronald Sinclair, MUS Ronald Stein. Golden State / American Releasing Corporation.

The Cast: Lloyd Bridges (Rex Moffet), Joan Taylor (Anne Libeau), Lance Fuller (Armand), Morgan Jones (Macy), Paul Birch (Sheriff), Lou Place (Carrom Bentley), Paul Dubov (Ben), Jonathan Haze (Tom Chandler), Gene Marlowe (White Star), Dick Miller (Tall Tree), Chester Conklin (Mooney), Jean Howell (Mrs. Chandler).

The Story: At the turn of the century, the Apache Peace Treaty has put an end to the bitter fighting between the white man and the Indian. Almost. The Apaches have been placed on reservations and although most are willing to abide by the treaty there is still much hostility between the two races. And when a small town bordering one of the Apache reservations experiences a series of vicious crimes, the irate citizens blame the Apaches and threaten reprisal raids. Rex Moffet, a Government agent, is sent to investigate. He arrives just in time to stop a knife fight between a young hothead named Tom Chandler and a beautiful half-breed girl named Anne Libeau. When Rex tries to help her, he encounters heavy opposition from the townspeople. It seems that Anne's brother Armand is suspected of being one of the Indians responsible for the recent attacks. Later Rex encounters Anne swimming naked in a lake and tries to explain that he's only trying to keep the peace but Anne is suspicious of the White Man. In spite of herself she falls in love with Rex and when she

87

learns that Armand is the leader of the outlaws and that Rex is riding into one of his traps, Anne is forced to turn against her brother to save him. Rex and Armand end up on top of a cliff—Rex armed with a wooden stick and Armand with a knife. Armand plunges to his death, an Apache massacre is avoided, peace is restored, and Rex and Anne take the first step toward true interracial relations.

Behind the Scenes: This was one of the pictures Roger Corman made as part of a three-picture contract with the American Releasing Corporation. It marked the film debut of actor Dick Miller, who became a regular in Roger's subsequent pictures. Miller had come from New York to be a writer but his buddy, Jonathan Haze, knew Roger was looking for actors so he introduced Dick as an actor. And Miller was given a part as Tall Tree, an Indian.

"It was just like when I was a kid, playing cowboys and Indians, only now I was getting paid for it," Miller said. "A week later Roger asked me if I wanted to play a cowboy. I was naive, you know. I said, 'Are you making another picture already?' And he said, 'No. It's the same picture. You can be one of the people in the town. Put a hat on and nobody'll know the difference.' And he was right. Except at one point he wanted me to join the posse that ends up in a shoot-out with the Indians. I told him I could conceivably end up shooting myself."

Miller told David Everitt in his *Fangoria* interview: "I remember the horses were running through the street and they all took a shit. Everybody grabbed shovels and someone said, 'That's your job, every time they . . .' I said, 'Get outta here! I'm not going to shovel shit!' But after that I don't think there was ever a matter of doubling up on anything. Of course, you did things you didn't know you were supposed to do or not do. They were non-union pictures so everybody would clear the set, re-do the set, and . . . well, doing your own stunts was almost mandatory. Roger'd say, 'Well, you're going to come down there on your horse and you get shot, fall off the horse and go off the cliff.' You'd say, 'Sure, fine, let's do it.' And you did it. You didn't think twice."

The music for the picture was supplied by another newcomer, Ronald Stein, who'd come from St. Louis to find work in motion pictures and was down to his last dollar. Although things didn't particularly look hopeful, Stein told his wife that something "wonderful" was about to happen. That Sunday he got a call from Roger Corman around four o'clock in the afternoon. A few days before Stein had left a recording of his music at Roger's office on Sunset Boulevard. "We're going to give you a chance," Roger told him. "We don't have a lot of money. We can pay you four hundred dollars and and one and a half percent of the producer's profit and a credit as big as Dimitri Tiomkin's; a card all to yourself." Stein was asked to write a modern Indian score. He had no idea what that meant but he said he'd do it.

"That's when I first learned about the reduced orchestra that could be used for low budget pictures," Stein said. "You could use 22 or 24 men for a certain figure per man, which was lower than the scale they had to pay for larger orchestras when you had to use more men. That was a special deal for pictures that were budgeted under a hundred and fifty thousand dollars or something like that."

Half-breed Joan Taylor is in no mood for trouble from Jonathan Haze (foreground), in *Apache Woman* (American Releasing Corp., 1955).

Stein's contract called for thirty minutes of music which he was only given ten days to compose. When music editor Jerry Erwin timed it, it came to 29½ minutes.

"Don't worry about it," Erwin told him. "When you cut off the music at the end there's dissipation for a few seconds and there's always some down time between music, even when it begins. And there's pick-ups and other things so there'll be extensions...."

Erwin was right. Everything worked out just fine. Roger was happy and so were the folks at American International. For the next two years Ronald Stein composed music for practically every picture the company made.

Atlas. "Feared by Every Man, Desired by Every Woman!" 1960 C 79 min. PRO-DIR Roger Corman, SP Charles B. Griffith, DP Basil Maros, ED Michael Luciano, CHOR Barbara Comeau, MUS Ronald Stein. Filmgroup.

The Cast: Michael Forest (Atlas), Frank Wolff (Paraximedes), Barboura Morris (Candia), Walter Maslow (Garnis), Christos Esarchos (Indros), Andrea Filippidis (Talectos), Theodore Dimitriou (Gallus), Miranda Kounelaki (Ariana), Sascha Dario (Prima Ballerina), Sid Savage (Biggis Dikkis).

The Story: The armies of Thenis and Seronikos have been at war for months and they're starting to buckle under the strain. So they decide to settle the matter by having the best man from each side square off. The ruler of the Seronikos, an unscrupulous sadistic chap named Paraximedes, sends his equally unscrupulous lady, Candia, to persuade Atlas to fight for them. Having no idea what's actually going on, Atlas wins the fight and unwittingly makes it possible for Paraximedes to lay waste to the people of Thenis. Once he's aware that he's been duped, Atlas leads a rebel army against Paraximedes and sets things right again.

Behind the Scenes: Believe it or not, *Atlas* was the by-product of an international scandal that took place a year before the picture's release. In 1960 the United States sent a U-2 plane to spy on the Russians. When the plane was shot down, President Eisenhower claimed it was a weather ship, unaware that Francis Gary Powers, the pilot of the plane, was still alive in the Kremlin. And what Powers told the Russians didn't exactly jibe with Ike's account of things. In the end there was nothing for Ike to do but 'fess up. But it's okay for the United States government to lie and spy (and cheat and kill if it comes to it) because we wear the white hat. Right?

Roger Corman saw a film in this embarrassment and put Robert Towne to work on a script titled *I Flew a Spy Plane Over Russia* which Roger intended to make in Europe. But Towne wasn't able to whip the thing out fast enough so Roger switched gears and decided to make a muscleman movie in Puerto Rico instead. At the time, a Boston exhibitor named Joe Levine had made a fortune on a picture called *Hercules,* which he'd purchased for very little money from the Italians. Buying a picture was easier than making one and a lot less expensive. Which, in retrospect, is what Roger should have done. But he didn't. And after he and Chuck Griffith worked out a scenario for *Atlas,* Roger got involved with a producer in Greece who agreed to sink a pile of money into the project. Suddenly, *Atlas* became a BIG picture. The trades announced that it would be a roadshow attraction. But the deal fell through. Griffith was summoned to Greece to scale the script down to a $75,000 budget.

"We used local talent from around the town near Athens, and the picture was written in just a few days," Griffith told Dennis Fischer in an interview for *Midnight Marquee.* "There was a Greek cameraman and a Greek crew. Nobody knew left from right. The 'army' couldn't march. They tore the nose guards off their papier-maché helmets so that their relatives could recognize them in the picture and there was paper hanging down from their helmets. The tips of their spears were hanging down because they were made out of rubber which I had to have done at a tire shop around the corner of the set."

They couldn't get permits to shoot with actors in public buildings so most of the picture was shot around archeological sites. In the evenings, Roger and Chuck drank Turkish coffee in Constitution Square, which was the hot spot in Athens. Roger said, "We were having coffee there one night, wandering around, when we passed this nightclub that featured belly dancers. We went in, sat down, and this really good looking belly dancer came over and sat at our table. We were talking and laughing. The show was about to close and she said to me, 'I love you. Buy a bottle of champagne and you and I will go back to my apartment and have a wonderful time.' Sounded good to me. So I ordered a bottle which was brought to me along with a bill for a hundred dollars. I told the guy who brought the bottle to take it back. The upshot was they took the bottle back and she fell out of love with me immediately."

When the picture was in the can it was obvious it wasn't roadshow material so Roger gave a cover story to the trades. He said, and I quote: "Exhibitors with box office acumen we respect indicate the dangers of pricing pictures out of the market. They admit the occasional success of roadshows but point out that they are interested in long-run attendance increase over extended periods instead of spot bonanzas. In effect, the roadshow oasis may be a mirage."

Certainly in the case of *Atlas* it would have been.

Attack of the Crab Monsters. "From the Depths of the Sea . . . A Tidal Wave of Terror!" 1957 B&W 62 min. PRO-DIR Roger Corman, SP Charles B. Griffith, DP Floyd Crosby, Underwater DP Maitland Stuart, ED Charles Gross, TITLES Paul Julian, MUS Ronald Stein. Los Altos/Allied Artists.

The Cast: Richard Garland (Dale Drewer), Pamela Duncan (Martha Hunter), Russell Johnson (Hank Chapman), Leslie Bradley (Karl Weigand), Mel Welles (Jules Deveroux), Richard Cutting (James Carson), Beach Dickerson (Ron Fellows and The Crab), Tony Miller (Stan Sommers), Ed Nelson (Quinlin and The Crab), Charles B. Griffith (Tate).

The Story: Scientists come to a remote island in the Pacific to study the effects of nuclear fallout on plant and animal life. "Strange," one member of the expedition notes, "we can see only a small part of the island from this spot yet you can feel lack of welcome. Lack of abiding life, eh?" The pilot of the plane agrees. "I felt the same when I came here to rescue your first group. I not only knew that they were gone but they were lost, completely and forever, body and soul." Karl Weigand, the leader of the group, thinks the previous party may have met with foul play. Soon his worst suspicions are confirmed. Giant crabs, mutated by atomic radiation, pick off Weigand's group one by one. The crabs have the ability not only to absorb the knowledge of their victims' brains but to talk in their voices as well. And the damn things are near impossible to kill because they're made of free atoms; a mass of liquid with a permanent shape. The crabs can also send out arcs of heat to melt and fuse chunks of the island. The crabs slowly whittle the island to one small corner. In the end there's only one crab and three people left to fight the final duel. Having earlier discovered that electricity can disintegrate the monster, one brave soul climbs to the top of a power line and rides the pole as it whacks the crab in the head, sacrificing himself to save the others.

Behind the Scenes: In 1954 a movie called *Them* came out and sort of took everybody by surprise, including Jack Warner whose studio made it. At the preview, Warner expressed his displeasure by telling his entourage that he didn't want to see another like it.

Them was the first movie to suggest the possibility that radiation could cause giant mutations, in this particular instance an army of 25-foot ants. Warner may have thought it was utter nonsense but audiences loved it, so much

Top: "We're right here, professor!" says Crab as he reaches for Mel Welles; bottom: Pamela Duncan, Russell Johnson, Richard Garland and Leslie Bradley try to save Welles—from *Attack of the Crab Monsters*.

Opposite: Leslie Bradley has fallen victim to the monster mollusk, in *Attack of the Crab Monsters* (Allied Artists, 1957).

so that for the next six years *Them* set the pattern for dozens of science fiction films about giant insects and other life forms. *Attack of the Crab Monsters* was one of these films, and one of the few to radically vary the formula.

Roger Corman wanted suspense or action in every scene of *The Crab Monsters.* His writer, Chuck Griffith, ably supplied it. It was typical for the mutated monsters in these films to eat people (or suck them dry) but in Griffith's scenario they also absorb the knowledge. Every meal raises the crab's I.Q. a couple of points. In essence, each victim becomes a part of a collective whole, working for the survival of the crab.

There are moments when *Crab Monsters* takes on the characteristics of an old fashioned ghost story when the voices of the victims call to their friends.

Griffith was in the middle of his screenplay, then called *The Attack of the Giant Crabs,* when he saw *The Silent World* (1956), which was full of incredible underwater scenes. Griffith was blown away and decided to write a lot of underwater scenes into his script, then promised Roger he'd shoot the stuff himself at the bargain price of $100. A couple of months later Roger telephoned to say the actors were on their way over to Griffith's place so he could teach them to scuba dive. Having forgotten the whole business, Griffith phoned Jonathan Haze who got there fifteen minutes ahead of the actors to give Griffith a crash course in scuba diving.

Filming went smoothly until Griffith had to sink the large crab prop that Roger had built for $400. It was a silly looking thing with a bizarre, almost human face which was hollowed out so that someone could crawl beneath and propel it. And as it was made of Styrofoam, it proved to be nearly impossible to submerge. When they finally managed, the arms broke off and shot to the surface. And the eyes kept peeling off.

Russell Johnson, who's actually the hero of the picture, recalled very little about the making of *Crab Monsters* except that it was shot during the winter time. "We were all in our swimsuits," said Johnson, "at the beach, freezing to death." Mel Welles, the guy who gets his hand chopped off, remembered having fun. "It was like a comic book," he remarked. "I think it was the least colorful Roger Corman picture in terms of behind the cameras because it went basically the smoothest."

Released by Allied Artists on a double bill with *Not of This Earth, Attack of the Crab Monsters* (according to Roger Corman) was the highest grossing low budget film of 1957.

Bloody Mama. **"When It Comes to Killing, Mama Knows Best!"** 1970 C 90 min. PRO-DIR Roger Corman, SP Robert Thom from a story by Robert Thom and Donald A. Peters, DP John Alonzo, ED Eve Newman, MUS Don Randi. American International.

The Cast: Shelley Winters (Kate "Ma" Barker), Diane Varsi (Mona Gibson), Bruce Dern (Kevin Dirkman), Clint Kimbrough (Arthur Barker), Alex Nicol (George Barker), Michael Fox (Roth), Scatman Crothers (Moses), Stacy Harris (McClellan), Pamela Dunlop (Rembrandt), Robert De Niro (Lloyd

Barker), Robert Walden (Fred Barker), Lisa Jill (young Kate), Steve Mitchell (sheriff).

The Story: It's the middle of the Great Depression and Kate Barker is tired of being poor. And from all indications she'll always *be* poor since her husband isn't exactly an overachiever. So Kate leaves him, taking her four worthless sons with her and with their help becomes a notorious outlaw and killer. "You had everything and we had nothing and it ain't fair," Kate screams as she sprays a pack of cops with machine gun bullets. The Barker Gang is into everything — robbery, murder, kidnapping, rape. It all comes to an end at their hideout when federal agents give Ma and her boys a more than ample dose of their own medicine.

Behind the Scenes: From the skimpy plot synopsis you might conclude that not only haven't I seen this movie but I was too lazy to even do a little digging for someone else's account of it — but the truth is, I've done both. Essentially, *Bloody Mama* is a collection of incidents that could be juggled in almost any order, except for the beginning and the end. The focus of this film seems to be on the characters rather than a plot. Roger Corman called it an examination of "the dynamics of a very strong, unified family."

The real "Ma" Barker was a God-fearing woman named Arizona Clark Barker who took her four boys to church every Sunday and taught them how to kill and steal during the week. She died in 1935, at her Oklawaha, Florida, hideout during a shootout with federal agents. Her son Freddie was killed with her.

Characters like Ma Barker have always been ripe material for filmmakers, who are usually a little reckless with the truth in their accounts. Gangster films practically kept Warner Bros. open during the 1930s. The Kefauver investigation in the early 1950s briefly revived the gangster film but it was *Bonnie and Clyde* in 1967 that gave the genre a face-lift and new life. It was unusually violent but the most controversial aspect of it was that it presented the two gangsters in a sympathetic light.

Roger Corman's *Bloody Mama* is one of the movies that benefited from *Bonnie and Clyde's* success, but unlike its benefactor, its portrait of gangster life is a lot less sympathetic. Bonnie and Clyde were presented not as ruthless killers but as two rather ignorant people who have no idea what they're getting into when they embark on a life of crime. Corman's characters are ruthless, incestuous, and sadistic.

Just about the time this movie was supposed to go into production, Bobby Kennedy was murdered. And Martin Luther King shortly before him. Public opinion seemed to suggest, in light of those events and the public outrage of the war in Vietnam, that the last thing anybody needed was another violent crime movie where murders were choreographed with the loving care of a ballet. American International scrapped the project "due to excessive violence inherent in the story." AIP waited patiently for a couple of months then proudly announced that "shooting" had begun. The critic from *Motion Picture Herald* thought the only thing wrong with Corman's offering was the humorous end titles, which said: "In memory of all mothers."

Top: Shelley Winters gives Robert Walden a bath; bottom: Winters sits by while son Robert De Niro sniffs glue—from *Bloody Mama* (AIP, 1970).

It did quite well at the boxoffice:

The Milgram Theater, Philadelphia (13 days)	$37,126
Center theater, Little Rock (14 days)	$20,195
Riviera theater, Knoxville (13 days)	$15,781
State theater, Memphis (13 days)	$ 8,011
Jefferson theater, Beaumont (7 days)	$13,992
Coronet theater, Atlanta (13 days)	$16,342
Miami Multiple (13 days)	$92,405

A Bucket of Blood. "You'll be *sick, sick, sick* . . . from LAUGHING!" 1959 B&W 66 min. PRO-DIR Roger Corman, SP Charles B. Griffith, ED Anthony Carras, ART DIR Dan Haller, DP Jack Marquette, MUS Fred Katz, Saxophone Solo Paul Horn. Alta Vista/American International.

The Cast: Dick Miller (Walter Paisley), Barboura Morris (Carla), Antony Carbone (Leonard De Santis), Julian Burton (Maxwell Brock), Ed Nelson (Art Lacroix), John Brinkley (Will), John Shaner (Oscar), Judy Bamber (Alice the awful), Myrtle Domerel (Mrs. Surchart), Burt Convy (Lou Raby), Jhean Burton (Naolia), Alex Gottlieb (singer), Bruno Ve Sota (art collector).

The Story: Walter Paisley is a good-hearted but simple-minded little guy. He works as a busboy at a beatnik coffee house called The Yellow Door. More than anything Walter wants to be an artist. He's inspired by the pompous poet Maxwell Brock who makes speeches about art and artists. "Life is an obscure hobo," Brock says, "bumming a ride on the omnibus of art. . . . What is not creation is graham crackers." Walter couldn't agree more. The only problem is, Walter has no talent, except for maybe clearing tables and even that he can't seem to do to the satisfaction of his boss, Leonard De Santis. But at the expense of the landlady's cat, Walter gets his chance to see what it feels like to be an artist. To be . . . famous. Somehow, the cat becomes trapped in the wall of Walter's apartment and in his efforts to free it he accidentally stabs the animal with a knife.

Walter's beside himself with grief until he remembers more of one of Brock's ridiculous poems: "Let them die and by their miserable deaths become the clay within his hands, that he might form an ashtray or an ark." Walter gives Brock's poem a literal translation and covers the cat with clay, knife and all, and takes it to the Yellow Door. "Why'd you stick a knife in it," his boss asks. "I didn't mean to," Walter innocently replies. "Just got carried away, huh?" De Santis remarks. The cat is put on display at the Yellow Door and Walter becomes a minor celebrity. One of his fans slips him a pack of heroin out of appreciation.

Walter has no idea what he's been given but the undercover cop who saw the exchange does. He follows Walter home and tries to arrest him. Walter is frightened and whacks the cop across the skull with the edge of a frying pan. Not knowing what else to do, Walter covers the body with clay and shows it to De Santis and Carla, Walter's secret love. So secret even Carla doesn't know it. De Santis is shocked by Walter's new creation for in the interim he's discovered the truth. The cat had been knocked on the floor which chipped a piece of the clay, revealing the fur beneath. De Santis is ready to call the police when an art collector offers him $500 for the cat. De Santis gives $50 to Walter and pockets the rest, his guilt overcome by greed. And Walter, afraid of being forgotten, stalks new victims for his "statues." But his glory days come to an end the night De Santis has an art show at the Yellow Door in Walter's honor. Carla refuses Walter's marriage proposal, his idol, Maxwell Brock, turns out to be a money grubber after all, and someone discovers Walter's horrible secret. The police chase Walter to his dingy little apartment where they find him hanging by his neck, covered in clay.

Behind the Scenes: "The only people for me are the mad ones . . . the ones who never yawn or say a commonplace thing," wrote Jack Kerouac of the society drop-outs who called themselves the Beat Generation. Kerouac's book, *On the Road*, written in three weeks, became the group's leading spokesman.

The "beatniks" were the 1950s version of the "hippies" of the 1960s, a group of people who'd become disillusioned by war and the industrial revolution. They abandoned the American Dream and began looking for one of their own. They smoked dope, wore sandals, listened to jazz, and spouted free form poetry. For the most part, these bohemians were ignored by the media except as a subject for humor. The *Helen Trent* radio show added a beatnik character to the program, and a television show called *Dobie Gillis* featured Bob Denver as Maynard G. Krebs, a comical beatnik who blanched at the mere mention of work. Motion pictures all but ignored the subculture except for an occasional glimpse of it which was wildly distorted. Only *A Bucket of Blood*, written by Charles Griffith and directed by Roger Corman, took an honest look at the beatnik lifestyle.

It was shot in five days for something like $40,000 or $50,000 and was Roger Corman's first attempt at comedy. Ultimately it served as the blueprint for the better-known *The Little Shop of Horrors*, also written by Griffith. And both movies were made to take advantage of a standing set.

American International had just finished making *Diary of a High School Bride* (1959) and the sets were still up at the Kling Studios. Since Roger owed AIP another movie, he had Griffith look over the sets so he could tailor a script for them. In a few days Griffith handed Roger thirty pages of a horror-comedy called *The Yellow Door*. The story was a variation of *The Mystery of the Wax Museum* (1933).

The movie was sent out as part of a double feature package but by the time it reached the bigger cities, *A Bucket of Blood* slipped into second feature status and passed through town virtually unnoticed. Few critics bothered to review it. And a preview audience hooted it. One guy declared "This picture stinks!" at the top of his lungs while someone else cried out, "A bunch of Hollywood nuts made this one."

American International offered the following suggestions for promotion:

The first thing that should be set up in your lobby is a giant BUCKET, that is tipped to the side and has the appearance of red fluid dripping.

This can be done with some art or possibly just filling the bucket with red dye.

Giant cut-outs of a bucket should be mounted on your marquee.

Paths of "red drippings" should lead from various strategic points of the city to your theater.

Make some sort of arrangement with your local Red Cross to have a tie-in with A BUCKET OF BLOOD, whereby they would get enough volunteers to fill many buckets. This could even be tied in with your local newspapers.

Use special red spots on your displays as well as any other accessories, such as red drapes, red lights and even a possible red kleig light in front of your theater.

Feature a special BLOOD DRINK, and for those patrons who might have thin blood, give them a red candy pill, representing a blood builder and energy pill for witnessing A BUCKET OF BLOOD.

Have contests such as how many BUCKETS OF BLOOD would a human be able to fill? How many different type blood factors are there?

Run another contest in your local newspaper, asking persons to write in as many feature titles that have the word BLOOD in it, i.e., BLOOD ALLEY, KISS THE BLOOD OFF MY HANDS, BLOOD ISLAND.

Even though the movie sort of came and went, it was nearly impossible not to make money on it because so little had been spent to make it. Which is why Roger asked Griffith to write another comedy and (according to Mel Welles) Griffith came up with a vampire story called *Cardula* about a Dracula-type movie critic. Roger didn't like it so Griffith wrote another one called *Gluttony* which contained cannibalism. That being against the production code at the time, Roger asked for another one which turned out to be *The Passionate People-Eater*, the original title for *The Little Shop of Horrors*. *Creature from the Haunted Sea* was the last comedy in what is now called Corman's comedy trilogy.

But none of them, in this author's opinion, was more successful than *A Bucket of Blood* (originally announced as *The Living Dead*) even though Griffith himself prefers *Little Shop*.

Carnival Rock. "Roarin' Rockin' Action!" 1957 B&W 75 min. PRO-DIR Roger Corman, SP Leo Lieberman, DP Floyd Crosby, ED Charles Gross, Jr., ART DIR Robert Kinoshita, TITLES Bill Martin, MUS Walter Greene, Buck Ram. Howco.

The Cast: Susan Cabot (Natalie Cook), Brian Hutton (Stanley), David J. Stewart (Christy Christakos), Dick Miller (Ben), Iris Adrian (Celia), Jonathan Haze (Max), Ed Nelson (Cannon), Bruno Ve Sota, Chris Alcaide (Slug), Horace Logran (M.C.), Yvonne Peattie (Mother), Gary Hunley (Boy), Frankie Ray (Billy), Dorothy Neumann (Clara), Clara Andressa (Cleaning Lady #1), Terry Blake (Cleaning Lady #2), The Platters, David Houston, Bob Luman, The Shadows, The Blockbusters.

The Story: Christy Christakos is in danger of losing his nightclub, which he operates in conjunction with a carnival. He's $3,000 in debt, business is

Jilted David Stewart (left) sets fire to the club when he learns that Brian Hutton and Susan Cabot are planning marriage; from *Carnival Rock* (Howco, 1957).

terrible, yet all Christy can think about is the new singer he's hired, Natalie Cook, even though his best friend Ben warns Christy that the end is near. But Christy won't listen to his friend, anymore than he listens to Natalie when she tells him that she's in love with someone else. And when Christy is told that this "someone else" is in Natalie's dressing room Christy wants to break the door down.

· "You go in there now and she'll hate you for the rest of her life," Ben says. Christy waits until the next morning to confront Natalie but, as usual, he won't listen to the truth. And so Natalie's forced into cruelty to make her point. "I gotta live my life," she screams. "You're old. Fifty years old. And I'm young." Hurt and angry, Christy's parting shot is: "What I want, no one else will have. I promise you that."

Natalie's lover, Stanley, is convinced that the only way to solve the problem is to get rid of Christy. With the help of Max, who runs "The Wheel of Fortune" concession, Stanley plans to cheat Christy out of his club. But Stanley decides he can't go through with it. He wants to back out of the deal but Christy insists on cutting cards for the club when he realizes who Stanley is. Of course Christy loses and then the fool takes a job as the club's comic. Under Stanley's management the club prospers and on the eve of his marriage to Natalie, Christy comes to Natalie's dressing room, still in his clown make-up. "Please, once again I ask you to leave this boy," he pleads.

"Please, Christy, I don't want to hurt you. I never did," she says compassionately. But Christy's not interested in what she needs or wants and tells her that she'll never marry Stanley. "In the end," he says, "you will belong to me." He waits for her after the show, grabs her and sets fire to the club. Stanley rescues them both and Ben leads Christy away, to New York where Ben's brother needs help running a television station. "He was a good man," Ben tells Natalie and Stanley. "He'll be a good man again." One can only hope that Ben's loyalty does not obscure his judgment to the point of putting Christy in charge of that television station.

Behind the Scenes: Roger Corman was quite excited by the fact that he was able to sign David Stewart for the role of Christy Christakos, as the actor had then recently won the Toni Award for his performance in Tennessee Williams' *Camino Real*.

"What Roger didn't know about David Stewart," said Dick Miller, "was that he'd won the award for playing a homosexual. It had nothing to do with great acting ability or anything to do with his part. That's like letting Gene Autry do *King Lear*."

In addition to his not being a particularly good actor (at least he's certainly not good in this picture), David Stewart was a method actor. And to get into his role he'd run around the set and do push-ups before each scene. In addition to those antics he had to go to other extremes that made him something less than popular with the other performers as well as the crew.

On the first day of shooting, during a scene between Stewart and Dick Miller in which the two actors were supposed to have an intense argument, Stewart hauled off and slapped Miller across the face. "Hey!" Miller said. "What are you doin'? This is pictures. You can miss me by a foot and it's gonna look good."

So they rehearsed the scene a few times but Stewart just didn't "feel it" without the contact. Roger, who was intimidated by his award winning star, pulled Miller to one side and persuaded him to let Stewart slap him once again. Only this time they'd get it on film and that would be the end of it. The slap across the ear that Stewart delivered left a ringing in Miller's ear for six months.

During another scene between Miller and Stewart, Miller was supposed to pull him away from Susan Cabot's dressing room and slam Stewart against the wall. But Stewart, who outweighed Miller by 70 or 80 pounds, wouldn't let go of the knob which kept coming off in his hand. Patiently, the propmen kept nailing the door back into place. "The knob is not real, Mr. Stewart," they told him. "Don't try to turn it. *Make believe* you're turning it." And each time that Miller slammed him against the wall, Stewart's head banged into it. Finally, Miller concluded that the only way he could drag the man away from the door was to sink his fingers into Stewart's arm and pull. And this time when Stewart's head hit the wall it struck the nail that a disgruntled grip had put there for that very purpose.

"You're bleeding," Miller told him. "I can *use* that pain," Stewart replied. A few days later Stewart showed Miller the bruises on his arm where Miller had grabbed him. Miller apologized for being so rough. "It's all right," Stewart told him. "I used the pain."

Later on, Stewart played a scene with Jonathan Haze where he was supposed to suffer a heart attack after seeing the woman he loved with another man. Stewart handed Haze a straight pin and asked Haze to stick him in the leg with it. Haze complied with his request and after the scene the pin had to be removed with a pair of pliers.

"Now there's a follow-up to all of this," Dick Miller said. "A couple of years later I was doing a *McCloud* and I was working with one of the finest actors in the business: Joseph Wiseman. Marvelous, brilliant actor. Maybe one of the ten best in the business. We're shooting on the Universal lot at night and David Stewart's name came up. And I started telling him the story about this idiot, this moron, this asshole, this imbecile. I go on and on and Wiseman looks at me and says, 'You know David Stewart is dead.' It turned out that he'd died of a heart attack three or four months prior to this night. And then Wiseman says, 'David Stewart was my dearest friend.' And I felt like crap. All night long I kept looking over at Wiseman. When we finished shooting we all went back to the trailers to change and he says, 'Come on in the car with me.' We got in the car and I said, 'Joseph, I really gotta apologize for what I said. I don't even know how to say this to you.' He said, 'Well, I don't know how to say this to you but I don't know who David Stewart is.'"

Creature from the Haunted Sea. "**What Was the Unspeakable Secret of the SEA OF LOST SHIPS?**" 1961 (1959) B&W 63 min. PRO-DIR Roger Corman, SP Charles B. Griffith, DP Jacques Marquette, ED Angela Scellars, MUS Fred Katz. Filmgroup.

The Cast: Antony Carbone (Renzo Capeto), Betsy-Jones Moreland (Mary-Belle), Edward Wain (Sparks Moran), Edmundo Rivera Alvarez (Colonel Tostada), Robert Bean (Jack), Sonya Noemi (Mango).

The Story: During a revolution on a small island in the Caribbean, loyalists steal the National Treasury in order to finance a counter-revolution. To get the treasury off the island they enlist the aid of a smalltime hood named Renzo Capeto who agrees to take the revolutionists and the national treasury to safety in his boat. Among Renzo's cohorts are his girlfriend, Mary-Belle, her brother Jack, and Sparks Moran who is, unbeknownst to them, a secret service agent. Renzo intends to steal the treasury and do away with Colonel Tostada and Major Casa Grande and their small squad and blame their deaths on a mythical sea monster.

A real monster, however, lurks in the waters through which the boat must travel. It kills some of the soldiers and Renzo concludes the best way to get the treasury is to sink the boat and come back for the chest later. They land on an unpopulated island and use it as a base from which to search for the treasure. The monster is furious with this invasion of his privacy and picks them off one by one until only Sparks Moran and his girlfriend are left.

Behind the Scenes: Roger was in Havana with Bernard and Larry Woolner, hoping to make a movie for Cuban Color Films, when Fidel Castro took over the town. The sound of machine gun fire in the middle of the night and the report the next morning that people had been gunned down in the streets sent Roger and the Woolners back to New Orleans where things were a little safer. This horrendous event was the inspiration for *Creature from the Haunted Sea*, packaged with Filmgroup's *The Devil's Partner.*

Roger had gone to Puerto Rico to make two pictures back to back, *The Last Woman on Earth* and *The Battle of Blood Island*, then decided to stay an extra week and make a third movie. He telephoned Chuck Griffith to write a horror comedy. Griffith said he couldn't come up with anything in the amount of time Roger was giving him (Griffith says three days, Roger says six) but Roger cajoled him, told him how great the other comedies had been *(A Bucket of Blood, The Little Shop of Horrors),* and Griffith ended up mailing the script to him in pieces with a part for Roger to play—Happy Jack Monahan. It was, by design, the most difficult role in the movie. "Brando would've had trouble with it," Roger remarked. He wisely gave the part to his boom man, Bobby Beam.

Beam and Beach Dickerson made the "Creature for $150 out of oil cloth, army helmets, steel wool, and ping-pong balls.

The Day the World Ended. **"Attacked by a Creature from Hell!"** 1956 B&W/Scope 82 min. PRO-DIR Roger Corman, EXEC PRO Alex Gordon, SP Lou Rusoff, DP Jock Feindel, ED Ronald Sinclair, SPFX Paul Blaisdell, MUS Ronald Stein. Golden State/American Releasing Corporation.

The Cast: Richard Denning (Rick), Lori Nelson (Louise Maddison), Adele Jergens (Ruby), Touch Connors (Tony), Paul Birch (Jim Maddison), Raymond Hatton (Pete), Paul Dubov (Radek), Jonathan Haze (stage two), Paul Blaisdell (Mutant).

The Story: A narrator explains that the world as we know it was wiped out by a nuclear war. But even though humankind had done everything in their power to destroy themselves, God had intervened and in His infinite wisdom has spared a few, though He clearly demonstrates a lapse of judgment by sparing a sociopathic hood named Tony and his sleazy lady friend Ruby, who are the first to find the secluded home of a retired naval captain named Jim Maddison. Maddison's home is a fortress, stocked with food and supplies and powered by its own gas generator. Maddison's been preparing for this day for quite some time but he's only got enough supplies for himself, his daughter Louise, and Louise's fiancé who they presume was killed in the blast.

Shortly after Tony and Ruby burst into the place a geologist named Rick stumbles in carrying Radek, who has been exposed to too much radiation. An

The Day the World Ended (American Releasing Corp., 1956): top, Corman gives instructions to Adele Jergens; bottom: Richard Denning and Lori Nelson rehearse.

old prospector named Pete arrives with his donkey, leaving Maddison to wonder how he's going to feed them all. Worse still, Radek appears to be evolving into the man of the future as his body adapts to a world poisoned by radiation. Then a stranger staggers into the valley in an even more advanced state of mutation than Radek. There are more like him in the hills, the stranger says shortly before he dies. A lot more. And stronger.

The strongest of the lot turns out to be Louise's fiancé, who's been transformed into a three-eyed, four-armed, crusty-skinned monstrosity that telepathically calls to Louise and lures her from the house. Once in the woods the creature carries her away. Rick tries to rescue her but he's no match for the mutant, even with a rifle. Fortunately, God intervenes again and the pure rain water He sends down destroys the mutant who can only live in contamination. The water acts like acid. In the end only Rick and Louise are left to repopulate the world.

Behind the Scenes: The grotesque looking creature for this film was the handiwork of monster-maker Paul Blaisdell who, together with his wife Jackie, supplied many of the beasties and unusual props for Roger Corman's early productions. Blaisdell also enjoyed portraying the monsters he made which, because he was only five foot two, often created problems. As a general rule of thumb, monsters were rather tall, so Blaisdell made Marty (his nickname for the mutant) a head taller which meant that in order to see he had to look through the mouth. Which meant that the mutant's chest was level with Blaisdell's chin.

"I knew there was going to be a problem when the time came for me to carry Lori Nelson," Blaisdell remarked. "She was five feet tall and I think she weighed a hundred pounds. I weighed a hundred and forty-two pounds. I said, 'Okay, I can lift you right off the ground, Lori, if you'll take a big swing at me and say, 'No, no, you beast!' or whatever and hook your arm over the back of my neck.' Now, if you ever see that scene again you'll see that Lori's doing it. I said, 'Now just hold on tight and up we go.' And everything worked out fine until my foot landed in a gopher hole. Karl Brainard and his buddy Dick Rubin had done a terrific job of smoothing the ground out but I guess they didn't see that hole. I told Lori, 'I gotta take a fall. I'm going over on my back. You can land on my rubber chest so let's not worry about it—let's just dooooooooo-iiiiiittttt!' I hit the ground and Lori landed on my chest, just the way we'd planned. And because it was made of rubber she bounced which made her giggle. And the more she giggled the more she bounced.

"As far as I'm concerned, in that picture, I think Lori did a beautiful scene when I was supposed to wiggle my antenna and send radio waves to make her leave the house and she got up out of bed hypnotized. Those big, beautiful eyes, wide open, staring. Everybody thought Lori did a beautiful job on that scene. Cause you'd swear from her acting that she was clear out of this world. As far as having a sense of humor goes, Lori posed with me for Bill Clarey, the still photographer, for a publicity photo where we're doing a soft-shoe dance. And I still have an eight by ten photograph of it that I wouldn't give up for the world. And speaking of photographs, you know the one that Lori keeps in a frame beside her bed in the movie, which is supposed to be her with her fiancé before he developed a third eye. Look closely the next time you watch the movie and you'll see the guy in that photo is Roger Corman."

On the subject of Roger Corman, Blaisdell had this to say: "I believe he was getting (now I say I *believe* this, I don't know for sure, but I believe he was getting) a fixed rate to do a picture; so many thousands of dollars. Now, he could do the picture in two days or two hundred days, but he'd still get the same amount of money. So, he would start a panic and do it in two days. From a business point of view there's nothing wrong with that. But from the standpoint of theatrics and narrative technique, Shakespeare he ain't. I do have some admiration for Roger. I did like to see some of the pictures he went on to do like *Fall of the House of Usher* and stuff like that which was really good; not the grade B stuff he hammered and tried to rush out for AIP."*

But since it was economically imperative for Roger to "hammer" out his productions, Paul Blaisdell's ability to design and create monsters and props with remarkable efficiency and speed made him one of the most valuable members of the Corman team. Yet, when both Roger and American International moved on to bigger budgeted films in the early sixties, Blaisdell fell out of favor and was more or less forgotten by everyone but his most devoted fans until recently, when a Japanese company began manufacturing a line of impeccably accurate monster models. Blaisdell's creations have proven to be the most popular of the lot. It's unfortunate that he didn't live long enough to enjoy his resurgence. Paul Blaisdell died of cancer in 1983. He'd spent his later years in seclusion, wondering why Hollywood had left him behind.

His credits include: *The Beast with 1,000,000 Eyes, The Day the World Ended, The She-Creature, It Conquered the World* (all 1956), *The Amazing Colossal Man, Invasion of the Saucer-Men, The Cat Girl, Not of This Earth, Voodoo Woman, From Hell It Came* (all 1957), *Attack of the Puppet People, Earth Vs. the Spider, It! the Terror from Beyond Space* (all 1958).

Five Guns West. "The Story of Five Reckless Men!" 1955 C 78 min. PRO-DIR Roger Corman, SP R. Wright Campbell, DP Floyd Crosby, ED Ronald Sinclair, MUS Buddy Bregman. Palo Alto/American Releasing Corporation.

The Cast: John Lund (Govern Sturgess), Dorothy Malone (Shalee), Touch Connors (Hale Clinton), Paul Birch (J.C. Haggard), James Stone (Uncle Mime), Bob Campbell (John Morgan Candy), Jonathan Haze (William Parcel Candy), Jack Ingram (Stephen Jethro), Larry Thor (Southern Captain), Jack Bohrer, Lionel Place, William Taylor.

The Story: Desperate for men during the last days of the War Between the States (a title plate informs us), the South found it necessary to offer pardons to outlaws to carry out special assignments. Strange dark figures rode under the flag of the Confederacy, and when this picture opens we are introduced to five of them: Bill Candy, who robbed and murdered four people; John Candy, who killed two lawmen during his attempt to free his brother Bill from jail; J.C.

This reminiscence is from an interview with Paul Blaisdell by the author.

Haggard, blamed for the death of two lawmen and three of his own men when he drove cattle to New Orleans in defiance of the law; Hale Clinton, who shot an unarmed man during a card game; and Govern Sturgess, supposedly another cutthroat, but who is actually a Confederate officer.

These men are supposed to ambush a stagecoach carrying a spy named Stephen Jethro who has absconded with $30,000 in Confederate gold. The ambush point is a waystation called Downey Springs on Union turf, deserted except for a young woman named Shalee and her worthless, drunken uncle. Shalee is quite an attraction, especially to Bill, who forces himself on her and, when she refuses him, begins to strangle her until his brother intervenes. "You shouldn't walk around alone," John warns her. "My brother's funny. He gets ta wantin' things. Wantin' can be a bad thing sometimes. Can boil up in a man's guts like cactus spines. Man's gotta rid himself of it." With little else to do while they're waiting for the stage, Hale Clinton also makes a pass at Shalee and is no more successful than Bill. "You got a lot to learn about patience," J.C. tells him. "I'm patient enough when the chips are on the table," Hale replies. "I just want the game to get started."

When the stage finally arrives, and the soldiers escorting it are killed, the group learns that Jethro has already deposited the gold with Wells Fargo in San Francisco. Naturally, everyone but Govern Sturgess wants to ride with Jethro to Frisco so he can draw out the money, but Govern Sturgess insists on taking the spy back to the Confederacy and that's when the bullets start flying. First to go is Bill, who never did like just sittin'. (Throughout the picture Bill says things like "I don't like this sittin'" and "I'm gettin' sick of this hangin' around" which is pretty suicidal stuff for a picture as talky as this one.) Brother John slips under the house and tries to kill Sturgess through the floor but Sturgess gets the drop on him and the gambler. J.C. thinks better of the whole thing and rides away as soon as the trouble starts. Sturgess takes Jethro back with a promise to Shalee that he'll return.

Behind the Scenes: *"Five Guns West* was the first picture that Roger directed," said Jonathan Haze who played the role of Bill Candy, a psychopathic killer. "It was written by a friend of mine, Bobby Campbell, who wrote a good part for me and himself. I staged all the fights in it. And if I stage a fight, and I'm in it, I never lose. Which was funny because Mike Connors was in the picture only he was Touch Connors in those days, and he was this big guy, you know, and I was this little guy, but I'd lick him in all the fights and I think that kind of ticked him off."

Haze told Sharon Williams in *Filmfax:* "Here I was, a kid from Pittsburgh who had *maybe* ridden a pony in the park, and suddenly I was riding horses.... I got Roger to make a deal to send me, Bobby Campbell and Touch Connors out to Fat Jones' ranch for two weeks.... Fat had his son-in-law take us out into a field up there and work us out on the horses. It turned out his son-in-law was Ben Johnson. So, at any rate, we learned to ride and we did the picture. A bunch of Easterners doing a western."[1]

---

1. *Sharon Williams, "Jonathan Haze Interviewed,"* Filmfax, *vol. 1, no. 5, p. 36.*

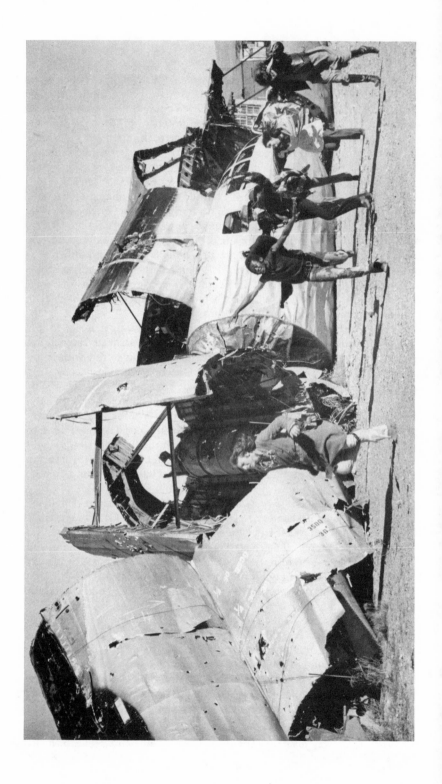

Gas-s-s-s! Or It Became Necessary to Destroy the World in Order to Save It. **"Lay a Little Fun on Yourself!"** 1970 C 79 min. PRO-DIR Roger Corman, SP George Armitage, DP Ron Dexter, ED George Van Noy, ART DIR David Nichols, MUS Country Joe and the Fish, Barry Melton. American International.

The Cast: Robert Corff (Coel), Elaine Giftos (Cilla), Pat Patterson (Demeter), George Armitage (Billy the Kid), Alex Wilson (Jason), Alan Braunstein (Dr. Drake), Ben Vereen (Carlos), Cindy Williams (Marissa), Bud Cort (Hooper), Talia Coppola (Coralie), Country Joe and "The Fish" (F.M. Radio), Lou Procopio (Marshall McLuhan), Jackie Farley (Ginny), Phil Borneo (Quant), Bruce Karcher (Edgar Allan Poe).

The Story: At a defense plant in Alaska, a mysterious gas which speeds up the aging process is accidentally released. Everyone over 25 dies within a matter of days. Coel and Cilla learn that Dallas is going to be a police state and decide to look elsewhere to start a new life. They travel across Texas and New Mexico and experience a series of bizarre encounters. They find that the kids are simply repeating the patterns and prejudices of their parents and elders before them. Coel and Cilla, along with Carlos, Marissa, Hooper and Coralie, try to find a commune established in an old Indian pueblo, Acoma, in New Mexico. They arrive at a drive-in where hippies and young people abound. Coel makes love with a beautiful young blonde on the roof of the drive-in, which Cilla seems to accept. F.M. Radio, the leader of the only rock group around, is like a god to the kids at the Lone Star Drive-In, a role which he enjoys even when the voice of God interrupts him from time to time. Later, the group is captured by Jason and the Nomads (not be to confused with Jason and the Argonauts or the Jason that keeps hanging around that summer camp that stays open in spite of its inability to deliver the fun and frolic expected of such camps), a football team that terrorize everyone they meet. Finally, Coel, Cilla and the gang end up in the hands of Marshall McLuhan and by this time Coel has decided to change the image of his little group in the hope of fitting in, only to discover the "middle classes" are now dressing in "Angels" colors. They escape from the middle class with the help of a black lady named Ginny and finally reach the commune.

Behind the Scenes: In the cutting room, Roger is with UCLA's George von Voy running a sequence from *Gas-s-s-s* through the moviola. The Texas warriors are looting a store. According to Digby Diehl ("Roger Corman: The Simenon of Cinema"), Roger asks, "'George, why did you cut off the beginning of this scene, where they throw rocks through the showcase window in that store?' 'Well I just thought that the sight of those rocks bouncing off the window sort of destroyed the illusion of the scene, Roger,' replied von Voy in an amused tone. 'The rocks bounced off the glass?' said Roger incredulously. George nodded. 'Well, I guess that wouldn't be too good.'"

Gas-s-s-s (AIP, 1970) presented newcomer Ben Vereen (second from left).

Gunslinger. "Hired to Kill the Woman He Loved!" 1956 C 83 min. PRO-DIR Roger Corman, SP Charles B. Griffith, Mark Hanna, DP Fred West, ED Charles Gross, MUS Ronald Stein. Santa Clara/American Releasing Corporation.

The Cast: John Ireland (Cane Miro), Beverly Garland (Rose Hood), Allison Hayes (Erica Page), Martin Kinsley (Gideon Polk), Jonathan Haze (Jake Hays), Chris Alcaide (Joshua Tate), Dick Miller (Jimmy Tonto), Bruno Ve Sota (Zebelon Tab), William Schallert (Scott Hood), Chris Miller (Tessie-Belle), Margaret Campbell, Aaron Saxon, George Opperman, Paul McGuire, Susan Cummings.

The Story: When a Texas marshal is murdered, his widow—Rose Hood—assumes office. And she remains the only real opposition to Erica Page's plans to illegitimately purchase as much property as she can, which she's been doing ever since she learned the railroad's coming to town. Erica hires Cane Miro, a gunslinger, to take care of the troublemakers, which include the sheriff. But Cane falls in love with Rose and kills Erica instead. Compelled by duty, even though she loves him, Rose shoots Cane in a showdown.

Behind the Scenes: For years Chuck Griffith told the story of how *Gunslinger* came about. Roger Corman took him to a western titled *Three Hours to Kill* and told him to write the same picture with a twist—change the lead from male to female. Except Griffith said it was a Randolph Scott western and Randolph Scott never made a picture called *Three Hours to Kill*.

"Well," said Griffith, "it was *a* Randolph Scott western and Roger was going to shoot for three days at Ingram's Ranch in Topanga Canyon." (It's a mobile home park now.) "It had a town street with a few acres of scrub around it. The usual bullshit. And the other three days were going to be shot out at Iverson's Ranch out past Chatsworth. So I went out to Ingram's and copied the names off the signs to use for the characters' names. That way they wouldn't have to re-do the signs. By then I knew where Roger was at. And I had a look around the land and I figured out that if you looked this way and that you could write the exteriors of the whole picture there and save thirty minutes a day each way, which was a whole shooting day on a six day picture. Roger was delighted. We shot the whole thing at Ingram's. That was going to be the last six day picture. It went seven. Roger was very bitter."

One of the reasons the picture went a day over schedule was because it rained almost every day.

"It wasn't bad rain," Griffith added. "We didn't use lights anyway, just reflectors. And there was nothing to reflect so it was all subtle. It actually gave the picture a more interesting look."

Both female leads suffered casualties. Allison Hayes fell off her horse and broke her arm. And Beverly Garland....

"I was supposed to run down these stairs, leap on my horse and ride out of town," Miss Garland recalled. "The first time I did it I went right over the horse. The second time I twisted my ankle 'cause I was in these awful boots. But I got on the horse and finished the scene. The next day I couldn't get my boot on because my foot was the size of a football. Of course, I had to finish the picture. There were only a couple of days left and Roger couldn't replace me. With Roger you always worked. I mean, you could have one eye hanging and he'd just shoot you from another angle. You really had to be a trooper. But he was a brilliant man. When you went on location with Roger you knew that if the director died, and the script got lost, and the cameraman broke his neck, the picture would still get made 'cause Roger knew how to do everything. And he did it well. So, anyway, Roger called this doctor. I don't think he was a real doctor. Maybe a horse doctor or something. He gave me a shot of novocaine in my ankle bone that almost sent me through the roof. They had to slit my boot to get it on my foot which made Roger crazy because I think he probably rented it or something. Anyway, they taped the boot on my foot and I worked all day. Fight scenes, of course, that's all I had left to do. Fight scenes. After that I couldn't walk for a week."

Even the less vigorous moments of the film held potential for disaster. A love scene between Beverly and John Ireland was transformed into a scene out of *The Naked Jungle*. The two were sitting in a tree, chilled to the bone, when they were attacked by an army of red ants.

Nothing seemed to go right. Roger was traumatized by the experience. It was his last western.

The Haunted Palace. "What Was the Hideous Thing in the PIT That Came to Honor Her?" 1963 C-Scope 85 min. PRO-DIR Roger Corman, EXEC PRO James H. Nicholson, Samuel Z. Arkoff, SP Charles Beaumont based on "The Strange Case of Charles Dexter Ward" by H.P. Lovecraft, DP Floyd Crosby, ED Ronald Sinclair, ART DIR Daniel Haller, MUS Ronald Stein. Alta Vista/American International.

The Cast: Vincent Price (Joseph Curwen/Charles Dexter Ward), Debra Paget (Ann Ward), Lon Chaney, Jr. (Simon Orne), John Dierkes (Jacob West), Leo Gordon (Ezra Weeden), Elisha Cook (Peter Smith), Frank Maxwell (Marinus Willett), Milton Parsons (Jabez Hutchinson), Cathy Merchant (Hester Tillinghast), Guy Wilkerson (Leach), Harry Ellerbe (minister), Darlene Lucht (woman), Barboura Morris (Mrs. Weeden), Bruno Ve Sota (bartender).

The Story: Charles Dexter Ward comes to a small New England fishing village to claim his inheritance, the house of his great-great-grandfather, Joseph Curwen. He's given a cool reception by the locals, the reason for which is eventually explained by a sympathetic doctor named Willett. "One hundred and fifty years ago a man named Joseph Curwen moved to this village and built this palace," Willett says. "His first wife died in childbirth. So he selected the most beautiful woman in the village and took her for his mistress. Unfortunately, she was engaged to marry an Arkanite named Ezra Weeden.... Well, according to legend, a number of strange things occurred when Curwen moved into the village. Terrible noises were heard in the night.... Young girls were said to have disappeared from their homes, to be gone until dawn and then reappear with no memory of their whereabouts.

"Weeden wasted no time in placing the blame directly on his doorstep.... He claimed Curwen was a warlock. Then, one night the people of this village marched on this palace, dragged your ancestor into the yard and burned

Leo Gordon (center) thinks Vincent Price (far left) should fry. John Dierkes (far right) and Frank Maxwell (third from right) are among the many who agree — from *The Haunted Palace* (AIP, 1963).

him. . . . Curwen put a curse on the village. He vowed he would return. It was thought he'd gained possession of a book called *Necronomicon* — enough secrets to give a man absolute power, it contained formulas through which one could summon the elder gods, the dark ones from beyond who once ruled the world."

The doctor recommends that Ward leave the village which Ward ultimately decides to do until he becomes possessed by the spirit of Curwen. One by one the ancestors of the men who killed the warlock are murdered. "I'll not have my fill of revenge until this village is a graveyard," Curwen tells his henchmen. "Till they have felt as I have the kiss of fire on their soft bare flesh." Curwen succeeds in resurrecting his dead wife, then plans to mate Ward's wife Ann with a thing from Hell when the villagers storm the palace and set fire to the place. Believing Ward is back in possession of himself, the doctor helps him to safety. "I don't know how I can ever repay you for what you've done, Dr. Willet," Curwen says. "But I intend to try."

"The moral is that you can't keep a keen warlock down — and who would want to, when he's so debonair a chap as Price, telling an unwilling but admiring visitor to his torture chamber 'Ah, yes, Torquemada spent many a happy hour here, a few centuries ago,'" said the *New York Herald Tribune*.

Behind the Scenes: This project was first conceived while Roger was working on *The Premature Burial* and at that time he'd planned to use the two principals from that picture—Ray Milland and Hazel Court—along with Boris Karloff. It was going to be titled *The Haunted Village*. By the time Roger was ready to make the picture, Milland and Court were dropped in favor of Vincent Price and Debra Paget. Karloff had taken ill while he was working on a picture in Italy so he was replaced by Lon Chaney. Then AIP insisted on changing the title to *The Haunted Palace* which was the title of an Edgar Allan Poe poem. In spite of the fact that the film was based on a story by H.P. Lovecraft, AIP wanted to sell it as another Poe movie because they were having such a great success with their other Poe pictures. Then producer Irwin Allen tried to stop them from using the title, on the basis of a prior claim. Obviously he had none.

"I usually go to the theater to see the films that I've scored just to see if what I accomplished came out the way it should for the effect in the audience," said Ronald Stein who composed the wonderfully eerie music for the picture. Stein told Randall Larson in *CinemaScore*: "The first night *The Haunted Palace* came out I went to a small theater on Hollywood Boulevard and I was sitting toward the back, and in front of me was sitting a little girl and what looked like her parents on either side. And, I don't know if there was too much theme, but about the last time Vincent Price walks down this hall (Roger Corman often has endless halls that people have to walk down to get places!) and while he was doing that the theme came in again . . . and it's about the third time you've heard that theme, and the little girl said out loud, 'Oh! That *music!*' Well, that made my evening, because she meant it in a kind of excruciatingly electrifying or exotic way."[1]

House of Usher. **"In the Tradition of *Wuthering Heights* and *Diabolique* . . . a Motion Picture You Will Never Forget!"** 1960 C-Scope 80 min. PRO-DIR Roger Corman, EXEC PRO James H. Nicholson, SP Richard Matheson based on Edgar Allan Poe's "The Fall of the House of Usher," DP Floyd Crosby, ART DIR Daniel Haller, ED Anthony Carras, SPFX Pat Dinga, MUS Les Baxter. Alta Vista/American International.

The Cast: Vincent Price (Roderick Usher), Mark Damon (Philip Winthrop), Myrna Fahey (Madeline Usher), Harry Ellerbe (Bristol), Bill Borzage, Mike Jordan, Madajan, Ruth Oklander, George Paul, David Andar, Eleanor Le Faber, Geraldine Paulette, Phil Sylvestre, John Zimeas.

The Story: Philip Winthrop arrives at the brooding Usher mansion to collect his fiancée, Madeline Usher who, he is told, is ill. Her brother, Roderick, is against the marriage. He warns Winthrop that a history of madness runs in the Usher family. But after a few hours of listening to Roderick plead with him to leave without Madeline, Winthrop is convinced that the only hope for her sanity is to get her out of the house. On the morning of their departure, Winthrop finds Madeline dead on her bed. At least, he thinks she's dead. It's only

1. *Randall D. Larson, "The Film Music of Ronald Stein",* CinemaScore, *no. 13, p. 54.*

The crew — Chuck Hannawalt (left), Roger Corman, Harry Reif and Jack Bohrer — on *House of Usher* (AIP, 1960).

after she's been buried that he learns from Bristol the butler that she suffers from cataleptic fits. Winthrop confronts Roderick with the possibility that he buried his sister alive and after being badgered Roderick confesses that he did just that.

"But she's dead now," he assures Winthrop who races to the crypt and finds a trail of blood leading away from the coffin. And then he finds Madeline. She *is* crazy now and she tries to strangle him then goes after Roderick. During the struggle a violent storm shakes the house, causing a split in a fissure. The house catches fire and begins to sink. Winthrop watches helplessly as a chunk of the roof, engulfed in flames, falls on Madeline and Roderick. Bristol drags Winthrop to safety then races back into the inferno to die. As Winthrop walks away the house sinks into the mire.

Behind the Scenes: *House of Usher* was a winner. If it hadn't been, American International would have been out of business. They sank over three hundred thousand bucks into it, more than triple the budget of any movie they'd ever made. Television had forced them into it. The quality of television programming had gone up. It was in color now and a lot of familiar faces were popping up. To compete, AIP had to spend more money. They had to hire a name actor, shoot it in color and CinemaScope, and do the best they could to make it look more expensive than it was. But who exactly decided that an Edgar Allan Poe movie would be the safest bet is anybody's guess.

Charles Griffith was hurt that Roger didn't ask him to write it. He'd written Roger's best movies and it seemed to him that he was being given the short end. But AIP wanted to put up the best possible front. Along with the name actor they hired a name writer, Richard Matheson.

"It was irritating," Griffith remarked, "because I saw Roger was making a value judgment based on how much money people were making and *he* was the one making policy. He said that no screen writer who gets less than fifty thousand a script is any good."

Griffith has been interviewed a number of times and he usually has little good to say about his days with Roger Corman, criticizing the way the movies were made, their short schedules, their tight budgets, and the derivative nature of their scripts. Angrily he recounts episodes where Roger "played it safe" instead of trying something a little unconventional, yet when Griffith produced, directed and wrote his own movies for Columbia he did exactly what he accuses Roger of doing. He admits he copped out but for some reason it makes him no more tolerant, which seems a little unfair if not downright hypocritical. And it should be noted that even though the movies Roger made from Griffith's scripts may have been far from the writer's vision they were hardly what you'd call conventional. At least, some of them. It would have been interesting to see what Griffith would have come up with for *House of Usher*. When he was finally asked to write a Poe movie he turned in a three hundred page comedy supposedly based on *The Gold Bug*. Sam Arkoff wasn't impressed.

But the critics were impressed by *House of Usher*. *The New York Tribune* called it "a restoration of finesse and craftsmanship to the genre of the dread." *The Los Angeles Examiner* said Roger deserved an accolade for achieving the impossible: "a film that kids will love that never once insults adult intelligence." The movie played for months, as opposed to AIP's usual hit-and-run operation.

I, Mobster. "The Life of a Gangster!" 1958 B&W 80 min. PRO Gene Corman, DIR Roger Corman, SP Steve Fisher from the novel "I, Mobster" by J.H. Smyth, DP Floyd Crosby, ED William B. Murphy, ART DIR Daniel Haller, MUS Gerald Fried and Edward L. Alperson. 20th Century–Fox.

The Cast: Steve Cochran (Joe Sante), Lita Milan (Teresa Porter), Robert Strauss (Black Frankie), Celia Lovsky (Mrs. Sante), Lili St. Cyr (herself), Jeri Southern (Jeri), John Brinkley (Ernie Porter), Yvette Vickers, Grant Withers (Paul Moran), John Mylong (Mr. Sante), Wally Cassell (Cherry-Nose), Robert Shayne (Senator), Frank Gerstle (District Attorney), Dick Miller, Frank Wolff, Walter Maslow, Dave Tomack.

The Story: Joe Sante, a second generation Italian-American, starts out in a slum neighborhood as a collector for bookies, advances to pushing narcotics, is promoted by businesslike murder to eminence in the syndicate and finally becomes a crime czar, only to wind up before a Senate Rackets Investigating Committee. The publicity renders him valueless to the underworld and he is liquidated by his most trusted henchman. Along the way, he disgusts his hard-

Steve Cochran (left) and Robert Strauss in a scene from *I, Mobster* **(20th Century–Fox, 1958).**

working father and breaks his mother's heart. He murders his dope-addicted brother and cheapens the woman who loves him.

    Behind the Scenes: In May of 1950, an obscure Tennessee legislator named Estes Kefauver organized a Special Committee to Investigate Organized Crime, which was televised to some 20 million captivated viewers. As questions were fired at the parade of colorful mobsters, theater attendance dropped drastically until some clever theater owners had the sense to pipe the political sideshow on their screens for free. What they lost in ticket sales they made up for at the snack bar. The framing device for *I, Mobster* is obviously patterned after the Kefauver hearings.

The Intruder. 1962 B&W 80 min. PRO-DIR Roger Corman, EXEC PRO Gene Corman, SP Charles Beaumont based on his novel, DP Taylor Byars, ED Ronald Sinclair, MUS Ronald Stein. Pathe American/Filmgroup.

The Cast: William Shatner (Adam Cramer), Frank Maxwell (Tom McDaniel), Beverly Lunsford (Ella McDaniel), Robert Emhardt (Verne Shipman), Jeanne Cooper (Vi Griffin), Leo Gordon (Sam Griffin), Charles Barnes (Joey Green), Charles Beaumont (Harley Paton), Katherine Smith (Ruth McDaniel), George Clayton Johnson (Phil West), William F. Nolan (Bart Carey), Phoebe Row (Mrs. Lambert), Bo Dodd (sheriff), Walter Kurtz (Gramps), Oceo Ritch (Jack Allardyce).

The Story: Adam Cramer, a member of the reactionary Patrick Henry Society, arrives in a small Southern town to stir up the white citizens into opposing integration of the local schools. Cramer ingratiates himself with the townspeople and persuades them to harass black youngsters attending the previous all-white school. Cramer's only articulate opponent is a newspaper editor named McDaniel. Cramer charms his way into the bed of Vi Griffin, a lonely woman married to a traveling salesman. When her husband Sam returns, the guilt-ridden woman runs away and Sam senses that Cramer is responsible.

In the meantime the town's mood becomes increasingly more violent. A black minister is killed when a bomb is tossed into his church. McDaniel loses an eye in a confrontation when he leads black students into the school. Cramer warns McDaniel's teen-aged daughter Ella that he will kill her father unless she accuses a young black, Joey Green, of attempted rape. The frightened girl agrees and a lynch-hungry mob lashes the boy to a schoolyard swing. But Ella confesses her lie and the crowd, furious and ashamed, withdraws, leaving Cramer without support.

Behind the Scenes: Of all of Corman's films, *The Intruder* is certainly his most personal picture, perhaps his *only* personal picture, and it was, in every respect, a daring picture to make.

"We filmed it in St. Charles, Missouri," said actor Leo Gordon who played Sam Griffin in the film. "They told us to pack up and get out with a police escort. Hard-nosed, goddamn people. The bartender wore a pistol in his belt and had a blackjack in his pocket. All of them looked and sounded like Slim Pickins."

Corman risked his own money and more or less risked his life to make what was essentially a noncommercial film. I asked him why.

"I simply wanted to make the film. I was interested in the subject. I've been a life-long liberal, or a man of the left wing of the political spectrum. I was intensely concerned with the civil rights movement and I wanted to make a film about it. I didn't expect to make a great deal of money but on the other hand I didn't expect to lose. But, indeed, it was my first loss. I don't know how many films I'd made before — ten, fifteen — and they'd all been successes. This was the first one that lost money. The reviews were wonderful. I can still remember after all these years one of the papers said: 'This motion picture is a credit to the entire motion picture film industry.' Which is very nice to have but as I say it was the first film that lost money.

"I think the subject was unpopular in the country at the time and because it was unpopular the film didn't get played. Although the reviews were very good and it won a couple of awards at secondary film festivals (although it went to the Venice Film Festival and some major festivals as well) I think ultimately the film was not as good as it might have been, although I'm very pleased with it. It was shot in three weeks under extraordinarily difficult conditions in the American South where we were being harassed both by the law and the citizens.

"I think I was letting my personal feelings come too strongly to the surface so it became too obviously a message picture. Too preachy is a better way to say it. After that I've made films of varying degrees of seriousness in which I attempted to make certain statements, but I've always clothed those statements. Going back to my Stanislavski training as an actor, they talked about the text and the subtext, the text being the surface manifestation, the subtext being the unconscious meaning. In *The Intruder* both the text and the subtext were the same. I'd not studied enough, did not know enough at the time to realize dramatically that was wrong.

"Since then, and this may be somewhat of an excuse for commercial intentions, I've attempted to maintain my personal beliefs as a subtextural element in filmmaking while the surface will be something more commercial, more exciting. A few years after *The Intruder* I did *The Wild Angels* and *The Trip,* both of which on the surface were exciting and were quite successful, having to do with the youth counter-culture of the period. Underneath, at least to me and to some critics because both of those films did go to film festivals, there was a meaning that was important to me. So after *The Intruder,* I followed that path.

"I remember seeing a cartoon once, I don't know where, years ago, and it showed all of these Elizabethan writers sitting around a tavern, and one of them is saying, 'I say do what Shakespeare does. Give 'em entertainment.'"

It Conquered the World. "Every Man Its Prisoner . . . Every Woman Its Slave!" 1956 B&W 68 min. PRO-DIR Roger Corman, EXEC PRO James H. Nicholson, SP Lou Rusoff, Charles B. Griffith (uncredited), DP Frederick West, ED Charles Gross, SPFX Paul Blaisdell, MUS Ronald Stein. Sunset/American International.

The Cast: Peter Graves (Paul Nelson), Beverly Garland (Claire Anderson), Lee Van Cleef (Tom Anderson), Sally Fraser (Joan Nelson), Russ Bender (Pattick), Jonathan Haze (Manuel Ortiz), Dick Miller (Neil), Karen Kadler (Ellen Peters), Charles B. Griffith (Pete Shelton), Paul Blaisdell (It!).

The Story: A creature from Venus takes up residence at Elephant Hot Springs cave, just outside the sleepy little town of Beechwood, intent on taking over the world. It enlists the support of the key authority figures in the area by implanting control devices in their brains. This It does by producing little bat-like kamikazes that deliver the devices to the backs of their victims' necks the way bees leave their stingers. And the way this creature knows who to control is with the help of Tom Anderson, a scientist who believes the alien has come to save mankind from destroying itself.

Beverly Garland gets her first glimpse of the invader from Venus in *It Conquered the World* (AIP, 1956).

Both Anderson's wife Claire and his best friend Paul Nelson try to convince him that he's playing on the wrong team. In desperation Claire goes to the cave with a shotgun to kill the thing. Meanwhile Paul's trying to talk some sense into Tom so he doesn't have to kill him. "How could he care anything about you?" Paul says. "He doesn't like. He doesn't dislike. He merely reasons, concludes, and uses." Then, over the ham radio that Tom uses to talk to the thing, they hear Claire's screams as the creature crushes her to death. Now Tom knows the truth. He gives Paul a list of the names of everyone who's under the creature's control and while Paul's gunning all of them down Tom goes to the cave with a blowtorch. "I made it possible for you to come here," Tom tells It. "I made you welcome to this earth. You made it a charnel house." Tom shoves the torch into one of the creature's eyes.

But before he can get away the thing crushes him as It's last act. "He learned almost too late that man is a feeling creature," Paul laments over Tom's corpse. "And because of it the greatest in the universe. He learned too late for himself that men have to find their own way, to make their own mistakes. There can't be any gift of perfection from outside ourselves. And when men seek such perfection they find only death, fire, loss, disillusionment, the end of everything that's gone forward. Men have always sought an end to toil and misery. It can't be given. It has to be achieved. There is hope. But it has to come from inside, from man himself."

Behind the Scenes: Science fiction films of the 1950s are notorious for their unconvincing special effects and silly looking monsters but none were more ill conceived than the one Paul Blaisdell designed for Roger Corman's *It Conquered the World*. Because of its shape and unusual appearance *It* has earned a lot of nicknames over the years: the Tee-Pee Terror, the Cucumber Critter, the Carrot Monster. The writer of the film referred to it as Denny Dimwit. Blaisdell affectionately called it Beulah.

"I kept thinking it wasn't finished," said Beverly Garland. "That they were still working on it and when they were done it would be much better somehow. That it would *emerge*. But it never did."

For some reason, Roger takes the blame for Beulah: "Actually, the original idea for that design was mine and I was playing too much back to my early physics classes. Again, this was a long time ago and I don't remember exactly, but to the best of my knowledge, it was supposed to have come from a very big planet. Therefore, obviously, it would have a very heavy gravity; any creature on such a planet would be built very low to the ground. I believe it was scientifically correct, except that when the thing was built, I realized that it was very unfrightening *because* it was so low to the ground. There's something to the concept of fear in looking up to something bigger or taller."

Blaisdell, however, accepts full responsibility himself. According to an interview with Carl Del Vecchio in the *Beverly Garland Fan Club Journal*, Blaisdell was responding to Jim Nicholson's request for something "really different." He told Del Vecchio: "Venus was considered a hot, misty place, given more to the growth of vegetation than animal life. Consequently, intelligent life evolving on such a planet would be more plant-like than mammalian. So I figured we could have a hyper-intelligent mushroom if I could design and build it."

Before constructing the real thing, Blaisdell built it in miniature and took it to Nicholson's home. Nicholson took one look at it and started laughing. "Paul," he said, "you've really done it again. I never thought you'd come up with something so far-out as this!"

The full-size version was built in Blaisdell's studio, in his home in the Topanga Canyon. He used quarter-inch plywood for the frame, covered it with panels of foam rubber, sealed the rubber with contact bond cement and sprayed it with red lacquer. Then he highlighted it with black lacquer. But it looked too smooth so Blaisdell took a hammer to it to give the skin some texture.

And then he couldn't get it through the door.

"I felt like the idiot who built a yacht in his basement," Blaisdell confessed. "I had to take her apart, take her outside, and put her back together again. She was subsequently transferred to the studio in a pick-up truck."

Two days before the picture was supposed to go into production Roger took a look at the script and discovered it didn't make any sense. It had been written by Sam Arkoff's brother-in-law Lou Rusoff. Roger called Chuck Griffith.

"I met him at somebody's house. Mark Hanna's house. Or Roger's house. I remember sitting in a small living room with this script Lou Rusoff had written and I was dropping the pages on the floor like a radio script," Griffith recalled. "I couldn't make heads or tails of what the picture was about. Of course it had to be done immediately so I just sat down and did it without re-reading anything and sort of made it up as I went along. It was really awful. It got some good reviews though because they called it a statement against communism in all the trades."

Beulah was transported to Bronson Canyon for her first big scene.

"She was left out in the open air for the first day of shooting when Roger Corman was having a panic and had all the grips running all over the place, and I'm afraid they trampled all over Beulah's front arms which wrecked the arm and hand controls," Blaisdell complained. (Griffith: "Beverly kicked it over. It came up to her Adam's apple.") "Well, at least I could still get in her and raise the arms. I could reach out with them but no more tricks like taking a handkerchief out of your pocket (which I did with Jim Nicholson). Beulah was thoroughly busted. Well, somebody remembered the script and said, 'Let's get her into the cave.' She was supposed to stay in a niche and menace anyone that came close. But when she wanted to do her outside mischief, she sent out the little fliers which I also designed and made. And they were little Venusian bats if you will. A lot of people thought they were as much fun as Beulah was. Beulah was supposed to stay in the cave but she did not. She just got kicked out of the cave and pushed around. Actually, it wasn't getting pushed, it was me propelling her from inside. Fortunately, I had built casters underneath her. Heavy casters, like the kind you'd use on a piano, so that she could easily be moved from place to place. But as much as I could move her while I was inside of her, she was never designed to be mobile and she looked awkward. But that was all right with Roger. Roger had to get the movie done. Had to get it done as fast as possible. So whose decision was it to bring it into the daylight? Well, that was Roger's decision. Because Roger forgot to get the generator to work the lights in the cave in Bronson quarry. So the only light we had was near the mouth of the cave."

Since there are a number of scenes in the movie that were photographed inside the cave, and they're all well-lit, one can only assume that Blaisdell's recollection of this particular point is questionable.

Blaisdell continued: "My favorite still photographer, Bill Clarey, managed to get a shot of me being menaced by Jonathan Haze. And Jack did a good job. He looked quite desperate and menacing with his G.I. helmet and his bayonet. In the last fading daylight that could illuminate the mouth of the cave, Jonathan Haze, who was one of the soldiers, along with (I believe it was) Dick Miller—they were the comedy relief in the show. Well, Jack charged me and let out a Confederate war whoop with great enthusiasm and let me (or should I say Beulah) have it right between the eyes. Fortunately, I had borrowed a G.I. helmet from Danny Knight who was one of the soldiers. And I had that slammed on top of my head and I was down as far as I could get inside of Beulah. But that bayonet came right through, of course, the foam rubber and the plywood framework, and it went screeching off the top of my helmet. I kept my mouth shut until Roger yelled 'Cut!' Then I said, 'Hey, Jack.' He says, 'Yeah, Paul.' I said, 'Next time will you aim a little higher?' He says, 'Okay.' But Roger got that in one take. In a hurry. As usual. So they just let it go. But as I said, Bill Clarey did get a beautiful shot of that, with Jonathan Haze in a silhouette, and the last light of the setting sun shining in through the cave in Bronson quarry."

Actor Dick Miller told David Everitt in *Fangoria* magazine that he broke his ankle making the picture: "I was a G.I. fighting . . . it looked like an upside-down ice-cream cone monster. . . . I kept yelling, 'Fire and fall back!' There was some extra behind me with a bayonet on the end of his rifle and every time I stepped back he hit me with that bayonet. About the third or fourth take, I realized the bayonet was under my helmet, instinctively, I didn't see it, I just felt it. As I stepped back, sure enough, it hooked my helmet from underneath and I had taken a funny step to get out of the way because I just instinctively knew something was wrong and I broke my ankle doing it. If I hadn't, I probably would've gotten the bayonet through my head. I remember they kept shooting. They'd stand me on one leg and push me past the camera."

Beulah was hit with several explosives which were supposed to simulate bazooka blasts. Roger was in such a hurry to set up the next shot he didn't notice that something unusual was happening.

"Smoke was coming out of the eyes and the mouth and underneath," Miller said. "It looked terrific. So I said, 'No! No! Don't cut!' And Roger yelled 'Cut, I said!' And I said, 'No! Don't!' and we got in this big screaming match. Then he saw what was happening and looked at the camerman and said, 'Did we get that?' And the cameraman said, 'No. You said to cut.' And Roger said, 'Shit!'"

At the end of the picture, Beulah is finally done in by Lee Van Cleef who burns her eye out with a blowtorch. The script called for a close-up of the empty socket oozing blood. Since it was a black and white picture, chocolate syrup was used for the blood.

"I was inside Beulah with a grease gun loaded with Hershey's syrup waiting for Roger to give me the go-ahead," Blaisdell said. "And when he did I squeezed the trigger and nothing happened. So I squeezed it again. Still nothing. What had happened was we'd taken so long to do the shot that by the time we were ready the syrup had turned into a Hershey bar in the barrel of the gun. Of course, by this time Roger's screaming for me to do something so I grabbed the trigger with both hands and gave it everything I had and the next thing I knew I was covered with chocolate. The thing backfired. I told Roger to cut and I crawled out from underneath Beulah and wiped the syrup from my eyes and saw that the gun had not only backfired but apparently I had succeeded in clearing the barrel as well. Because there was chocolate all over Bronson quarry. On the ground, on Roger, and on the cameraman. Well, it took a while but we cleaned ourselves up and went down the road for a bite to eat. We stopped in at this little place and I said, 'Hey, fellas. I think they have a special dessert today. Chocolate cake.' Ha. Ha. Ha."*

The Last Woman on Earth. **"They Fought for the Ultimate Prize!"** 1960 C 71 min. PRO-DIR Roger Corman, SP Robert Towne, DP Jacques Marquette, ED Anthony Carras, ART DIR Floyd Crosby, MUS Ronald Stein. The Filmgroup.

The Cast: Anthony Carbone (Harold), Betsy Jones-Moreland (Evelyn), Edward Wait (a.k.a. Robert Towne as Martin).

The Story: It had been at least ten years since I'd seen this picture when I sat down to write about it, so I went to several different reviews and articles about the picture to refresh my memory. And I have come to this conclusion: either those people hadn't seen the picture in a long time either or there isn't a whole lot to say about it. I recall that there were three people in Puerto Rico. One of them was either a gangster or a gambler and according to the pressbook he was on the lam from the New York police although I don't remember that being part of the plot. Anyway, the gambler has two companions: his slightly alcoholic lady friend and a whining lawyer who's an intellectual snob. The three of them go scuba diving and when they return to the city they find nothing but corpses. While they were underwater the end of the world happened somehow. "A bigger and better bomb, an act of God, what's the difference?" the lawyer says, probably echoing the sentiments of the screenwriter. All the sources tell me that the woman starts to get a hankering for the lawyer. Finally, she runs off with the jerk but the gambler or the gangster catches up to them. The two men duke it out. During the lengthy battle the lawyer goes blind and dies. "I killed him," the gambler notes. And then, as if possessed by the spirit of the lawyer, he asks the lady, "Will we never learn?" "He didn't think so," she replies. "Let's go home," he says. "Where's that?" she asks. "Help me find out," he replies and they walk out of the church, both sounding like the lawyer.

Behind the Scenes: This movie has the distinction of being written by Academy Award winner Robert Towne. He was, in fact, writing *The Last Woman on Earth* as it was being filmed, the way Raymond Chandler once wrote *The Blue Dahlia* (1946). The result, however, was something less than satisfying on both counts.

Since Roger needed to fly Towne to Puerto Rico where the movie was shot, he put Towne to work as an actor. He's billed as Edward Wein and can be seen in *Last Woman* and *The Creature From the Haunted Sea,* filmed back-to-back.

Jacques Marquette was the photographer of both movies. He'd worked with Roger before on *A Bucket of Blood* and had proven himself to be both fast and good. He remembered arriving in Puerto Rico, taking one look at the house Roger had rented for the cast and crew, and immediately checking into the Caribe Hilton.

*Paul Blaisdell's reminiscences are from an interview with the author.

The Little Shop of Horrors. "The Flowers That Kill in the Spring, Tra-la!"
1960 B&W 70 min. PRO-DIR Roger Corman, SP Charles B. Griffith, DP Archie
Dalzell, ED Marshall Neilan, Jr., ART DIR Daniel Haller, MUS Fred Katz.
Santa Clara/Filmgroup.

The Cast: Jonathan Haze (Seymour Krelboing), Jackie Joseph (Audrey),
Mel Welles (Gravis Mushnik), Myrtle Vail (Winfred Krelboing), Dick Miller
(Fouch), Leola Wendorff (Mrs. Shiva), Charles B. Griffith (thief, voice of
plant).

The Story: The sign in the window of Gravis Mushnik's Florist Shop reads:
LOTS PLANTS—CHEAP. Unfortunately, Skid Row isn't exactly an ideal location until Mushnik's moronic but well-meaning gofer crosses a Venus Fly-Trap
with a Buttercup and invents a new hybrid that begins attracting customers by
the droves. Normally the penny-pinching Mushnik treats Seymour pretty shab-
bily but when it looks like the plant, Audrey, Jr. (named after Seymour's dim-
witted but sweet girl friend), might be his ticket out of Skid Row, Mushnik insists the boy call him Dad. "Oh, look Dad. It's dying," Seymour notes and
Mushnik quickly replies, "Who you calling Dad? Who? Who?" Unless
Seymour can figure out a way to keep the plant alive he'll lose his job.

Quite by accident Seymour discovers the plant needs blood and so
Seymour squeezes as much as he can from his fingers. The next morning
Audrey, Jr., has doubled in size but by evening so has its appetite.
"FEEEEEEED MEEEEE," the plant demands but Seymour's fingers are dry.
Seymour wanders into the night, not knowing what to do and absently begins
pitching rocks in the train yard. He accidentally hits a bum in the head. The
bum stumbles dazedly in front of a passing train. Confused and frightened,
Seymour carries the corpse back to Mushnik's and feeds the evidence of his
crime to the plant, witnessed by Mushnik when he returns to the shop to fetch
his wallet. Mushnik considers calling the police but the plant is attracting too
much business.

When a thief breaks into the shop one evening and threatens to kill
Mushnik if he can't produce more money than he has in the cash drawer,
Mushnik tells the thief to look in the plant. "How do I get it open?" the thief
asks. "Just knock," Mushnik replies. The plant makes quick work of the bandit.
But the number of disappearances in the area have not gone unnoticed by Sgt.
Joe Fink and his partner Frank Stoolie, who begin questioning everyone on Skid
Row. They happen to be in Mushnik's place when the plant blooms. In each
bloom is the face of one of its victims. Seymour tries to kill the plant but it gets
the best of him and Seymour becomes another of the blossoms.

Behind the Scenes: Once again this was a film inspired by a standing set.
In fact, according to Roger, it was also the product of a bet. A fellow showed
him a storefront set and asked him if he could use it. Roger said he didn't have
a project in mind but if the guy could leave it up for a couple of weeks not only
would Roger make a picture on it but do it in two days.

"Roger shot for two days on the stage and I directed the exteriors, which
took two days and four nights," said Charles Griffith. "I used skid-row bums
for my crew."

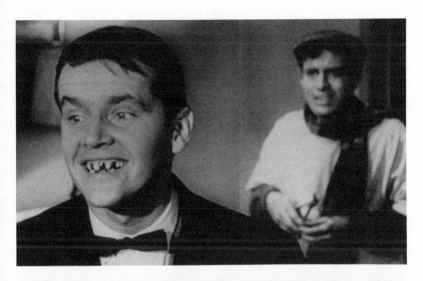

The Little Shop of Horrors (Filmgroup, 1960): top, Jack Nicholson (front) is delighted that Jonathan Haze pulled so many of his teeth; bottom, Haze gives his people-eating plant its first meal.

For ten cents a shot, Griffith hired a chief electrician, a first assistant director, and several bit players. "We had them doing all kinds of things — shooting craps, stabbing each other, falling down.... Mel Welles had fifty pages of dialogue to do each day. There was ad-libbing. Roger didn't know they'd be able to do that."

Over the years, *Little Shop of Horrors* has developed a cult following and is probably better and more fondly remembered than any of Roger's more prestigious productions. It was one of two American films to be shown at the Cannes Film Festival the year of its release and a few years back it was the inspiration for a popular off–Broadway musical written by Howard Ashman, who saw the picture when he was 14 years old. "It was late at night and it was showing on some local station and I thought it was the wittiest thing I had ever seen," Ashman said fondly. Years later, when the idea of turning it into a musical struck him, Ashman screened the picture for his agent who thought it was boring and unfunny. But the show proved to be a success and in 1986 Roger Corman signed a deal with Warner Brothers who turned Ashman's play into a movie. No picture ever gave Roger a better return.

Machine Gun Kelly. **"Without His Gun He Was Naked Yellow!"** 1958 B&W 80 min. PRO-DIR Roger Corman, EXEC PRO James H. Nicholson, Samuel Z. Arkoff, SP R. Wright Campbell, DP Floyd Crosby, ED Ronald Sinclair, ART DIR Daniel Haller, MUS Gerald Fried, El Monte/American International.

The Cast: Charles Bronson (George "Machine Gun" Kelly), Susan Cabot (Florence Eckert), Morey Amsterdam (Michael "Fandango"), Jack Lambert (Howard), Wally Campo (Maize), Bob Griffin (Vito), Barboura Morris (Lynn Rayson), Richard Devon (Apple), Ted Thorp (Teddy), Mitzi McCall (Harriet), Frank De Kova (Harry), Shirley Falls (Martha), Connie Gilchrist (Ma), Michael Fox (Clinton), Larry Thor (Drummond), George Archimbeault (Frank), Jay Sayer (Phillip Ashton).

The Story: George Kelly has a tough reputation. But hiding behind the machine gun is a pussy cat, a guy so frightened of dying that the sight of a coffin causes him to botch up a bank robbery, in which one of his men dies. After that, George decides bank jobs are too risky. Kidnapping's safer. So he and his lady friend Flo set their sights on a rich man's daughter and hold the kid and her nanny for ransom. But the cops surround the hideout before they have a chance to collect. And the reason the cops were able to find them was because George wanted a guy named Fandango to pick up the money. It never occurred to George that Fandango might still be sore because George held him against a leopard's cage and let the animal tear off his arm. When George sees all the cops that Fandango brought with them he wants to surrender but Flo wants him to shoot it out. "You were peddlin' watered down gin when I picked you up," she tells him contemptuously. "I gave you the machine gun, the name, the reputation, the backbone.... You know why? Because you were dumb enough and scared enough. I could use you, make you do anything I wanted you to. You were my gunhand.... I could have had fifty better than you. And I still

Charles Bronson as the notorious *Machine Gun Kelly* (AIP, 1958), a role originally intended for Dick Miller.

can. Only they wouldn't push around so easy." But, George asks, "Why die for nothin'? Just to show that we got some guts? Flo, I don't want to show mine with my life spillin' out of 'em." But Flo wants to go out in a bang so George finally knocks her to the floor before she can start trouble. The cops break in and one of them taunts Kelly. "You got a tough name, Kelly. Why didn't you shoot it out?" "Cuz I knew you'd kill me," Kelly replies simply. The cop grabs his arm. "Come on along, Pop-Gun Kelly."

Behind the Scenes: In real life George Kelly actually did start out as a small-time bootlegger where he would no doubt have stayed had it not been for his ambitious wife Kathryn, who, as the film suggests, pushed him into the big time. And he did get caught for a kidnapping but it wasn't a little girl, it was an Oklahoma oilman.

R. Wright Campbell was asked to write a fictionalized account of Kelly and told that Dick Miller would be playing the lead. Shortly before the picture went into production, Dick Miller was told that he would not be involved in the project and was given the money to buy him out of his contract. Twelve years later he found out why.

It was after Jim Nicholson had severed his connection with American International to go into independent production. Nicholson had an office on Sunset and Dick Miller stopped by one day to drop off some scripts. Although the two had never been close they started talking about old times and one thing led to another and it was then that the story about why Miller had been scratched from *Machine Gun Kelly* came out. Bobby Campbell wanted his brother, William, to get the part and to this end he began making phone calls and sending telegrams from New York. At first, Campbell suggested that Miller (who was supposed to be his friend) was all wrong for the role. Finally, Campbell insisted that only his brother could play it and, in fact, he was tailoring the script to fit him. The whole thing became too much for Nicholson, Arkoff and Roger Corman and they decided to put an end to it by giving the role to Charles Bronson.

"I thought about it many times," Miller said. "I walked away from a lot of parts but this one walked away from me and I really wanted it. I think it would have done for me the same thing it did for Charly."

The Masque of the Red Death. "Can You Face the Horror Behind the Black Door?" 1964 C-Scope 90 min. PRO-DIR Roger Corman, SP Charles Beaumont, R. Wright Campbell from a story by Edgar Allan Poe, ART DIR Daniel Haller, Robert Jones, DP Nicholas Roeg, ED Ann Chegwidden, MUS David Lee. Alta Vista/American International.

The Cast: Vincent Price (Prince Prospero), Hazel Court (Juliana), Jane Asher (Francesca), David Weston (Gino), Patrick Magee (Alfredo), Nigel Green (Ludovico), Skip Martin (Hop Toad), John Westbrook (Man in Red), Gay Brown (Senora Escobar), Julian Burton (Senor Veronese), Doreen Dawn (Anna-Maria), Paul Whitsun-Jones (Scarlatti), Jean Lodge (Scarlatti's Wife), Verina Greenlaw (Esmeralda), Brian Hewlett (Lampredi), Harvey Hall (Clistor), Robert Brown (Guard), David Davies, Sarah Brackett.

The Story: Prince Prospero encounters murmurs of rebellion from the villagers of Esteban when he comes to announce his grand ball. Encouraged by an old woman's prophecy that the day of their deliverance is at hand, a couple of peasants, Gino and Ludovico, criticize Prospero publicly and he orders them sentenced to death. Ludovico's daughter Francesca, who is also Gino's fiancée, pleads for their release. Prospero offers her a choice of lives but her decision is delayed when Prospero learns that the Red Death is sweeping through the town. He quickly returns to the safety of his castle, taking Francesca, Ludovico and Gino with him.

The two men are flung into dungeons while Francesca is given jewels and gowns and instructed in the ways of the Court by Juliana, Prospero's "companion." Francesca learns that Prospero is a follower of Satan and hopes to draw her into his cult. Gino and Ludovico are brought before the assembled guests in the banquet hall to provide amusement. Each is ordered to cut himself with a dagger; there are two and one is dipped in poison. Ludovico lunges swiftly at Prospero who steps aside and stabs Ludovico with his sword. Gino is freed but only to return to his village where the Red Death is rampant, but he vows to return to rescue Francesca. Juliana meanwhile calls on all the evil spirits to give her strength and is killed for her trouble. Prospero takes her death lightly

Vincent Price as Prospero in *The Masque of the Red Death* (AIP, 1964).

since he has been grooming Francesca to take Juliana's place anyway and assembles his guests for the commencement of the Masque Ball. But the arrival of a figure in red puts a damper on the festivities, killing everyone who crosses his path. When Prospero looks into the face beneath the cloak he sees himself just before he dies. Gino and Francesca are reunited.

Behind the Scenes (from the pressbook):

"Over two miles of Corridors were built in sections spreading over three stages for scenes in which Jane Asher runs terrified through the Palace in which she is held prisoner by Prospero in . . . 'The Masque of the Red Death.'

"Director Roger Corman explains the psychological motives for the corridors: 'If you search for the most chilling moment of any horror film you will usually be able to relate it to a scene in which some character is seen in a long corridor, either running away from or approaching some unspecified object of unparalleled terror. The moment *before* this revelation of the actual nature of that "thing" holds the fear.

"'In "The Masque of the Red Death," it is the unexpected sounds in the castle late at night, in one sequence, which arouse Francesca from her sleep and prompt her to run, terrified, to find their source. The frightened figure arouses fear in those watching — and the terrified flight is probably even more alarming in itself than anything which could lie at the end of it.'

"Other scenes in which the same carefully-executed run of terror is seen occur when Jane, her hair streaming wildly behind her in a panic-stricken flight along dark corridors, comes face to face with a masked figure who suddenly steps out from behind a draped curtain. Fear is quieted when the mask reveals the smiling face of a practical joker, and provides another brief temporary lull between the shudder-tactics of the story.

"Final moments of terror-on-the-move arise when Prospero first runs to find, and later flees from the Man in Red who has appeared at the Masque Ball. At first uncertain of his identity, Prospero searches the Palace to demand his identity. Later, realizing that Death has come to claim another victim he runs wildly from his pursuer through the halls and corridors of the Palace.

"Ten torture chambers were built for dungeon scenes showing the dreaded areas of the Palace where Prospero's victims are subdued by force. The chambers were accessorized with thumb-screws, iron maidens, racks, man-traps, flails and torture chains.

"Three hundred feet of cobwebs were thickly spread with a plastic fluid over the sets for scenes in the dark, dark dungeons.

"Pints of 'Blood' were used by make-up artist George Parteton for the scenes of the Masque Ball where the dancers are stricken by Red Death and break into a macabre Dance of Death.

"Another extra dimension of reality was brought to the scenes in which Prospero (Vincent Price) comes face-to-face with himself, immediately before he meets his own Red Death, by the use of real blood, given by a local hospital, and used for the close-up filming of scenes of transfixing horror."

Naked Paradise. "**Temptation and Terror in a Savage Land of Wild Desire!**" 1956 C 71 min. PRO-DIR Roger Corman, SP Charles B. Griffith, Mark Hanna, R. Wright Campbell (uncredited), DP Floyd Crosby, ED Charles Gross, Jr., MUS Ronald Stein. Sunset/American International.

The Cast: Richard Denning (Duke Bradley), Beverly Garland (Max McKenzie), Lisa Montell (Lani), Leslie Bradley (Zac Cotton), Dick Miller (Mitch), Jonathan Haze (Stony Gratoni), Carol Lindsay.

The Story: In Hawaii three small-time hoods hold up a sugar plantation on payroll day but before they can escape from the island a storm moves in and destroys their getaway boat. Zac Cotton, the leader of the group comprised of his mistress, Max McKenzie, and Zac's two henchmen, Stony and Mitch, charters a boat owned by Duke Bradley. But weather prevents sailing, giving Duke time to discover they're thieves and for Max to fall in love with Duke. In fact, love is in the air. Mitch falls for one of the local ladies and one of the local ladies falls for Stony.

Unfortunately for Mitch, Lani, the woman he's crazy about, already has a boyfriend whom Mitch ends up killing. And Zac ends up killing the rather porky woman who has her sights set on Stony and then has to kill Stony when he protests. During the confusion Duke and Max try to make a break for it and Duke might have been able to swim for help but he gives up when Max is captured.

Richard Denning and Beverly Garland in *Naked Paradise* (AIP, 1956).

To teach Duke a lesson, Zac fishes him out of the water with a meat hook. Duke gets even by shoving Zac's kisser into the boat's propeller.

Behind the Scenes: "Bob Campbell had written the original on that," Chuck Griffith said, referring to the script for *Naked Paradise*. "I don't know what stopped him but it was incomplete and I really used Bob's story and wrote a script on top of it. You know the story. We did it four times. The second time was when Roger was in South Dakota and he needed a horror script fast. It was always fast. So he wanted *Naked Paradise* again only with a monster, which I kept in a cave away from the rest of the people so he couldn't mess up the structure of the story. Everything was the same: the crooks were waiting to get away in an airplane, the gangster's moll falls for the rented hero and there's the speech about security*; everything was the same. We used it again for *Creature from the Haunted Sea* and *Atlas*."

*The speech: "Now wait a minute. Who knows what a tramp is? If she is a girl who has to give for what she gets —— well, I guess that makes her just about like everybody else. Every woman I've ever known and every girl I've ever talked with thought love was great but they always put one thing above it . . . security. That's first in line every time. Cash, check, furs or furniture, what's the difference?"

"*Naked Paradise* was wonderful because Roger took us to Hawaii to film it," Beverly Garland said. "We were on the island of Kauai and stayed at the Coca Palms. It was the only time I remember going first class on one of Roger's pictures."

"Then he got a deal on a Boy Scout Camp on the other side of the island," Jonathan Haze recalled with less fondness. "All of the crew and some of the actors were taken out of the hotel and moved to this camp. Roger went with us to prove he was no better than the rest of us. I did it for a couple of nights and I finally said to him, 'Roger, I can't do this. If you want me to act in the movie then I gotta be in a hotel where I don't have eight grips snoring in my ear all night. I don't want to go to sleep at nine o'clock at night. I don't want to have to sit in the toilet to read my script. I want to live like a human being. If you can do this, Roger, you do it. You stay here. But I'm going back to the hotel."

In *Fangoria,* AIP's vice president Sam Arkoff told Tom Weaver about his role in the film:

"We went over to Hawaii—me, my two kids and my wife, Jim [Nicholson] with his wife and three kids. Roger told me one day to come over to where he was shooting and he gave me this one line to read to Richard Denning: 'It's been a good harvest, and the money is in the safe.' Now *that's* a key line. That was my first and last role; I've never been asked back into any of 'em since!"

Two years after its release the picture was given a new title—*Thunder Over Hawaii.* And it was this new title that was used to refer to the film by everyone that I interviewed. I wondered why and finally asked Dick Miller about it. He explained: "It was released as *Naked Paradise* and they didn't think that was a classy enough title after they viewed the picture. And they decided to make it *Thunder Over Hawaii* as an action title. Roger does that today. He releases a picture in Georgia or someplace then pulls it back and changes the title. He says, '*Stick It Up Charlie* is no good. We gotta give it another name. *Butterflies Are Free.*' This was the first time *that* happened. When people asked me what I was doing I would say [quietly] '*Naked Paradise.*' I was ashamed of the title. I thought they'd think it was a porno film or something.

"Actually, *Naked Paradise* is a great title. But he didn't think it had enough action to it. He thought *Naked Paradise* kind of gave it a romantic quality. You know, tropical islands and some kind of idyllic love story. And he wanted something with a little more action to it.

"*Thunder Over Hawaii* is an action title. *Thunder* over anything is an action title. *Over Arizona, Over New York, Over New Mexico.* Everybody worked in a *Thunder Over* picture. And it took me years because I always used to say *Naked Paradise.* And I'd get the opposite thing. People would say, 'Yes, it was released as *Naked Paradise* but now it's called *Thunder Over Hawaii.*' I knew that. And it did turn out to be a good picture. And I got some good reviews on it. We had real sneaks in those days. We used to go out in the toolies someplace, some little theater and show it and get a reaction.

"Marketing was Roger's forte. He knew what he was doing. These little sneaks really meant something to him. What they liked. What they didn't like. And he went along with it. He'd say, 'We'll cut out that scene' if he could afford to cut it out, if the whole picture wasn't 68 minutes or something. I was standing in the lobby and Beverly Garland, who I admired greatly, said: 'You really walked away with that one. You really come out looking great.' I said, 'You're kidding.' And she said, 'No. No. You're really good.' And she said it loud enough and with enough enthusiasm and I think Roger picked up on it. And very shortly after the picture was released (not the next week, you know, but a month later or so) I got *Rock All Night,* which was my first starring picture."

"Somewhere in This World Stalks a Thing That Is. . ."
Not of This Earth. 1957 B&W 67 min. PRO-DIR Roger Corman, SP Charles B. Griffith, Mark Hanna, DP John Mesall, ED Charles Gross, SPFX Paul Blaisdell, TITLES Paul Julian, MUS Ronald Stein. Los Altos/Allied Artists.

The Cast: Paul Birch (Paul Johnson), Beverly Garland (Nadine Storey), Morgan Jones (Harry Sherbourne), William Roerick (Dr. Frederick Rochelle), Jonathan Haze (Jeremy Perrin), Dick Miller (Joe Piper), Ann Carol (Davanna woman), Tamar Cooper (Joanna Oxford), Roy Engel (Sgt. Walton), Pat Flynn (Officer Simmons), Gail Ganley and Ralph Reed (teenagers), Harold Fong (Chinaman).

The Story: On the planet Davanna, prolonged atomic warfare has created a race of people whose blood is literally evaporating in their bodies. Which means they need daily transfusions. Looking for fresh blood, and hoping to find a cure, one of these aliens comes to earth. Using the name Paul Johnson, and sporting a pair of thick dark glasses to conceal his egg-white eyes which can burn right into a person's brain, the alien seeks help from Dr. Frederick Rochelle. Johnson hypnotizes Rochelle so that he'll work on a cure without discussing the matter with any of his colleagues. Rochelle gladly lends Johnson his nurse, Nadine Storey, so she can give Johnson his necessary daily transfusion of blood.

Nadine's boyfriend, a policeman named Harry Sherbourne, doesn't like the set-up at all. Johnson seems like a cold fish to him and Johnson's chauffeur is a two-time loser named Jeremy Perrin. Both Nadine and Jeremy become suspicious of Johnson and do a little snooping. Behind a secret panel they find a strange machine which, unbeknownst to them, is a matter-transmitter which Johnson has been using to teleport live human specimens back to Davanna. Meanwhile, a female Davannian arrives to inform Johnson that the specimens he sent arrived squashed so he needs to send more ASAP. The alien is also in need of an immediate transfusion so the two break into Rochelle's office for some blood, unaware that Rochelle has been experimenting with blood from a rabid dog.

The woman staggers into a hospital and dies. Since the dark glasses she's wearing are identical to Johnson's, and her blank eyes indicate she's from

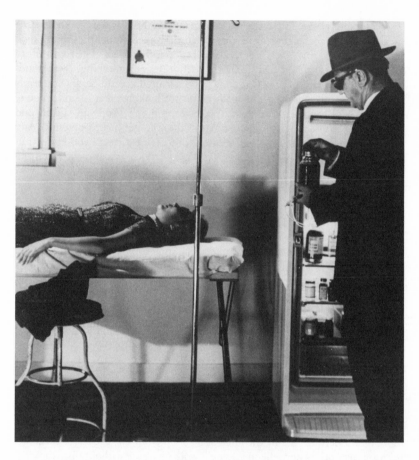

Ann Carol is about to get a transfusion of rabid blood from an unidentified actor filling in after Paul Birch walked off the picture. From *Not of This Earth* (Allied Artists, 1957).

another planet, Harry puts two and two together and heads for Johnson's place. Johnson returns home and catches Nadine and Jeremy at the matter-transmitter. He fries Jeremy's brain with his X-ray eyes and chases Nadine through the woods. Harry catches up to Johnson and turns on his siren. Johnson can't stand loud noises, loses control of his car and plummets over the side of a mountain road to his death. But as Harry and Nadine walk away from his grave, another stranger approaches sporting dark glasses.

Behind the Scenes: Supposedly, this picture came about because Chuck Griffith told Roger it was time to do another science fiction picture. Roger asked if Griffith had anything particular in mind and Griffith said, "Yeah. A guy with X-ray eyes that zaps people." It took him a month to write it. His wife at the time was a nurse and she gave him a lot of the information he needed to make the medical gobbledygook more believable. It was the first science fiction film to contain mental telepathy and matter transmitting.

"It had other things that didn't get shot," Griffith said. "You know, during the war it was illegal to sell yellow margarine because of the butter interests. So they'd sell white margarine in a plastic bag with a yellow food capsule inside. I had something like that in *Not of This Earth* where the invader broke a capsule and mixed it in a bathtub full of water that turned into a big dog. I wanted a Great Dane to be dressed in a monster suit with a crocodilian mouth on it and everything."

Instead, Paul Blaisdell designed a jellyfish-like thing that flew through the air. In one of the most gruesome moments in 50s sf films, Blaisdell's creature envelopes the head of William Roerick who plays Dr. Rochelle in the film, and as he struggles to remove it, a trail of blood oozes from his head which is completely covered by the creature, and collects in a pool on the desk in front of him. Blaisdell told Carl Del Vecchio in the *Beverly Garland Fan Club Journal* that he also created the matter-transmitter: "Rog just wanted a teleportation machine, so I said, 'Okay, you get a teleportation machine.' I didn't have much time to build it and I wish I could have designed it better. I would have liked it to look a lot jazzier than it did, but there was no time. At least you got the framework and the lights, as you know from seeing the movie. So I guess, such as it was, it did the job. But wouldn't we all like to see it done better if we didn't have to have it ready 'yesterday' for Rog?"

As well as being one of the first films to contain matter-transmitting and mental telepathy, *Not of This Earth* may have also been one of the first pictures to use contact lenses as part of its make-up, specifically to create the white-eyed alien, as worn by actor Paul Birch.

"Roger had Paul wearing contact lenses," Blaisdell said. "I'm not talking about the ones you slap on your cornea, I'm talking about the full-size ones which can become very painful after a few hours. And Roger just had Paul sitting around between takes all ready to go. A couple of hours passed and Birch felt like his eyes were burnt holes in a blanket. Then, he took the lenses out and his eyes hurt so bad he couldn't see straight."

Birch finally got so angry about it that he and Roger got into a fight over it, on the front lawn of the house where much of the picture was filmed.

"It was a farce and came to nothing really," Chuck Griffith remarked. "They took off their glasses and squared off ... pushed and shoved and so on."

Which ultimately led to the actor walking off the picture. Fortunately for Roger, most of Birch's scenes were in the can. A stand-in was used in a couple of sequences and since Birch wore the dark glasses through most of the film, it was easy to palm off a substitute. (The double was used when Johnson first enters Rochelle's office. He sits in the reception room and reacts adversely to a loud noise. Later, he's the one who accidentally gives the rabid blood to the woman from Davanna.)

"I really believe Roger can get around just about anything," Beverly Garland said.

Richard Denning and Peggie Castle discuss old times while Dick Miller tries to eavesdrop, in *Oklahoma Woman* (AIP, 1956).

The Oklahoma Woman. "Queen of the Outlaws, Queen of Sin!" 1956 B&W 71 min. PRO-DIR Roger Corman, EXEC PRO James Nicholson, SP Lou Rusoff, DP Fred West, MUS Ronald Stein. Sunset/American International.

The Cast: Richard Denning (Steve Ward), Peggie Castle (Marie "Oklahoma" Saunders), Cathy Downs (Susan Grant), Tudor Owen (Ed Grant), Martin Kingsley (Bill Peters), Touch Connors (Tom Blake), Jonathan Haze, Dick Miller, Bruno Ve Sota.

The Story: After serving a stretch in prison, Steve Ward decides to reform and live a peaceful life on a ranch left to him by his grandmother in Oklahoma. During his absence, Steve's girl Marie has become wealthy and powerful through unscrupulous means. Marie offers Steve a seat in the senate but Steve wants no part of her offer or her once he realizes what she has become. Instead he falls for his neighbor, Susan Grant, whose father happens to be Marie's main opposition.

Tom Blake, Marie's top gun, is jealous of Steve since Marie's still in love with him and figures he'll have a better chance with Marie if Steve is out of the way. So he decides to kill two birds with one stone. He murders Susan's father and pins the blame on Steve. The townspeople are ready to lynch Steve but Susan manages to beat a confession out of Marie by engaging her in a knock-down, drag-out fight that destroys Marie's saloon as well as her chances for victory.

Behind the Scenes: Cathy Downs, the leading lady in John Ford's male-dominated western *My Darling Clementine,* expected star billing in this picture but Roger Corman signed Peggie Castle to play the title role and she also expected star billing. A compromise was reached in which Peggie would get star billing provided her name was in the same size typeface as Cathy's and that Cathy would get star billing in another American Releasing Corporation film. It took two years but finally, in 1957, Cathy starred opposite Glenn Langan in Bert I. Gordon's *The Amazing Colossal Man,* which was a project originally assigned to Roger Corman under the title *The Amazing Nth Man.*

The Pit and the Pendulum. **"The Greatest Terror Tale Ever Told!"** 1961 C-Scope 85 min. PRO-DIR Roger Corman, EXEC PRO James H. Nicholson, Samuel Z. Arkoff, SP Richard Matheson based on Edgar Allan Poe's short story, DP Floyd Crosby, ED Anthony Carras, ART DIR Daniel Haller, SPFX Pat Dinga, MUS Les Baxter. Alta Vista/American International.

The Cast: Vincent Price (Nicholas/Sebastian Medina), John Kerr (Francis Barnard), Barbara Steele (Elizabeth Medina), Luana Anders (Catherine Medina), Antony Carbone (Charles Leon), Patrick Westwood (Maximillian), Lynn Bernay (Maria), Larry Turner (young Nicholas), Mary Menzies (Isabella), Charles Victor (Bartolome).

The Story: Francis Barnard comes to the castle of Nicholas Medina to learn the cause of his sister's death. Elizabeth, he is told, became obsessed by the torture devices in the Medina basement and one day they found her locked in an iron maiden, having gone completely mad. "The blood of a thousand men and women were spilled within these walls," Nicholas tells Francis, who knows that Nicholas is the son of Sebastian Medina, the most infamous member of the Spanish Inquisition. But Francis believes that his sister was made of stronger stuff and can't imagine her being influenced by atmospheres much less be the victim of them. And he detects an air of guilt about Nicholas that Nicholas's sister, Elizabeth, tries to explain.

When Nicholas was a child he was, against their father's orders, snooping around the basement when their father walked in with their mother, Isabella, and Sebastian's brother, Bartolome. Hiding in the shadows, the ten-year-old Nicholas watched as his father struck Bartolome with a hot poker, screaming one word over and over: Adulterer! And then, he turned on Isabella, accusing her of vile debauchery with his brother, cursing her as faithless, and promising her the agonies of hell in payment for her infidelity. And there, before Nicholas's very eyes, his mother was tortured to death. Later, the family doctor, Charles Leon, drops another bombshell. Isabella was not tortured to death. She was walled up in her tomb while yet alive. "From that day forth the very thought of premature interment was enough to drive your brother into convulsions of horror," Dr. Leon explains. Nicholas believes that Elizabeth may have been interred prematurely . . . because of what happened to his mother many years ago."

The Pit and the Pendulum (AIP, 1961): opposite, top, Vincent Price mugs his way down another corridor; bottom, Corman checks out the pendulum one last time to make sure it won't slice his star. This page, top, Larry Turner receives instruction from Corman; bottom, Price (left) battles Patrick Westwood as terrified Luana Anders watches.

And now, the doctor believes someone is using that fear to drive Nicholas mad, making him believe that Elizabeth's ghost haunts the castle. But Francis is still not convinced. He believes that Nicholas is the one *pretending* that Elizabeth is haunting him by playing the harpsichord at night, leaving Elizabeth's trinkets behind. And when Elizabeth's old room is wrecked and Francis finds a secret passage leading to Nicholas's room, he accuses Nicholas of the act. By this time Nicholas is so distraught and confused he thinks Francis might be right. But it's actually Dr. Leon and Elizabeth who are the culprits—an elaborate scheme by two clandestine lovers to drive the unwanted husband out of his mind. They eventually succeed but the whole thing backfires.

Seeing them together in a lover's embrace, Nicholas becomes his father and Elizabeth and Leon in his mind are Isabella and Bartolome. And into this insanity steps Francis Barnard who fills in for Bartolome when Leon accidentally falls to his death trying to escape. Nicholas konks Francis on the head and straps him to a table beneath a razor-sharp pendulum which slowly descends with every swing. Fortunately Catherine arrives in time with one of the servants. Nicholas is killed, Francis is saved and they leave the torture chamber which Catherine declares will remain locked forever. They don't notice Elizabeth, her mouth gagged, locked in the iron maiden.

Behind the Scenes: According to the pressbook, the pendulum used in the climax of this picture was eighteen feet long, with a realistic rubber cutting blade, and weighed over a ton, rigged from the top of the sound stage, suspended thirty-five feet in the air. It was constructed under the supervision of Ross Hahn, Jr., who worked from Dan Haller's designs.

"I found that such a pendulum actually was used during the Spanish and German Inquisitions," said Haller. "At first we tried to use a rubberized blade and that's why it got stuck on Kerr's chest. We then switched to a sharp metalized blade covered with steel paint. The problem was to get it in exactly the right position so it would slash John's shirt without actually cutting him. To guard against this we put a steel band around his waist where the pendulum crosses. He was a good sport about it but I noticed him perspiring a good bit and no wonder. That pendulum was carving out a fifty-foot arc just above his body."

The Premature Burial. **"Within the Coffin I Lie . . . ALIVE!"** 1962 C-Scope 81 min. PRO-DIR Roger Corman, SP Charles Beaumont, Ray Russell from Edgar Allan Poe's short story, DP Floyd Crosby, ED Ronald Sinclair, ART DIR Daniel Haller, MUS Ronald Stein. Santa Clara/American International.

The Cast: Ray Milland (Guy Carrell), Hazel Court (Emily Gault), Richard Ney (Miles Archer), Heather Angel (Kate Carrell), Alan Napier (Gideon Gault), John Dierkes (Sweeney), Dick Miller (Mole), Brendon Dillon (minister).

The Story: Guy Carrell's fear of being buried alive completely cripples his ability to live. He cancels his wedding plans and when his fiancée, Emily Gault, shows up unexpectedly to ask for an explanation, Guy tells her about the death of his father when he was 13: "The doctors said it was a heart attack. There was a funeral. And he was sealed in this vault. That night I heard him crying out. A pitiful, desperate cry. I begged with them, I pleaded with them. 'He's alive! He's alive!' I said, but no one would believe me.

"Can you possibly conceive it? The unendurable oppression of the lungs, the stifling fumes of the damp earth, the rigid embrace of the coffin, the blackness of absolute night. And the silence, like an overwhelming sea. And then . . . invisible in the darkness but all too hideously real to the other senses, the presence of the conqueror worm." Guy's sister Kate says all the business about their father is balderdash, a product of Guy's overactive imagination. The wedding proceeds as planned but Guy can't shake the belief that like his father he'll one day be buried alive. He constructs a tomb and a coffin with various escape devices but still his dreams are tortured by images of his gadgets proving faulty. His friend, Miles Archer, had hoped that Guy's marriage to Emily would brighten Guy's outlook but when he realizes such is not the case he warns Emily that Guy's fear might actually cause him to have a seizure.

Emily goes to the tomb Guy has constructed for himself, where he spends nearly all of his time, and has it out with him. "You don't fear burial alive because you're already buried alive," she tells him. "What is it you're afraid of? Being locked in the tomb? Well, you've been locked in a tomb for months. This tomb. And I've been your widow." She threatens to leave, so Guy burns the tomb and returns to the house, but he can't shake his fear.

Miles insists that the only way Guy can rid himself of this nonsense is to exhume the body of his father and prove once and for all that he was not buried alive. But when the coffin is opened the corpse inside indicates a struggle after burial and Guy collapses. Emily's father, Dr. Gideon Gault, declares him dead and Guy's worst fear becomes reality. Unable to move, he's conscious during his funeral and watches as they lower his coffin into the earth. He's rescued by the grave-robbers who've been hired by Dr. Gault, who plans to experiment on Guy's corpse. Guy kills the grave-robbers, Dr. Gault, and buries Emily alive. Miles tries to interfere and Guy is about to stab him with a shovel when he, Guy, is shot in the back by his sister. Miles is understandably confused until Kate explains that Emily had desecrated their father's tomb by planting a phony corpse. It was all an elaborate plot to kill Guy for his money, which Kate knew but held her tongue because she was afraid Guy wouldn't believe her unless she had some proof, which is a pretty lame excuse for doing absolutely nothing. But the real puzzlement is how Guy figured the whole thing out during his premature burial.

Behind the Scenes (from the pressbook): "The vivid imagination of Edgar Allan Poe, set in words by the master of the terror tale and brought to the motion picture screen by American International Pictures in 'The Premature Burial,' receives added dimension in the motion picture through the efforts of a brilliant young California artist.

"An integral part of AIP's filmization of the famed Poe story . . . are the weirdly terrifying paintings seen in the film. They are the product of the imagination and skill of Los Angeles painter Burton Shonberg whose four beautiful works for the terror tale took almost three months to complete.

Top: Ray Milland is about to bury Hazel Court alive; bottom, Corman looks at electric device that Milland will use to kill Alan Napier (rear); Court is at left—from *The Premature Burial* (AIP, 1962).

"Shonberg was first 'discovered' and commissioned by Roger Corman . . . to paint portraits of the Usher family for his first Poe picture, 'The House of Usher.' Shonberg's work caused so much favorable comment that Corman commissioned him again to do the art work for 'The Premature Burial.'

"The young artist lives and works in Los Angeles. His product covers a wide range of subjects, with a preference for portraits. He is a studious young man whose main interests are painting and philosophy."

The Raven. **"The Macabre Masterpiece of Terror!"** 1963 C-Scope 86 min. PRO-DIR Roger Corman, EXEC PRO James H. Nicholson, Samuel Z. Arkoff, SP Richard Matheson supposedly based on a poem by Edgar Allan Poe, DP Floyd Crosby, ART DIR Daniel Haller, ED Ronald Sinclair, SPFX Pat Dinga, MUS Les Baxter. Alta Vista/American International.

The Cast: Vincent Price (Erasmus Craven), Peter Lorre (Adolphus Bedlo), Boris Karloff (Scarabus), Jack Nicholson (Rexford Bedlo), Hazel Court (Leonore Craven), Olive Sturgess (Estelle Craven), Connie Wallace (maid), William Baskin (Grimes), Aaron Saxon (Gort), Jim Jr. (the Raven).

The Story: Erasmus Craven is idly passing the time one evening by amusing himself with his own magic when he's interrupted by the tapping of a raven at his window. He bids the bird enter, then asks, "Who sent you to me? Are you some dark winged messenger from beyond? Answer me monster. Tell me true. Shall I ever hold again that radiant maiden whom the angels call Lenore?" To which the bird unexpectedly replies, "How the hell should I know? What am I, a fortune teller?" The bird turns out to be a rather unpleasant, chubby little fellow named Adolphus Bedlo who was turned into a bird by a sorcerer named Scarabus. Erasmus knows Scarabus well since he was a rival to his father for the head post of the Brotherhood of Magicians.

By right the post belongs to Erasmus but being of a peaceful nature he's chosen to live more or less in seclusion since the death of his father, leaving the evil Scarabus unchallenged. Erasmus returns Bedlo to his rightful form. And that's when Bedlo notices the painting of Leonore, Erasmus's dead wife. Bedlo swears the woman is alive in the castle of Scarabus. And indeed she is. She'd faked her death, after becoming bored with Erasmus, in order to enjoy Scarabus's wealth and power.

Bedlo turns out to be part of a plot to lure Erasmus to the castle so that Scarabus can learn the secret of the magician's hand manipulations. Scarabus threatens to harm Erasmus's daughter, Estelle, unless Erasmus reveals his power and it's then that Erasmus realizes it's time to take action. He challenges Scarabus to a duel to the death. The two magicians duel all right but not to the death. Erasmus proves to be the more powerful of the two and with the castle in flames, Erasmus, Estelle, Bedlo and his son Rexford escape, leaving Lenore to bicker with Scarabus.

Behind the Scenes: This was the fifth Edgar Allan Poe film that Roger Corman made and the fourth written by Richard Matheson, who told Roger from the outset that he was getting burned out and the only way he could get through another script was by playing it for laughs. Roger was getting a little

Aaron Saxon is about to chop off Peter Lorre's head as Corman (right) directs *The Raven* (AIP, 1963); Lorre will escape, however, as this is a comedy.

weary himself and told Matheson to go ahead. By the time Peter Lorre and Vincent Price finished with it, the laughs were even broader. When the picture was shown to the Breen Office they not only approved it but praised it. Roger was quite pleased.

Rock All Night. "Some Have to Dance . . . Some Have to Kill!" 1957 B&W 65 min. PRO-DIR Roger Corman, EXEC PRO James H. Nicholson, SP Charles B. Griffith based on "The Little Guy," TV play by David P. Harmon, DP Floyd Crosby, ED Frank Sullivan, ART DIR Robert Kinoshita, MUS Buck Ram. Sunset/American International.

The Cast: Dick Miller (Shorty), Abby Dalton (Julie), the Platters and the Blockbusters (themselves), Robin Morse (Al), Richard Cutting (Steve), Bruno Ve Sota (Charlie), Chris Alcaide (Angie), Mel Welles (Sir Bop), Barboura Morris (Syl), Clegg Hoyt (Marty), Russell Johnson (Jigger), Jonathan Haze (Joey), Richard Carlan (Jerry), Jack De Witt (Philippe), Bert Nelson (Bartender), Beach Dickerson (The Kid), Ed Nelson (Pete).

The Story: Because of his short stature, Shorty walks around with a chip on his shoulder that continually gets him into trouble. At a nightclub where the Platters are appearing Shorty lasts two numbers ("I'm Sorry" and "He's

Mine") before his temper gets him bounced out. He wanders into the Cloud Nine where a small-time, hip-talking agent, Sir Bop, is about to unveil his newest discovery, a nervous singer named Julie. Even with the encouragement of the bar's owner, Al, her nerve gives out and she performs miserably for her audition. Not wanting to be humiliated, Sir Bop makes her try again with the same results.

Suddenly a man rushes in with the news of a dual murder during a robbery attempt down the street and sees the men responsible, Jigger and Joey, sitting at the bar. The guy makes a break for the door but Jigger guns him down, then threatens to kill anyone who makes a false move. He forces Julie to sing again to make everything appear to be normal for the police when they come to search the place. This time, in spite of the pressure, Julie performs beautifully, but the police aren't fooled and surround the building.

Joey and Jigger threaten to shoot their way out until Shorty taunts them and they decide to take Julie and one of the other female patrons as hostages. And none of the patrons will stop them. The Kid, a boxer who according to his manager has the "killer instinct," is yellow; Angie the truck driver can't face guns even though his girl is one of the hostages; a guy named Jerry declines to earn the protection money Al's been paying him. Which leaves only Shorty. He slams Jigger into a wall and takes his gun. Jigger's partner, Joey, happily gives up. The police take them away along with Jerry since Al has decided he doesn't need Jerry's brand of protection. And Julie decides she doesn't want to sing and leaves with Shorty instead.

Behind the Scenes: The inspiration for this film was a standing set and the availability of a singing group called the Platters who'd placed a number of hit records on the charts, among them "Only You," "The Great Pretender," and "My Prayer." American International told Roger he could have the group if he could come up with a picture for them before they went on tour. Which gave Roger two weeks. He bought a 25-minute television piece called "The Little Guy" which he'd seen on Jane Wyman's show and handed it to Charles Griffith to expand into an hour. Naturally, Griffith's new version was to center around the Platters. Then, two days before production there was a change in the Platters' schedule and they were only going to be available for a day. Griffith had to rewrite the script so that it would no longer favor the singing group and he only had 48 hours to do it.

"I took a pair of scissors and cut the script into pieces," Griffith said. "I added about twenty percent additional characters. I pasted what I could use from the original script on the new pages. At the same time Roger got Buck Ram [the Platters' manager and chief song writer] to throw a bunch of songs together. I didn't know what the songs were going to be. Buck Ram claimed credit for the writing. Who would want to go to all the trouble to lie to take credit for a piece of shit like that? The Sir Bop character that Mel Welles played was written for Lord Buckley."

"Dick Buckley was a guy I used to write for," Mel Welles explained. "He was an outrageous comedian that talked in hip talk and yet looked like an English Lord. But, as usual, Dick was kind of flakey about his movements and

Dick Miller (left) and Russell Johnson in *Rock All Night* (AIP, 1957), filmed in five days.

his disappeared. So I decided to play the part myself. Nobody else could. In those days nobody else understood hip talk. The only people that ever used any kind of hip words on television were Frank Sinatra and Steve Allen and they used words like *dig*. And that was it. So we're right in the middle of the beat generation and beatniks were the only ones who understood the language and Roger got very scared that nobody would understand the picture. So I wrote the first dictionary of hip talk — *The hiptionary*. There were five million of those sent out with the picture as a move for everybody to be able to understand not only what I said, but there was a lot of hip talk in the picture. If I'd have done that for a major studio, I would get the royalty off that. I didn't even get ten dollars for it. And I was, at the time, really the nation's authority on hip talk."

Griffith said: "We had a group called The Blockbusters. Dick Miller called them The Ballbusters. And The Platters, of course. They did two songs. We had a crane for that. It was the first time I saw Roger use a crane. They had to move the nightclub tables out of the way so the crane could get into the shot. It was very elaborate."

"There's a guy named Bert Nelson [who plays the bartender]," Welles added. "He was a bouncer at The Interlude nightclub and I got him a job in the picture. Later, Bert went to Europe because he was into muscle building and he wanted to play in those gladiator pictures, those Steve Reeves type things. Today, he lives in Germany and he's a multimillionaire. He opened up an Italian restaurant in Berlin and now he owns a chain of Italian restaurants in Europe. And half of an Italian frozen pizza business. And he's a Jewish kid from the south."*

The Saga of the Viking Women and Their Voyage to the Waters of the Great Sea Serpent. "The Raw Courage of Women Without Men Lost in a Fantastic Hell-on-Earth!" 1957 B&W 70 min. PRO-DIR Roger Corman, EXEC PRO James H. Nicholson, SP Lawrence Louis Goldman from a story by Irving Block, DP Monroe P. Askins, SPFX Jack Rabin, Irving Block, MUS Albert Glasser. Malibu/American International.

The Cast: Abby Dalton (Desir), Susan Cabot (Enger), Brad Jackson (Vedric), June Kenney (Asmild), Richard Devon (Stark), Betsy Jones-Moreland (Thyra), Jonathan Haze (Ottar), Jay Sayer (Senja), Gary Conway (Jarl), Lynn Bernay, Sally Todd, Mike Forrest.

The Story: A thousand years ago, in the North Atlantic, a group of women set out to sea in search of their men, who have failed to return from a hunting excursion. The women's longboat is caught in a deadly vortex and only Desir, the tribe's leader, Enger, their priestess, Asmild, Thyra and Ottar (the only man in the outfit) survive. They're washed ashore in a land inhabited by a bloodthirsty lot called the Grimaults, ruled by a ruthless man named Stark and his weakling son, Senja. Stark and his men take the women captive and attempt to seduce them with wine and "merriment" but the women aren't interested. Furious, Stark orders them to a rock quarry where the Viking men are doing slave labor. Stark wants to burn Desir and her lover, Vedric, at the stake so maybe the other ladies'll give a little but Enger thwarts his plan by calling on help from the Gods. The Gods rain on the fire and fry Senja with a lightning bolt, giving the Vikings a chance to escape. The Grimaults chase after them, Stark now madder than ever over the death of his son, but before he and the Vikings can lock horns, a gigantic sea serpent intervenes and makes short work of Stark and his men. Vedric kills the serpent with a well-aimed spear and the Vikings head for home.

Behind the Scenes: A million dollar movie for a $1.98. That's how this

---

Griffith's and Welles' reminiscences are from interviews with both conducted by the author.

Top: Abby Dalton and Brad Jackson (right) paddle to escape the Grimaults; bottom: Richard Devon leads a less than sturdy crew in pursuit — *Viking Women and the Sea Serpent* (AIP, 1957).

Brad Jackson is about to give Richard Devon a sore throat, in *Viking Women.*

project was sold to Roger Corman and how he, in turn, sold it to American International.

Jack Rabin, who'd been in the special effects business for a decade or more, showed Roger some fancy illustrations of sea monsters and Viking warriors in mortal combat in the middle of a raging ocean and boldly claimed that for a very small sum of money, he could bring those drawings to life with his special effects know-how. But something got lost in the translation.

Locations for the film were Bronson Canyon in the Hollywood Hills, Iverson's Ranch in the San Fernando Valley, Cabrillo Beach and ZIV Studios on Santa Monica. The cost was the usual $60,000 or $70,000. Three days into production Roger knew he'd made a mistake. Everything seemed to be going wrong. On the first day the leading lady phoned in sick. As one of the first rules of low budget filmmaking is to move on, no matter what, Roger moved all the ladies in the cast up a notch and hired an extra to play the least important role. Roger was good at thinking on his feet. The film's second lead, Susan Cabot, thought it was one of Roger's best qualities, that and the fact he gave her the kind of meaty roles she never got when she was under contract to Universal, although there was a price to pay for it. A performer in a Corman film was asked to do things above and beyond what a major studio would have expected.

"I remember the scene where the Viking women set out to sea in search of their men," Susan Cabot told *Fangoria* magazine. The second the boat hit the water the rudder fell off. "There were, I believe, eleven girls in a Viking-type ship, and we were pulled out to sea, tugged by a rope attached to another boat. And the man who was towing us fell asleep. We started screaming at him, but the sound of the ocean drowned us out."

As the boat drifted out of the cove and around the side of the mountain, it began to sink. There was nothing to bail water with so Susan used one of her boots. A couple of surfers fortunately came to the rescue and pulled the boat to shore. It was a brief respite from danger as the tiny strip of land they were on was quickly disappearing beneath the tide. The options were limited. They were forced to climb the mountain.

The ladies had another bout with danger the afternoon they were supposed to come charging out of a cave on horseback. Nobody told them about the drop. Susan and Abby Dalton were in the lead. They managed to stop their horses in time and kept the others from going over as well, but there were some anxious moments when the horses were bunching together, pushing Susan and Abby closer to the edge.

"Come on. Come on," Roger yelled. "This will be an exciting scene."

One of the ladies yelled, "It's pretty dangerous, Roger."

"It's in your contract," Roger reminded her.

"It's in your hat," the woman replied.

Dick Devon, the film's villain, called it a disastrous film to work on. He was the one who found the restricted beach sign that someone had tossed in the bushes. One look at the water told Dick why: serious undertow. And he had a scene where he and some of the other actors were supposed to row out to sea in canoes. Dick didn't like the idea at all but Roger assured him that they wouldn't have to go very far. He'd cut as soon as they were a few feet from shore.

Sitting in the canoe, headed toward what he believed was dangerous waters, Dick needed more reassurance. He turned to the fellow behind him to double-check the game plan.

"He said to keep rowing until he yells cut and not before," the guy told him.

Dick was suddenly convinced that Roger had tricked him. That Roger had no intention of cutting the scene early at all. Fear and rage turned Dick into a wild man. He flung himself into the water while it was still only waist high and headed for shore, screaming obscenities at Roger. He hadn't gone far before a wave slapped him face down in the water. He tried to get up but the weight of the sheepskins and armor he wore held him down. He wondered if he would die. He fought his way to the surface, gasping for air. Once he'd had his fill and with death behind him, he remembered his rage again. He shook his fists high in the air and screamed, "If I ever get my hands on you, I'll strangle you."

Nobody could hear him above the noise of the surf, anymore than they heard Susan and Abby yelling for their lives, but his body language was clear enough. Roger was long gone by the time Dick staggered out of the water.

It may have been these delays that drove Roger to whip out 73 camera set-ups in a single day, his all-time record high. He moved so fast that day he told the cameraman not to bother with slates.

With equal swiftness, Jack Rabin and Irving Block completed their special effects. Close-up their sea serpent looked like an old rag. In the far shots it was Block's finger, covered with clay, with a fin stuck to it.

The movie was sold to the public much in the same manner as it had been sold to Roger, with a flashy illustration guaranteed to send expectations soaring. Rabin owned 15 percent of the picture. He never saw a dime. According to the accountant at AIP, who sent Rabin a report every year, the picture never went into profit. Which has to be the most fantastic thing about the picture, don't you think?

The St. Valentine's Day Massacre. "The Most Shocking Event of America's Most Lawless Era!" 1966 C 100 min. PRO-DIR Roger Corman, SP Howard Browne, DP Milton Krasner, ED William B. Murphy, ART DIR Jack Martin Smith, Phillip Jeffries, SPFX L.B. Abbott, Art Cruickshank, Emil Kosa, Jr., MUS Fred Steiner. 20th Century–Fox.

The Cast: Jason Robards, Jr. (Al Capone), George Segal (Peter Gusenberg), Ralph Meeker (Bugs Moran), Jean Hale (Myrtle), Clint Ritchie (Jack McGurn), Frank Silvera (Sorello), Michael Guayini (Patsy Lelordo), Joseph Campanella (Weinshank), Richard Bakalyan (Scalisi), David Canary (Frank Gusenberg), Bruce Dern (May), Harold J. Stone (Frank Nitti), Kurt Kreuger (James Clark), Paul Richards (Charles Fischetti), Joseph Turkel (Guzik), Leo Gordon (Heitler), Milton Frome (Adam Heyer), Mickey Deems (Schwimmer), John Agar (O'Bannion), Celia Lovsky (Josephine Schwimmer), Tom Reese (Newberry), Jan Merlin (Willie Marks), Alex D'Arcy (Aiello), Reed Hadley (Hymie Wiss), Gun Trikonis (Rio), Charles Diekop (Salvanti), Rico Cattani (Anselmi), Alex Rocco (Diamond), Barboura Morris, Jack Nicholson, Daniel Ades.

The Story: During prohibition, a racketeer named Al Capone controlled 10,000 speakeasies in Chicago. His office took up one whole floor of the city's Hawthorne Hotel and he had more than 700 men on his payroll. "Everybody calls me a racketeer," Capone once said. "I call myself a businessman. When I sell liquor, it's bootlegging. When my patrons serve it on a silver tray on Lake Shore Drive, it's hospitality."

Naturally, there were other "businessmen" who wanted to cut in on Capone's action and one of these was a former pickpocket and safe-cracker named Dion O'Banion. When O'Banion was killed, George "Bugs" Moran, with the help of the remaining O'Banions, became Capone's archrival. Ultimately, Capone tired of Moran and ordered Machine Gun Jack McGurn to get rid of the pests. McGurn outfitted a handful of gangsters in police uniforms and they entered a garage where O'Banion's men were waiting for a haul of hijacked hooch. Pretending to make a raid, the phony cops lined O'Banion's men against the wall and killed them with a blast of machine gun fire.

Behind the Scenes: Howard Browne, who scripted Corman's version of *The St. Valentine's Day Massacre,* was living in Chicago in 1929, working at the L.

Jason Robards in one of his least impressive performances, as Al Capone in *The St. Valentine's Day Massacre* (20th Century–Fox, 1966).

Kline department store. When he heard a radio news broadcast about the killing he took a streetcar to the 2100 block but couldn't get within five blocks of the place. Reading about the incident later in the newspaper, Browne found the story with pictures of the gangsters both fascinating and repelling. He had no idea that one day he'd be writing about it.

"Digging into dead people, people who died dramatically, can be kind of exciting," said Browne. "I could almost do a story on the research itself."

The event took place as follows: On February 14, 1929, Bugs Moran's gang was waiting for a shipment of hijacked bootleg whisky in a low, brick building marked S.M.C. Cartage company. There were Adam Heyer, proprietor of the phony carting firm, Moran's brother-in-law James Clark, a playboy optometrist named Reinhardt H. Schwimmer, Frank and Peter Gusenberg, John May and Albert R. Weinshank. Bugs Moran, his bodyguard, and his sales manager hadn't arrived yet. They were approaching the building, walking south on North Clark Street, when they saw what appeared to be a police car pull up near the hangout. Three men wearing police uniforms and two in plain clothes got out and entered the garage. Moran and his buddies took off.

Inside the building Moran's men were disarmed and lined up against the wall. The men in civilian clothes came out of hiding, one with a Thompson submachine gun, the other with a double-barreled sawed off shotgun. For 10 seconds the Tommy gun riddled the hoods with bullets and when Clark and May stirred the shotgun finished them off.

Frank Gusenberg was still alive when the real police arrived and when asked who did it he gasped, "Nobody shot me." He was dead three hours later.

Scalise and Anselmi, the triggermen in the massacre, once boasted they never missed mass a day in their lives.

To help promote the picture, 20th Century–Fox staged quite a show at the B & K Roosevelt Theatre in Chicago where the film premiered. There were ten antique cars, one carrying a wax figure of Al Capone, 20 ladies from the Gaslight Club in flapper-style clothes and newsboys hawking 5,000 copies of the 1929 front page of the *Chicago Daily News*.

The Secret Invasion. "The Daring Plan; The Staggering Odds!" 1964 C-Scope 95 min. PRO Gene Corman, DIR Roger Corman, SP R. Wright Campbell, DP Arthur E. Arling, ED Ronald Sinclair, ART DIR John Murray, SPFX George Bracknell, MUS Hugo Friedhofer. San Carlos/United Artists.

The Cast: Stewart Granger (Richard Mace), Raf Vallone (Roberto Rocca), Mickey Rooney (Terence Scanlon), Edd Byrnes (Simon Fell), Henry Silva (John Durrell), Mia Massini (Mila), William Campbell (Jean Saval), Helmo Kindermann (commandant), Enzio Fiermonte (Wuadri), Peter Coe (Marko), Nan Morris (Stephana), Helmet Schneider (captain), Giulio Marchetti (officer), Nicholas Rend (captain of the fishing boat), Crag March (Petar), Todd Williams (Partisan leader), Charles Brent (Monk), Richard Johns (wireless operator), Kurt Bricker (German naval lieutenant), Katrina Rozan (peasant woman).

The Story: In Cairo during World War II, British intelligence selects five convicts to rescue an Italian general from a prison in Dubrovnik. The five men are Richard Mace, the mad major, driven by the knowledge that history could not afford their failure; Roberto Rocca, the master criminal, destined against his will to be a hero; Terence Scanlon, the demolition demon, capable of blowing the crystal off a watch and leave it running; Simon Fell, the forger, as good with a pen as he was with a gun; John Durrell, the assassin, who didn't need a war to kill—with him murder was an instinct. These renegades must free General Quadri so he can turn his troops against their German allies and hopefully bring about the end of the war. Their reward for all of this is, of course, their freedom. And so they agree to give it a shot. Unfortunately they're captured by the Nazis and thrown into prison with the General who, they discover, is an imposter. The real general was killed. Durrell disguises himself as a Nazi and forces the fake general to address his troops then kills him before the imposter can tell the people to remain loyal to the Nazis. This turns the Italians against the Nazis and the mission proves to be a success after all.

Behind the Scenes: Gene Corman made a deal with United Artists to shoot a $600,000 picture in Yugoslavia. Peter Bogdanovich was involved in the project in its earliest stage; he was told it would be a cross between *The Bridge on the River Kwai* and *Lawrence of Arabia* ... but cheap. According to

William Campbell (left), Stewart Granger, Mickey Rooney (front), Henry Silva, Raf Vallone and Edd Byrnes in *The Secret Invasion* (UA, 1964).

Bogdanovich, the basic idea for the story came from one sentence in a history book. Bobby Campbell was hired to actually write the script, which resembled an earlier script he'd written for Roger, *Five Guns West*. Campbell's original title was *The Dubious Patriots*.

At first the folks at UA wanted the McGuffin (as Alfred Hitchcock called the thing that propelled the plot) to be a physical thing, like an ammo dump or a naval base but Roger felt that would make his picture too similar to *The Guns of Navarone* (1961). So he suggested that the McGuffin be a person—a partisan leader whose escape could lead to an uprising against the Nazis. In a letter to David Picker at UA, Roger added yet another twist on the plot. He proposed that the Nazis should be reluctant to kill the leader out of fear of making him a martyr, which leads them to substitute a lookalike to take his place.

Edd Byrnes was cast in the role of Simon Fell, the forger. He'd been television's most popular star in the late fifties, as the hip-talkin', hair-combin' Kookie on 77 *Sunset Strip*. When he heard that Raf Vallone, one of Italy's top leading men, was going to be one of his co-stars, Byrnes was sure the movie was going to be a hit. The two men sat together on the plane to Yugoslavia when Byrnes happened to glance in Roger's direction and noticed the stack of books on his lap. "There were titles like *How to Direct Motion Pictures* and *The Art of Motion Picture Directing* and things like that," Byrnes recalled. "I turned to Raf Vallone and said, 'This is going to be a great picture!' We were really worried. But it came out pretty good."

Stewart Granger was hired for the role that was originally written for Bobby Darin. Granger was one of MGM's top leading men in the 1950s, the studio's Errol Flynn. Roger said the actor caused "the worst experience" of his entire career.

"They paid Stewart Granger fifty thousand," said the film's assistant director, Chuck Griffith. "I ran into him in the market a couple of weeks ago [this was in 1985]. He started ranting about Roger. [Granger] was a captain in the script and he said, 'I have to be a major!' I think he rationalized it by saying he was too old to be a captain."

And at four o'clock in the morning, the Major felt he was entitled to whatever lines of dialog he took a fancy to and he took a fancy to one of the lines written for Edd Byrnes. When Byrnes protested, Granger threatened to walk off the picture. Roger wouldn't give in. Granger headed for the door. But he couldn't go far. They were on a boat.

"It's very sad to grow old," Granger once remarked. "It's depressing to watch anything deteriorate — particularly yourself."

It probably won't come as any surprise to learn that Roger managed to make a second feature while he was in Yugoslavia. He made a deal with some local filmmakers for a murder mystery called *Point of Terror*. Roger supplied the actor, William Campbell; the filmmakers supplied the rest. Roger was in England working on *The Masque of the Red Death* when he discovered it hadn't been such a good deal after all. *Point of Terror* turned out to be unreleasable. Roger asked Jack Hill to shoot some new scenes but Hill's California sequences didn't match the European locals and so the project was turned over to Stephanie Rothman to salvage. By that time, William Campbell wasn't available so Rothman had to devise an entirely new storyline to explain (or kind of explain) the new actor in Campbell's stead. In the original story, Campbell was an artist who painted nude women and then murdered them. In Rothman's version, Campbell is a vampire, capable of changing form.

The film was titled *Blood Bath* (1966), changed to *Track of the Vampire* for television.

She Gods of Shark Reef. "Beautiful Maidens in a Lush Tropical Paradise Ruled by a Hideous Stone God!" 1958 (1956) C 63 min. PRO Ludwig H.

Don Durant, Bill Cord, Lisa Montell and Jeanne Gerson in *She Gods of Shark Reef* (AIP, 1958), which sat on the shelf for two years awaiting release.

Gerber, DIR Roger Corman, SP Robert Hill, Victor Stoloff, DP Floyd Crosby, ED Frank Sullivan, MUS Ronald Stein. American International.

The Cast: Don Durant (Lee), Bill Cord (Chris), Lisa Montell (Mahia), Jeanne Gerson (Dua), Carol Lindsay (Hula Dancer), Beverly Rivera.

The Story: To finance his life of leisure in the Hawaiian Islands, a ne'er-do-well named Lee becomes a thief. Aided by one of the natives, he tries to steal a cache of guns but the two are caught by the night watchman. Lee crushes the watchman's skull with a length of heavy chain, then has to lay low. He convinces his brother, Chris, to help him escape. They set out for a distant island in an outrigger canoe but are overtaken by a storm that swamps their craft. They're rescued by some native women who take Lee and Chris to their village.

The two soon learn there are no other males on the island and all of the women are employed by the Company to pearl dive. The women believe their work is blessed by a stone god located beneath the waters off shore, on a shark infested reef. From time to time a young maiden is sacrificed to the god to keep things regular. Chris falls for a woman named Mahia and is content to spend the rest of his life on the island but Lee soon tires of it, steals some pearls and heads out to sea in the outrigger canoe. Chris chases after him and after a fight Lee ends up near the great stone god and is eaten by the sharks. Meanwhile,

Mahia is about to be sacrificed when Chris shows up in time to rescue her. They sail off for another island and a new life.

Behind the Scenes: This movie was filmed back-to-back with *Naked Paradise* for an independent producer named Ludwig Gerber, who supplied Roger with a script. Gerber spent a year and a half trying to sell this turkey but nobody was interested until he brought it to AIP, who sent it out as part of a combination with *Night of the Blood Beast.* Ronald Stein, who composed the score, told *The Denver Post* that it was "one of the worst films ever made." Stein said he wrote an hour's worth of music for it (it's only a 63 minute picture) because "it *needed* 60 minutes of music to save it."

Ski Troop Attack. **"They Turned a White Hell Red with Enemy Blood!"** 1960 B&W 63 min. PRO-DIR Roger Corman, SP Charles B. Griffith, DP Andy Costikyan, ED Anthony Carras, MUS Fred Katz. Filmgroup.

The Cast: Michael Forest (Factor), Frank Wolff (Potter), Wally Campo (Ed), Richard Sinatra (Herman), Sheila Carol (Ilse), Roger Corman.

The Story: It's World War II. Five American grunts are wandering around the snow-covered mountains of Germany, on a mission that's so secret even they don't know what it is. The only thing they know for sure is that they're to avoid making contact with the enemy. And to this end they more than meet the challenge. There are a few brushes with some dangerous looking stock footage but nothing serious. The squad leader, Lt. Factor, takes a lot of verbal abuse from his sergeant who resents the fact that Factor is better educated than he is.

Then the boys stumble onto a secluded little cabin. They burst into the place and find a woman named Isle. They make fun of her German accent, tease her about her husband who's gone to war, slaughter her chickens, and generally give a poor account of themselves. Isle adds a little poison to their chow but Factor catches her in the act. But seeing as she's the only woman around, the guys let her continue to make their meals. Then she pulls a gun on them and they're forced to plug her.

Not burying her body proves to be a serious tactical error for the boys. Isle's corpse is discovered by the leader of a German ski troop. He and his men go after the culprits. Meanwhile, Factor and his men have finally gotten wind of their mission. They're to delay enemy troop movement by blowing up one of their bridges. Three G.I.s die before the mission is complete, leaving only Factor and his grumpy sergeant to hash over the time the idiot sergeant destroyed their only avenue of retreat.

Behind the Scenes: This one was shot in Deadwood, South Dakota, to take advantage of a right-to-work state, where Roger and Gene Corman could make a nonunion movie. They decided to split the cost of transportation by making two movies. Gene and director Monte Hellman shot their movie the first two weeks, then the cast and crew went to work on Roger's movie for another two weeks. It was not, as it turned out, an ideal place to be during the winter. The snow made it impossible to match scenes. And when the ski instructor that Roger hired to play the German squad leader broke his leg, Roger had to take the role. Not knowing any German, Roger faked the lines and hired an accountant to overdub a voice.

Between takes, waiting for his actors to get into position on top of a snow-covered mountain above him, Roger's ill-timed use of a bullhorn caused an avalanche. No one was hurt but it messed up Roger's shot. He'd wanted a shot of the troop skiing down a slope of virgin snow and when he realized what he'd done, that he'd waited an hour for nothing, there seemed to be only one thing left to do. He raised the bullhorn to his mouth and said: "Stop that snow!"

The Shock-by-Shock Confessions of a
Sorority Girl. "Smart ... Pretty ... and All Bad!" 1957 B&W 60 min.
PRO-DIR Roger Corman, EXEC PRO James H. Nicholson, SP Ed Waters, Leo Lieberman, DP Monroe P. Askins, ED Charles Gross, Jr., MUS Ronald Stein. Sunset/American International.

The Cast: Susan Cabot (Sabra Tanner), Dick Miller (Mort), Barboura O'Neill (Rita Joyce), June Kenney (Tina), Barbara Crane (Billie Marshall), Fay Baker (Mrs. Tanner), Jeanne Wood (Mrs. Fessenden), Margaret Campbell.

The Story: To be eligible for the inheritance her father has left her, Sabra Tanner must graduate from college. She takes her anger out on the other students, two in particular. One is Billie Marshall, a weak-willed girl whom Sabra easily dominates. Sabra forces Billie to do odd jobs for her and when she's dissatisfied with the results, whacks Billie's fanny with a wooden paddle. Rita, the other primary target of Sabra's hate, catches Sabra giving Billie a hazing and threatens to tell the Dean unless Sabra promises never to do it again.

Sabra immediately seeks revenge. She breaks into Rita's room and finds a box of letters written by Rita's father, who is in prison. Sabra asks Rita what she thinks her chances of becoming president of the student body would be if everyone knew her father was a jailbird. Then Sabra's mother cuts off her allowance. Shortly after, Sabra learns that another member of the sorority, Tina, is pregnant. Under the pretense of trying to help her, Sabra gets Tina to blackmail Rita's election manager and former student body president, Mort, claiming he's the father.

But Mort won't be blackmailed and eventually gets Tina to admit that he's not the father. Despondent, Tina tries to kill herself by jumping off a cliff during a beach party. Mort saves her and Tina spills the beans about Sabra. The incident compels Rita to risk exposure. She tells the other girls about the secret that Sabra is holding over her head. The rest of the sorority sisters confront Sabra, let her know she's not worth their trouble, and leave her to crawl back under the rock from which she came.

Behind the Scenes: "When I first starting directing I had no experience with actors," Roger has stated. "My education had simply not been in that area. I'd come from writing and production. After the first few films I found that I really needed some training in acting in order to communicate better with the actors. I went to Jeff Corey's acting class and studied with a number of people. The lead in *Sorority Girl* was Susan Cabot, who was a very dedicated method actress from New York. I remember there was an extremely emotional scene she

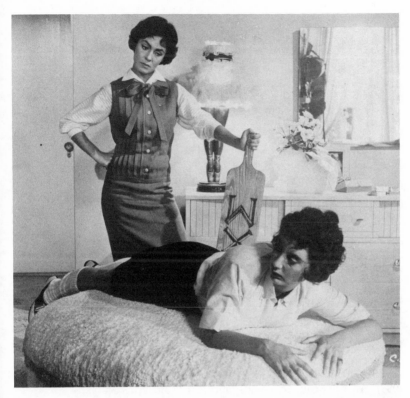

Susan Cabot prepares to paddle Barbara Crane, in *Sorority Girl* (AIP, 1957).

had to play around a swimming pool with an actress playing her mother. I was going to shoot the scene in a medium shot and a close shot. Utilizing what I had just learned in the class, I talked about the scene with Susan and we did the first take in a medium shot. And she was brilliant. She was really wonderful. The crew applauded and I went over and congratulated her. Then we set up for the close shot and although she was good, she was never able to reach the level of intensity she had in the medium shot. Of course, what you want is the close shot for the most emotional part of the scene but I left more of the medium shot than I had planned to. I learned a lesson and that was to let the performers know they needed to save something for the close shot and not use all of the emotion for the medium shot."

Swamp Women. "Scarlet Women Out to Get Every Thrill They Could Steal!" 1955 C 73 min. DIR Roger Corman, PRO Bernard Woolner, SP David Stern, DP Fred West, ED Ronald Sinclair, MUS Willis Holman. Woolner Bros.

   The Cast: Beverly Garland (Vera), Carole Matthews (Lee), Touch Connors (Bob), Marie Windsor (Josie), Jill Jarmyn (Billie), Susan Cummings (Marie).

Beverly Garland (left) and Carole Matthews in *Swamp Women* (Woolner Bros., 1955), AKA "Swamp Diamonds" and "Cruel Swamp."

The Story: Three tough broads—Josie, Billie and Vera—who call themselves the Nardo gang, are in prison for stealing diamonds. An undercover policewoman named Lee masterminds their escape hoping they'll lead her to the booty. They head for the Louisiana bayous and commandeer a boat belonging to a young geologist named Bob. They shoot Bob's guide, knock Bob unconscious and toss Bob's lady friend to the alligators. Bob becomes their prisoner as well as the cause of some bickering among the ladies who take turns making passes at him.

Lee does her best to protect Bob, which starts trouble with Vera, the toughest of the lot. "Look, if I bother you, go somewhere else," Lee tells Vera. Josie tries to intervene. "Look," Vera snaps, "nobody talks to me like that. I'll kill that dame." Billie makes her own pass at Bob. "What can I do for you?" he asks. "Anything you like," she replies. "What if I don't like?" Bob retorts. "You will," Billie says confidently. And that's when Vera pops up. "You dirty little dumb broad," she spits.

Once the diamonds are uncovered, Vera takes them and the guns and climbs a tree so she can snipe the rest of the gang. She's killed with a spear. Lee sets Bob free and the two of them hold Vera and Billie until the police can arrive.

Behind the Scenes: At the end of the film, when Beverly Garland was impaled with a spear, Roger said to her, "When you're killed, you have to drop." And since Beverly was about twenty feet off the ground in a tree she was naturally curious if anyone would be there to catch her. Roger assured her that there would be. So she threw all caution to the wind and did what Roger asked her to do. Three guys caught her. And when it was over Roger said, "You're really one of the best stuntwomen I have ever worked with."

Jonathan Haze was the stunt coordinator, as he was on several of Roger's pictures. "Most of the fight scenes between women somehow don't turn out right on the screen," Jonathan remarked. "Women don't have the same muscular coordination as men. On film, the gals look like they're either playing volleyball or patty-cake. This leads the audience to laugh, something that every producer fears in an action thriller."

Tales of Terror. "A Trilogy of Shock and Horror!" 1962 C-Scope 90 min. PRO-DIR Roger Corman, EXEC PRO James H. Nicholson, Samuel Z. Arkoff, SP Richard Matheson, DP Floyd Crosby, ED Anthony Carras, ART DIR Daniel Haller, MUS Les Baxter. Alta Vista/American International.

The Cast: "Morella" — Vincent Price (Locke), Maggie Pierce (Leonora), Leona Gage (Morella), Edmond Cobb (driver). "The Black Cat" — Vincent Price (Fortunato Lucresi), Peter Lorre (Montressor Herringbone), Joyce Jameson (Annabel Herringbone), Lennie Weinrib (policeman), Wally Campo (bartender), Alan DeWitt (chairman), John Hackett (policeman). "The Facts in the Case of M. Valdemar" — Vincent Price (Valdemar), Basil Rathbone (Carmichael), Debra Paget (Helene), David Frankham (Elliot James), Scotty Brown (servant).

The Stories: "Morella" — For 26 years following the death of his wife during childbirth, Locke has lived in seclusion. His daughter Leonora returns home, having been banished during infancy. She finds that Locke still harbors ill will, blaming her for her mother's death. Leonora tells Locke she has but a few months to live and his anger melts away. She tells him of her inability to form relationships and he recounts that last evening when Morella, in spite of her ill health, insisted on giving a party. Her mummified corpse remains in the house, in her old bedroom. And during the night her jealous spirit sucks the life from Leonora, then strangles her husband.

"The Black Cat" — Montressor Herringbone has little time for his wife until he discovers that she is having an affair with a much more civilized chap than himself named Fortunato Lucresi. Montressor invites the fellow over for a friendly drink, spikes the wine and when Fortunato awakens he finds himself chained to Montressor's basement wall, beside him the corpse of his mistress, Annabel, Montressor's wife. Worse still, Montressor is walling the both of them up. Fortunato can't believe this nightmare is real. "We'll have a good laugh about this," he says desperately. "*I* will," Montressor mutters. "*I* will." But Montressor's dreams are tortured by images of the people he's murdered and when the police arrive to investigate the disappearance of his wife, Montressor leads them straight to the cellar, confident they will find nothing. Perhaps they

A TRILOGY OF SHOCK AND HORROR!

"...and there was an oozing liquid putrescence ...all that remained of Mr. Valdemar." --POE

"I had walled the black monster up within the tomb!" --POE

"The winds of the firmament breathed but one sound within my ears and the ripples upon the sea murmured evermore...MORELLA" --POE

AMERICAN INTERNATIONAL presents

EDGAR ALLAN POE'S

TALES OF TERROR

in PANAVISION® and COLOR

Tales of Terror (AIP, 1962): top, Vincent Price (left), Jack Bohrer, Roger Corman and Basil Rathbone chatting between scenes; bottom, Corman gives direction to Peter Lorre and Joyce Jameson.

wouldn't have if Montressor hadn't accidentally imprisoned Annabel's black cat behind the wall. The animal cries out and the crime is revealed.

"The Facts in the Case of M. Valdemar" — Dying a painful death, an elderly man named Valdemar seeks relief by means of mesmerism at the hands of Dr. Carmichael who asks no fee for his services save a simple favor: the doctor wants to hypnotize the old man at the moment before death. When Valdemar dies Carmichael is able to keep his mind alive. Valdemar's wife Helene begs the mesmerist to free his hold but he will not do so until Helene agrees to marry him. Valdemar's rotting corpse rises from the bed and kills the evil doctor.

Behind the Scenes (from the pressbook):

"Neither glory, nor publicity, nor fame goes to the film editor for his key role in the final product that American movie audiences see on the screen — but it is his professional skill and experience that often makes the difference between just an ordinary and a good motion picture.

"That American International's newest color and Panavision thriller, *Poe's Tales of Terror* is as exciting as it is, is another tribute to the skill of film editor Anthony Carras. He also was the man behind the film scenes in AIP's previous Edgar Allan Poe hits, *House of Usher* and *The Pit and the Pendulum*.

"Detroit-born Tony grew up in New York City where he graduated as an aeronautical engineer. He moved on to Sikorsky Aircraft and then to Army-Air Force bombers for World War II as a captain.

"Vocational guidance experts uncovered his penchant and talent for the show business world, so Tony left airplanes behind and entered the famous incubator of entertainment, the Pasadena Playhouse. He graduated cum laude and became a director for television and stage plays.

"Utilizing his television and theatre experience, he switched to sound engineering and effects at 20th Century–Fox, working on *Not as a Stranger* and *Guys and Dolls*.

"Next step was American International Pictures as sound editor then as film editor, and this year he'll direct his first motion picture, *The Seafighters*.

"Tony not only is the 'picture doctor' for all AIP films, but he works hand in hand with producer, director and art director to evolve the many wonderful special effects that distinguish a fine film. One of his specialties is optics and he has helped originate many special optical effects to enhance the thrills of many pictures, with *Poe's Tales of Terror* one of the best examples of his art.

"The director in Tony still holds on and he is anxiously waiting for a chance to direct *The Seafighters*. . . .

"Tony is the father of five youngsters, owns a big home in eastern Los Angeles and prefers baseball, bowling and movies for his entertainment."

Top: Rathbone (center) watches as make-up artist does Price; bottom, the two in action.

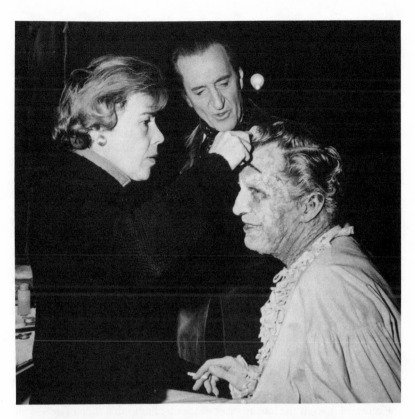

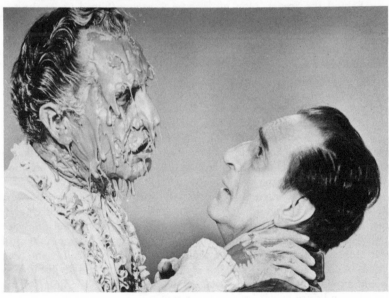

Teenage Caveman. "Prehistoric Rebels Against Prehistoric Monsters!" 1958 B&W C-Scope 65 min. PRO-DIR Roger Corman, SP R. Wright Campbell, DP Floyd Crosby, ED Irene Morra, ASSOC DIR Maurice Vaccarino, MUS Albert Glasser. Malibu/American International.

The Cast: Robert Vaughn (the boy), Leslie Bradley (symbol-maker), Darrah Marshall (the maiden), Frank De Kova (the villain), Joseph Hamilton, Robert Shayne, Beach Dickerson, June Jocelyn, Jonathan Haze, Charles Thompson, Ed Nelson.

The Story: In a barren, rocky land dwells a primitive, superstitious tribe, bound by the Law, a semireligious code that forbids them from going across the river to the lush lands beyond where there is much game and the promise of an easier life. When the symbol-maker of the tribe is hurt during a hunt, his son takes a small group beyond the river, where one of them dies in quicksand. Fearing the death was an omen of things to come, the others return home but the symbol-maker's son remains. When his father recovers he goes after the boy and brings him home. The tribe demands his death for breaking the Law but the father persuades them to simply forbid the boy to speak again until he becomes a man, at which time he is initiated into the tribe and takes a young maiden for his wife.

But the symbol-maker's son still dreams of the land beyond the river and again sets off in search of the truth. He finds prehistoric creatures in the form of stock footage from *One Million B.C.* and a monster (left over from *Night of the Blood Beast*) that turns out to be a mutated man who explains that the people of the tribe are the descendants of the survivors of the atom bomb and that he, the mutated man, is the lone survivor of another group that didn't fare as well.

Behind the Scenes: Most of *Teenage Caveman* (filmed under the title *Prehistoric World*) was shot at Bronson Canyon, located above Hollywood Boulevard off Franklin Avenue near Beachwood Drive. Once a mineral quarry, the cave and the canyon behind it have been used in hundreds of motion picture and television shows. But the location used for the sequence where actor Beach Dickerson drowns in a pit of quicksand was the Aboretum, just across the street from the Santa Anita Racetrack in Arcadia, about 20 miles from Hollywood, on an expansive chunk of land once owned by Lucky Baldwin, the site of dozens of jungle epics. Dickerson recounts his experience there:

"I was supposed to fall off a log into this water that was so filthy it almost made me throw up. So I held my breath and jumped in and started flailing around. Roger kneels beside me and says, 'I don't believe you're drowning. You're not convincing me.' Well, of course I didn't want to stick my face in this gunk but I figured I might as well get it over with so I finally gave him what he wanted. I kicked and screamed and sank and floated to the top like a dead man. Then we went to Bronson Canyon and shot my funeral sequence. Everybody was sitting in a half circle and I was sitting in the wardrobe truck watching. Roger comes over to me and says, 'What are you doing here?' And I said, 'Well, I can't be out *there*. It's *my* funeral.' And he said, 'Bullshit. Who would recognize you anyway?' If you see the picture I'm in the front row in a bearskin and a frightwig, beating a tom-tom.

Teenage Caveman (AIP, 1958): "This water was so filthy it almost made me throw up," said Beach Dickerson (top); bottom, Robert Vaughn and Darah Marshall in a more arid moment.

Robert Vaughn, the *Teenage Caveman,* is attacked by Beach Dickerson in a bear suit.

"A couple of days later Roger was shooting a sequence where this character called the Man from the Burning Plains rides into camp and gets stoned to death. They brought in this scroungy old horse and I look around and ask, "Who's going to play the Man from the Burning Plains?" And then I saw them coming toward me with this bearskin and I thought, 'Oh, shit.' Because the ground I'm supposed to fall on is solid granite. I said to Roger, 'I'm not a stunt-man.' He said, 'You're just as capable of falling off a horse as anyone.' 'Yeah,' I said, 'and save you fifty bucks.' So I rode into camp wearing this ridiculous beard. I looked like Ulysses S. Grant in a bearskin. And they stoned me and I fell off the horse and I was great. We got the whole thing in one take. Then the cameraman tells Roger, 'I think I saw his underwear.' Roger was furious.

'You're wearing underwear!' he roared. 'How dare you?' I said, 'Of course I'm wearing underwear. I've got a bearskin around me for crissakes.' So we have to do it again.

"Then we went to Iverson's Ranch and they were going to do this scene where they hunt and kill this bear. I was waiting for the trainer to show up with the bear when I see this guy coming toward me with a bear suit. 'Oh, my God,' I thought. Of course it was hotter than hell and here I am in this bear suit on all fours. I was at the top of a hill and I couldn't see a thing and Roger yelled, 'Okay, bear. Come down the hill.' And I came down backwards cause I couldn't see anything. "What are you doing?" he screamed. "I can't see anything, for crissakes," I screamed back. "Well, what can we do? Think quick," Roger said. So I suggested they make a path for me to follow with a rope and I suggested they do it quick because I was roasting to death inside that suit. So here I come down this hill and Roger says, 'Okay, bear. Stand up.' So I stand up. 'Okay, you're a mean bear.' I growled. 'You're not mean enough,' he says so I growled and snarled and he keeps telling me I'm not mean enough and pretty soon we're screaming at one another until he thinks I'm mean enough and then he says to all these guys playing the hunters, 'Okay. Kill the bear.'"*

Teenage Doll. "Too Young . . . to Be Careful. Too Tough to Care. Now It's Too Late to Say 'NO'!" 1957 B&W 68 min. PRO-DIR Roger Corman, EXEC PRO Bernard Woolner, SP Charles B. Griffith, DP Floyd Crosby, ED Charles Gross, Jr., ART DIR Robert Kinoshita, MUS Walter Greene. Woolner Bros. / Allied Artists.

The Cast: June Kenney (Barbara Bonney), Fay Spain (Hel), John Brinkley (Eddie Rand), Colette Jackson (May), Barbara Wilson (Betty), Ziva Rodan (Squirrel), Sandy Smith (Lorrie), Barboura Morris (Janet), Richard Devon (Dunston), Jay Sayer (Wally), Richard Cutting (Phil Kern), Dorothy Neumann (Estelle Bonney), Ed Nelson (Dutch, Blindman), Damian O'Flynn (Harold Bonney).

The Story: Nan Baker, a member of the Black Widows gang, is found dead in an alley. The members of her gang suspect she was pushed off a railing by Barbara Bonney, a rival of Nan's for the affections of Eddie Rand, the leader of the Vandals. Hel, the leader of the Widows, wants to force a confession out of Barbara. Assuming that she'll run to Eddie, Hel decides to take up a collection. "Eddie'll sell his grandmother's teeth for a ticket to the burlesque and he'll sell Barbara Bonney for not much more," she tells the gang.

Meanwhile, Barbara goes home to change her torn and bloodied dress. Her mother Estelle knows she's in trouble and for the umpteenth time relates the story the no good bootlegger Estelle once knew. "Maybe someday you'll meet a man like that," Estelle says, assuming her daughter already has. "You'll know he's cheap and worthless and treacherous but you won't care. You'll do anything he wants, any time, and be glad for the chance to do it . . . and you must never, ever fall in love with one of them."

*Dickerson's reminiscence is from an interview with the author.

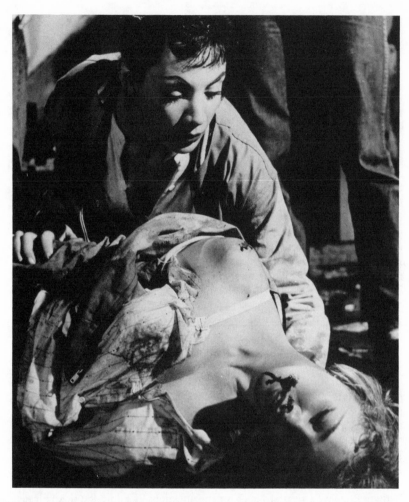

Squirrel (Ziva Rodan) finds the body of gang member Nan Baker in this scene from *Teenage Doll* (Allied Artists, 1957).

Sure enough, Barbara discovers that Eddie Rand is exactly the sort of scum that her mother warned her about. "You don't go looking for a con man and expect to find a boy scout," Eddie says glibly but ultimately promises to get her out of town. The rest of the gang disperses to set a trap for the Black Widows and their male counterparts, the Tarantulas, who they feel certain will come looking for Bonnie. Feeling sorry for herself, Bonnie reflects on the fact that she's done nothing to cause the trouble; that everything's happened *to* her. Nan's death was accidental, a result of Bonnie's trying to defend herself. "You did one thing wrong," Eddie tells her. "The worst thing anybody can do. You stepped out of your class."

Top: June Kenney finds momentary refuge in a deserted warehouse; bottom: Barbara Wilson is showing her father's gun to Fay Spain — from *Teenage Doll*.

Sure enough, the Black Widows and the Tarantulas come and during the rumble the police show up. Hel and a couple of the others chase Barbara into a warehouse where she runs into Eddie. "You got three choices," Eddie tells her. "You can go through that door to the Widows, you can go jump out the window to the cops and take a chance on the gas chamber, or you can go to Phoenix, change your name and learn to scuffle." "I'm afraid," she tells him. "So who isn't?" he replies. "Look, kid. You're lucky. You still gotta choice." In the end, Barbara decides to take her chances with the police.

Behind the Scenes: In his script, originally titled *The Young Rebels* (the title under which the film often appears on television), writer Charles Griffith conjured up a deadly weapon: "I invented something called a Potato Grenade which was a potato impaled on a peeler with razor blades stuck in it. The [Will H.] Hays [author of the 1930 Production Code] Office nixed the idea. In fact, we had to change the story so the gang hires someone else to do their dirty work for them. That really ruined it. We also had a very unsatisfactory ending because we couldn't figure out what the hell we could get away with."

This was another ten day picture, shot mostly at night, and was one of the grittiest juvenile delinquency pictures of the period.

While they were shooting the exteriors of a house, the next-door neighbor turned on her sprinklers in the hope that Roger would pay to shut them off. Roger sent the assistant director to ask the woman to increase the pressure since the glint of the water made a nice effect. The woman angrily shut them off.

To ease the anticipated criticism of the film, a prologue was added that said: "This is not a pretty picture.... It could not be pretty and still be true. What happens to the girl is unimportant.... What happens to the others is more than important, it is the most vital issue of our time. This story is about a sickness, a spreading epidemic that threatens to destroy our very way of life. We are not doctors ... we can offer no cure ... but we know that a cure must be found." In keeping with this tone, the pressbook offered the following suggestions:

"JUVENILE PANEL DISCUSSION. Many radio and television stations schedule panel shows in which high school boys and girls, in addition to an adult moderator, discuss the problems confronting teenagers. Spot a television slide or, if on radio, a transcription announcement immediately following any such show.

"INTERVIEW ON DELINQUENCY PROBLEM. Arrange with radio station or newspaper to provide time or space for teenagers to voice their gripes. Pinpoint the subject by asking a provoking question such as 'Do you believe that teenagers are basically bad? If so, who is responsible?'"

The Terror. "**From the Depths of an Evil Mind Came a Diabolical Plan of Torture ... Inconceivable ... Unbelievable!**" 1963 C 81 min. PRO-DIR Roger Corman, DIR (uncredited) Francis Ford Coppola, Monte Hellman, Jack Hill, Dennis Jacob, Jack Nicholson, EXEC PRO Harvey Jacobson, SP Leo Gordon, Jack Hill, ART DIR Daniel Haller, TITLES Paul Julian, ED Stuart O'Brien, MUS Ronald Stein. Filmgroup/American International.

The Cast: Boris Karloff (Baron Von Leppe), Jack Nicholson (Andre Duvalier), Sandra Knight (Helene), Dick Miller (Stefan), Dorothy Neumann (Eric's mom), Jonathan Haze (Gustaf).

The Story: Separated from his regiment somewhere on the Baltic coast, Andre Duvalier, an officer in Napoleon's army, falls from his horse and is awakened by the gentle lapping of the waves on the beach. A beautiful woman shows him to fresh water, then disappears into the pounding surf. When Andre attempts to follow her he is attacked by a hawk. Swept off his feet by the surf, he is knocked unconscious. He wakes to find himself in the home of a strange old woman and her half-witted, mute servant Gustaf. The hawk that attacked Andre turns out to be the old woman's pet.

Andre follows the hawk into the forest and again encounters the woman from the beach. She kisses him tenderly then vanishes into the woods. Andre tries to follow her but is stopped by Gustaf. For Andre was about to step in quicksand. The old woman tells Andre he can find the woman he seeks at the castle of Baron von Leppe. The description Andre gives to von Leppe fits the Baron's wife, who's been dead for twenty years. The Baron and his servant Stefan are most anxious for Andre to leave but Andre thinks something strange is going on and he's correct. The old woman from the forest had a son named Eric who was killed by the Baron. To revenge her son's death, she hypnotized a young woman (Helene from the beach) to impersonate the Baron's dead wife in order to drive him to suicide. "The Baron did return that night to find Eric with the Baron's wife and he did kill her," Stefan explains. "But in the struggle and in the fight it was not Eric that died. It was the Baron. I killed the Baron. He took the Baron's place . . . in mind as well as body." This revelation is too late to do Eric much good. He's already flooded the basement and drowned. And the innocent pawn in this game of death, Helene, unexplainably melts into muck.

Behind the Scenes: This is the picture that was touted as Roger Corman's three-day wonder, supposedly shot on a weekend on sets left over from *The Raven*. Actually, in some respects, *The Terror* took longer to make than any other Corman film.

As he went into his second week of production on *The Raven*, Roger was struck with the idea of making another picture on the sets for his own company, the Filmgroup.

"He called me up," said Leo Gordon. "Told me he needed scenes for Boris Karloff. He didn't have a story. Just Karloff, a couple of actors, and the damn castle."

When *The Raven* finished shooting on Friday, Roger told everyone to leave the sets till Monday. Then, over the weekend, Roger filmed the scenes Gordon had written for Karloff, Jack Nicholson and Dick Miller.

"I was in every shot, of course," Karloff recalled. "Sometimes I was walking through and then I would change my jacket and walk back. He nearly killed me in it. The last day he had me in a tank of cold water for about two hours." As the sets were being pulled down around their ears, Roger was dashing around with Karloff and the cameraman two steps ahead of the wreckers.

Sandra Knight as the mysterious catalyst in Corman's *The Terror* (AIP, 1963), filmed in order to take advantage of sets left over from *The Raven*.

Three months later Dick Miller got a call from Roger saying they were going to finish the movie. By then, Miller didn't know what he was talking about.

"It was hysterical," Miller said. "When you see the film you'll see me walk through a door and I'll gain twenty pounds. And my sideburns kept moving up and down. And, of course, my character kept changing because we never knew what we were supposed to be doing."

Several directors had a hand in the project: Francis Ford Coppola, Monte Hellman, Jack Hill. Hill related an amusing incident about the picture to Jeffrey Frentzen in *Fangoria* magazine: "Francis had this shot of Jack Nicholson and Sandy Knight coming down this hillside trail in the woods, and as they came around the corner of this hillside, thousands of butterflies were going to fly up in front of them. So he had guys out catching butterflies all set to go, and he called action, they let the butterflies go, and Jack Nicholson comes around acting like a fag, y'know, flapping his arms. And he says, 'Oh, is that a take?'"[1]

"That film is immortal," Nicholson remarked. "There's no question about it." Unhappily, next to his *Playboy* interview, Nicholson reports that *The Terror* is the most seen and discussed item of his career. He thought he was absurd in the part, dressed in Marlon Brando's wardrobe from Napoleon, too big in the shoulders. Peter Bogdanovich, who used scenes from *The Terror* in his film *Targets* (1971), warned Nicholson that if the picture was ever re-released it could destroy his career.

Tomb of Ligeia. "CAT or WOMAN or a Thing Too Evil to Mention?" 1965 C-Scope 79 min. PRO-DIR Roger Corman, SP Robert Towne, DP Arthur Grant, ART DIR Colin Southcott, SPFX Ted Samuel, TITLES Francis Rodker, ED Alfred Cox, MUS Kenneth V. Jones. American International.

The Cast: Vincent Price (Verden Fell), Elizabeth Shepherd (Lady Rowena Trevanion/Ligeia), John Westbrook (Christopher Gough), Oliver Johnston (Kenrick), Derek Francis (Lord Trevanion), Richard Vernon (Dr. Vivian), Ronald Adam (Parson), Frank Thornton (Peperel), Denis Gilmore (Livery Boy), Penelope Lee.

The Story: Verden Fell is burying his deceased wife Ligeia in an English country churchyard in 1821 when the local parson protests that the ceremony should not take place because the woman was not a Christian. Fell says that his wife will not rest because she's not really dead and quotes her philosophy: "Man need not kneel before the angels nor lie in death forever but for the weakness of his feeble will." Suddenly a black cat screeches and Ligeia's eyes open.

A few months later while on a fox hunt, Lady Rowena Trevanion wanders into the churchyard and finds herself staring unaccountably at the strange inscription on Ligeia's tombstone. The black cat hisses, her horse panics and she is thrown. She's carried away by Fell to his vast Gothic abbey. They're seen by Rowena's hunting companion Christopher Gough, who informs Rowena's father, Lord Trevanion. He comes in with a fox from the hunt which coincidentally was Ligeia's pet. The fox disappears during their conversation and Fell suspects the cat made off with it.

Rowena is attracted to Fell and some days later, as they are about to kiss, the cat darts between then and scratches Rowena's face. Later it lures her to the bell tower of the abbey where she is nearly killed. Once again she is rescued by Fell and eventually they marry. But Fell becomes like a stranger to her, curiously leaving her alone at night and soon Rowena begins having nightmares involving Ligeia and the cat. One night she finds the dead fox in her bed. Christopher Gough, hired by Fell to sell the abbey, suspects something is wrong and exhumes Ligeia's coffin, only to discover a wax effigy in place of a corpse.

Meanwhile, Rowena is losing her mind. In her bedroom mirror her image becomes Ligeia. She smashes the glass and discovers a secret passageway which

---

1. *Jeffrey Frentzen, "Not Just Another Cog in the Corman Factory," Fangoria, vol. 3, no. 45, p. 14.*

Tomb of Ligeia (AIP, 1965), Corman's final Poe film: top, Elizabeth Shepherd discovers a secret passageway behind the mirror; bottom, Vincent Price (foreground) tends to Shepherd after a nasty spill.

leads to Ligeia's corpse and to Fell, who apparently is suffering under the delusion that his wife is still alive. Rowena tries to bring him to his senses but the man is so confused that he thinks Rowena is Ligeia and to rid himself of her sets fire to the abbey, then tries to kill the cat which he also believes harbors Ligeia's spirit. Gough arrives in time to rescue Rowena but Fell dies in the flames.

Behind the Scenes (from the pressbook):

"You don't have to be an egg head to enjoy the new Poe terror film *Tomb of Ligeia* but an understanding of psychology helps, according to its director Roger Corman.

"While most movie fans are familiar with the menacing roles played by Vincent Price, Corman declares that enjoyment of the Poe films in which Price has been starring recently is greatly enhanced if you are acquainted with the philosophy of Sigmund Freud.

"'I went deeply into Freud when I first began interpreting Edgar Allan Poe stories for the screen,' he says. 'Poe was a writer obsessed with symbolism and Freud was the master of symbolism. In fact, Poe's whole world of ruined sanctuaries, brooding trees, cawing birds, cats, deaths and funerals was a symbolic one. As an American obsessed with Europe's decadence, he was himself symbolic of America's long, regretful farewell to the Europe it wanted to believe was all evil.'

"As a result, Corman makes what might best be described as a quality horror picture of the kind which attracts the egg head as well as the masses.

'Magnificently mounted and filmed in Color and Scope on location in a 100-year-old English abbey, *Tomb of Ligeia* is a screenplay developed by Robert Towne from a Poe short story which dramatizes incidents surrounding the life after death of a woman of such powerful will that her evil spirit terrorizes her widower and the girl he later marries."

Ligeia was Roger's final Poe picture, supposedly because the director was tired of repeating himself, but dwindling box office returns may have had something to do with it. He did vary his formula by shooting much of it outdoors. Vincent Price had always wanted to do a picture in a ruin so he was happy. But they weren't allowed to put furniture in the monastery because it was considered a national monument so some interiors were created at Shepperton Studios.

Alternate titles: *Lygeia, Last Tomb of Ligeia, Tomb of Lygeia, Tomb of the Cat, Ligeia, House at the End of the World.*

The Tower of London. "Half Man . . . Half Demon . . . He Turned a Nation into a Chamber of Horrors!" 1962 B&W 79 min. PRO Gene Corman, DIR Roger Corman, SP Leo V. Gordon, Amos Powell, James B. Gordon from a story by Leo V. Gordon and Amos Powell, DP Arch R. Dalzell, ED Ronald Sinclair, ART DIR Daniel Haller, MUS Michael Anderson. Admiral/United Artists.

The Cast: Vincent Price (Richard of Gloucester), Michael Pate (Sir Ratcliffe), Joan Freeman (Margaret), Robert Brown (Sir Justin), Justice Watson (Edward IV), Sara Selby (Queen), Richard McCauly (Clarence), Eugene Martin

(Edward V), Sandra Knight (Mistress Shore), Richard Hale (Tyrus), Donald Losby (Richard), Bruce Gordon (Earl of Buckingham), Joan Camden (Anne), Morris Ankrum (Cardinal).

The Story: As King Edward IV of England lies dying, his hunchback brother Richard plots to do away with everyone who stands between himself and the throne. To protect his two young sons until they're old enough to replace him, Edward appoints his other brother Clarence as Protector of the Realm. Richard stabs Edward in the back in the tower wine cellar with a knife bearing the queen's crest. Suspicious of his wife, Edward appoints Richard as Protector. Richard's first act in that position is to cast doubt on the boys' legitimacy. He tries to persuade the royal nursemaid, Mistress Shore, to lie for him, but the woman prefers to die on the rack rather than side with the creep.

The queen meanwhile is assured by her lady-in-waiting, Margaret, that Lord Stanley, Margaret's father, will offer military aid against Richard who, unbeknownst to his followers is suffering hallucinations, tormented by the ghosts of the people he's murdered. He strangles his wife believing her to be the spirit of Mistress Shore. Undaunted by this unfortunate accident, Richard holds Margaret hostage to prevent her father from moving against him, suffocates the young princes, and declares himself King. He is then haunted by their ghosts as well. Eventually he's forced to battle Lord Stanley. Wave after wave of stock footage brings Richard to his knees. His mind now completely gone, he battles his tortured conscience until his horse throws him and he lands on the battle-ax of a dead soldier.

Behind the Scenes (from the pressbook):

"Villainy is more rewarding than virtue as far as Vincent Price is concerned. . . . His latest screen villainies will be seen [in] *Tower of London*. In this Admiral Production for United Artists, the in-person gentle Vincent is a 100-proof villain, Richard III, one of history's meanest, unregenerate heels, and the man who reached the throne of England over the bodies of wife, nephews, brothers and friends.

"Recent roles in hit horror pictures, including the successful series of Poe translation to the screen . . . prove that Price is right for his latest role. Such experience in raising the hackles on the audience's collective neck was the warm-up for his portrayal of Richard, the Stonehearted.

"'Every trick of dastardy I ever learned,' Vincent says, 'was preparation for my role in *Tower of London*. Then we added some new, diabolic devices to fill out Richard's character as one of the 10 meanest men in the world.

"'I'd have to live in a fortress and drive to work in an armored car if people thought I was as horrible as the character I portray,' Price said. 'I'm grateful that people recognize the difference between me and Richard, for instance, and I'm glad that I'm one of the villains audiences love to hate.'

"Also in the large cast of *Tower of London* are Michael Pate, Joan Freeman, Robert Brown and Bruce Gordon, the latter no slouch at villainy himself, he being the 'Nitti' of TV's *Untouchables*.

"It was this Richard, incidentally, who, finally vanquished on the field of

Vincent Price as the evil Richard III is more in danger of bumping into the backdrop than of vanquishment by the nonexistent enemy — *The Tower of London* (UA, 1962).

battle, his supporters dispersed and death staring him in the face, uttered the immortal 'A horse, a horse; my kingdom for a horse.'"

The Trip. "A Lovely Sort of Death!" 1967 C 85 min. PRO-DIR Roger Corman, SP Jack Nicholson, DP Arch Dalzell, ED Ronald Sinclair, MUS The American Music Band. Roger Corman / American International.

The Cast: Peter Fonda (Paul Groves), Susan Strasburg (Sally Groves), Bruce Dern (John), Dennis Hopper (Max), Sali Sachse (Glenn), Katherine Walsh (Lulu), Barboura Morris (Flo), Caren Bersen (Alexandra), Dick Miller (Cash), Luana Anders (waitress), Tommy Signorelli (Al), Mitzi Hoag (wife), Judy Lang (Nadine), Barbara Ransom (Helena), Mike Blodget (lover), Susan Walter, Frankie Smith (Go-Go Girls), Peter Bogdanovich, Brandon De-Wilde.

The Story: Paul Groves is a director of television commercials. He's just finishing an assignment at the beach, when his wife Sally arrives to chide him about missing an appointment to sign their divorce papers. All of a sudden the tremendous pressures of his personal and professional life close in on him and Paul decides to drop a little acid in the hope of understanding himself. His friend John acts as his guide.

At first Paul's trip is cool, soothing. Brilliant colors, soft meadows, the sea. Everything is alive. Waves of energy and beautiful, breathing jewels are everywhere. Slowly, however, images of his wife and a blonde goddess named Glenn (who earlier confessed a strong sexual attraction to people on acid) appear. Paul feels as if he's dying and wants to take an antidote. John pleads that he hold on and get "with it." In his hallucination, Paul dies and attends his own funeral. Then he's expected to defend himself in front of a judge for his commerciality and lack of integrity. Paul becomes paranoid and takes refuge in a closet. When he emerges he thinks John has been murdered and runs from the house. Once the acid wears off, Paul is left wondering what to do next.

Behind the Scenes: The following excerpts are from *The Trip* pressbook and are therefore not to be believed for a microsecond. A detailed account of the making of the film can be found in Chapter 4 and should be read prior to tackling the following nonsense for a more enjoyable time.

"'As with many subjects of a controversial nature, writers seem to rush in so fast to take advantage of the commercial aspects of the situation that they lose all the originality the subject can provide. That was the case with LSD,' Corman explained.

"*The Trip*, Hollywood's first excursion into the psychedelic world, stars Peter Fonda, Susan Strasberg, Bruce Dern, Dennis Hopper and Salli Sachse.

"'I was extremely interested in the subject, but when I started reading LSD scripts, I found that all they had done was take the old narcotic formulae — the addiction, the suicides, the jumping out of windows — and changed the name of some other drug to LSD. That isn't what we wanted,' Corman continued.

Peter Fonda experiences his own death under the influence of LSD, on *The Trip* (AIP, 1967).

"Finally, Corman's insistence on a vivid, unconventional treatment of a new and vital subject bore fruit. Writer Jack Nicholson presented him with *The Trip*.

"It was LSD script number eight, but it was the magic number.

"'It not only was different. It was revolutionary. And we gave it the revolutionary treatment it deserves. We have filmed it with a vitally exciting young cast and more special photographic techniques than has been used in a Hollywood picture in many years.

"'And nobody jumps out of the window,' Corman concluded.

* * * * *

"To document his version of the reactions to LSD, Corman discussed the subject with more than 50 subjects who have taken the drug, some of them repeatedly. Voluminous notes were compiled, then checked, footnoted and interpreted by leading experts in the psychedelic field.

"Corman provided the final touch himself. He took a dose of LSD under medical supervision and incorporated his own experiences into the body of the subject matter.

"The result of this exhaustive study is *The Trip*.

"To implement Peter Fonda's journey into the psychedelic unknown, Corman utilizes graphically imaginative sets and costuming. The use of vivid color is striking as an integral part of Fonda's changing mood, sometimes diaphanous, sometimes hard and piercing as carbon steel. The result is presented through the eyes of a fluid, creative camera, making as full a utilization of the motion-picture technique as has ever been displayed in a film from Hollywood.

"'This will be a total film,' explained Corman in that the audience will be so included in the unfolding of the subject on the screen that they will be as near to totally integrated into the pictures' emotional impact as is possible in entertainment.

"'Although we will not attempt to delve into the pros and cons of the use of LSD in *The Trip*,' Corman continued, 'we will provide the audience with more experience than anyone has yet dared show on the subject. Then if anyone wishes to make a judgment on LSD they'll have something on which to base their decision.

"'What we will show is life even though to some it will be unreal, to others unbelievable and to a vocal few without excuse. What controversy *The Trip* stirs is not of our doing. We are merely communicating. When communications stops, can the death, not only of the medium, but of the society, be far behind?' inquired the producer."

The Undead. "Terror ... That Screams from the Grave!" 1957 B&W 75 min. PRO-DIR Roger Corman, SP Charles B. Griffith, Mark Hanna, DP William Sickner, ED Frank Sullivan, MUS Ronald Stein. Balboa/American International.

The Cast: Pamela Duncan (Diana Love/Helene), Richard Garland (Pendragon), Allison Hayes (Livia), Val Dufour (Quintus Ratcliff), Mel Welles

(Smolkin), Dorothy Neumann (Meg-Maud), Billy Barty (Imp), Bruno Ve Sota (Scroop), Aaron Saxon (Gobbo), Richard Devon (Satan), Dick Miller.

The Story: Two doctors, Quintus Ratcliff and Ulbrect Olinger, hire a prostitute for their experiment in regression. Under hypnosis, the prostitute, Diana Love, is taken back in time to the Middle Ages and her previous life as Helene, condemned as a witch and destined to die beneath the headman's axe at dawn. The experiment goes haywire when Helene, with Diana's help, escapes from her dungeon cell and takes refuge with Smolkin, the addlepated gravedigger she supposedly bewitched. Helen was framed by Livia, a real witch, who wanted Helene out of the way so she could have Helene's lover, Pendragon.

Ulbrect warns Quintus that his meddling with the past could drastically alter the future. This is of no concern to Quintus. Instead of trying to rectify the damage he may have caused he uses some electronic device to link his brainwaves with Diana's so that he too can travel back into the past as an observer. Meanwhile, Livia convinces Pendragon that the only way he can help Helene is by trading his soul to the Devil for her life. Pendragon goes with Livia to the Witch's Sabbath but before he can strike the bargain Quintus intervenes.

Helene is faced with an awkward dilemma. If she chooses to live out her life as Helene, she'll forfeit her future incarnations. All of the voices from her future beg her to let them live. In the end she runs to the chopping block as the sun peeks over the mountain. But when her head is severed, so is Quintus's link with the future. Dr. Olinger and Diana look at the chair in which he was sitting and see only his clothes. Quintus is trapped in the past with the Devil laughing in his face.

Behind the Scenes: In the early 1950s, Doubleday published a book by Morey Bernstein titled *The Search for Bridey Murphy*. Bernstein claimed to have hypnotized a woman named Ruth Simmons and regressed her to her former life as a saucy-tongued woman of Ireland named Bridey Murphy. Bernstein's book sold over 170,000 copies and for a while the subject of reincarnation was on everyone's lips. Roger Corman figured it was ripe material for a horror film.

"I told him that by the time we got the thing out it would be a dead issue," said the writer, Charles Griffith. "Then the Paramount movie based on Bernstein's book bombed so Roger changed the picture from *The Trance of Diana Love* to *The Undead* which is a zombie title. The whole thing was originally written in iambic pentameter, all of the stuff in the past. The scenes were separated by synclines done by the Devil. It was the best piece of writing I'd done up until that time or maybe since, I don't know. Roger loved it when he first read it. Then he showed it around and nobody understood it so he told me to translate it into English a couple of days before we had to shoot. And it was gone, you know. It was a mess then."

Mel Welles believed that it would have been one of the classic films of all time if Roger had shot the script as it was originally written. "It made that Medieval regression part come off very ethereal, very Hansel and Gretelish, and would have been very charming," Welles said. "Roger lost his nerve. Didn't want to do it. I remember all of us were very disappointed. Bruno Ve Sota

Dorothy Neumann (left) gives refuge to Pamela Duncan, who is running from the headsman's axe: *The Undead*.

especially. Also, casting Pamela Duncan and Richard Garland in the roles wasn't really terrific either."

"We worked out some fantastic make-up things," Dick Miller recalled. "And Roger shot 'em ass-backwards. I was a leper. There was this old Australian

The Corman Stock Company players in force: from left, Pamela Duncan, Richard Garland, Dorothy Neumann, Allison Hayes, Val Dufour, Richard Devon and Mel Welles, in *The Undead* (AIP, 1957). (Writing lower right is screenwriter Charles Griffith telling Mark McGee he enjoyed the interview.)

Top: Mel Welles knows where the runaway is but won't tell Allison Hayes; bottom, Hayes is about to chop Bruno Ve Sota's head off, as Billy Barty watches eagerly: *The Undead,* one of the more unusual films ever made.

make-up man and we worked out some effects with Kleenex where the skin just falls off. I created it. He was going to put sores on me. And I said, 'Why don't we do this thing with Kleenex.' You wet it and it looks like skin. Like a bad sunburn. And it was great. But Roger shot the make-up in a master shot. And then when my face is cleared up after I've sold my soul to the Devil he shoots this nice handsome shot of me. Me with my be-bop haircut trying to play a Medieval leper. It was unbelievable. He moves in for a close-up to show that my skin has cleared up. I said, 'You missed this fantastic make-up.' 'Well, we're not going to go back and get it. Forget it.'"

Chuck Griffith remembered another scene that was sabotaged by the film's quick shooting schedule wherein Bruno Ve Sota was supposed to get his head sliced off by Allison Hayes. "He was supposed to back up against the wall and she was supposed to swing an axe that went through the neck, right into the wall," Griffith said. "Then the body was supposed to slide down the wall, squirting blood, and the head was to stay on the axe blade, looking surprised. No attempt was made to do that. Bruno was really dying to do it."

Roger was shooting at such a rapid pace that at one point he told his cameraman to get a shot of a sunset and when he was informed that they'd run out of film he told the man to shoot it anyway.

"It was a very strange film," Roger said. "I haven't seen it for a long, long time. I was maybe a little too ambitious for ten days and seventy or eighty thousand dollars. This is one of the things I learned over the long-run: we were better off making a small picture for a small amount of money than trying to make a big one and cheat it."

Most of the picture was filmed inside Jimmy Petch's Sunset stage which was an old supermarket. The exteriors were filmed around a house designed by an art director in the 20s, somewhere on Carmenita in Beverly Hills.

The Undead was rich with fresh ideas. It's unique if nothing else but unfortunately it has the look and feel of a 50s television show, as do many low budget features of the period, but *The Undead* seems to suffer more from it. Still, it remains one of the most interesting of Roger's early pictures.

Von Richthofen and Brown. 1970 C 97 min. PRO Gene Corman, DIR Roger Corman, SP John and Joyce Corrington, DP Michael Reed, AERIAL PHOTOGRAPHY Peter Allwork, Peter Pechowski, Seamus Corcoran, ED George Van Voy and Alan Collins, ART DIR Jim Murankami, SPFX Peter Dawson, MUS Hugo Friedhofer. United Artists.

The Cast: John Phillip Law (Von Richthofen), Don Stroud (Roy Brown), Barry Primus (Hermann Goering), Karen Huston, Corin Redgrave, Hurd Hatfield, Peter Masterson (Oswald Boelcke), Robert La Tourneaux, George Armitage, Steven McHattie, Brian Foley, Ferdy Mayne.

The Story: Baron Manfred von Richthofen is a chivalrous German fighter pilot whom Canadian upstart Roy Brown has vowed to kill. Von Richthofen, whose bright red plane is dubbed "The Red Baron," becomes enraged when Brown instigates a sneak attack that destroys German planes and innocent hospital patients and staff. Von Richthofen leads a counterattack during which

On location in Ireland filming *Von Richthofen and Brown* (UA, 1971), the last film Roger Corman directed. Behind him is one of the World War I planes built for *The Blue Max* and also used in *Darling Lili*.

Hermann Goering, who thinks Von Richthofen's moral code is as foolish as Brown does, slaughters a group of nurses. When it is clear that Germany has lost the war, Von Richthofen is asked by his superiors to join in a plot to take over the postwar government, which he refuses to do. Instead he goes on one last mission giving Brown the chance he needed to shoot him down.

Behind the Scenes: This is one of those cases of which came first, the chicken or the egg? Did Roger want to make a movie about the German air ace

Von Richthofen and then luck into a deal whereby he could use all the planes from the multimillion dollar epic *The Blue Max** or vice versa? Originally Roger wanted Don Stroud to play Von Richthofen and Bruce Dern for Roy Brown but the money people at United Artists nixed Dern. When previewed, a nude love scene between UA choice John Phillip Law and actress Karen Huston caused laughter instead of the expected hushed excitement and was deleted.

War of the Satellites. "The Interplanetary War of the Future!" 1958 B&W 66 min. PRO-DIR Roger Corman, EXEC PRO Jack Rabin, Irving Block, SP Lawrence Louis Goldman from a story by Irving Block and Jack Rabin, SPFX Jack Rabin, Irving Block, Louis DeWitt, ART DIR Dan Haller, ED Irene Morra, DP Floyd Crosby, MUS Walter Greene. Allied Artists.

The Cast: Susan Cabot (Sybil), Dick Miller (Dave Boyer), Richard Devon (Van Ponder), Robert Shayne (Hodgkiss), Jerry Barclay (John), Eric Sinclair (Dr. Lazar), Jay Sayer (Jay), Mitzi McCall (Mitzi), Beach Dickerson, John Brinkley, Bruno Ve Sota.

The Story: The United Nations Rocket Operations is in serious trouble. Every satellite they send into outer space reaches a certain point then blows up. Opposition to the project mounts daily, given more fuel by an ultimatum from space, found by a couple of necking teenagers. Sent in a small rocket the message warns that if earth continues to explore outer space the planet will be obliterated. The head of the project, Dr. Van Ponder, is on his way to a U.N. meeting when some interplanetary force sends his car off the road and when the news of Van Ponder's death reaches the U.N. it looks as if the space program is doomed, in spite of an impassioned plea to continue by the doctor's assistant, Dave Boyer.

Only Van Ponder's sudden and shocking appearance at the meeting turns the tide and the committee votes to go ahead with the construction of three separate rockets, each of which will carry a piece of a new satellite which will be assembled in outer space. What nobody knows is Van Ponder *was* killed in that automobile accident and has been replaced by an alien in Van Ponder's form. Just before take-off Dave Boyer sees Van Ponder split into two separate selves and once the three rockets have made their rendezvous and the satellite has been assembled, Dave tells his lady friend Sybil and Dr. Lazar about his discovery.

Dr. Lazar insists that Van Ponder submit to a "routine" medical examination. The alien stalls long enough to develop a heart then unaccountably kills the doctor anyway. The alien splits in two again and while the one is out trying to sabotage the mission, the other, now equipped with a heart, is experiencing human feelings and wants to share them with Sybil. Dave manages to destroy the alien and take control of the satellite in time to alter Van Ponder's suicide course. In retrospect, it would have been less trouble if the aliens had simply killed Van Ponder and left well enough alone since it was Van Ponder's return from the dead that swayed the decision of the U.N. committee.

*Memorable only for its exciting plane fights, Jerry Goldsmith score and flashes of Ursula Andress undressed.

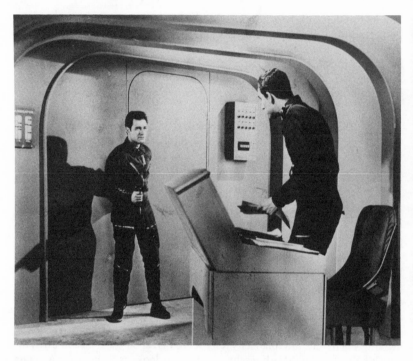

Dick Miller has the drop on alien-in-human-form Richard Devon, in *War of the Satellites* (Allied Artists, 1958).

Behind the Scenes: On October 4, 1957, soviet scientists put the first man-made satellite (Sputnik) into orbit around the earth. By May of the following year, *War of the Satellites* was in theaters to take advantage of the head-lines.

According to an interview with Roger Corman that appeared in *Kings of the Bs*, one of the best books on low budget filmmaking, Jack Rabin (who with his partner Irving Block cooked up stories to give their special effects company something to do) came to Roger with the idea to do a satellite picture the day following Sputnik's launch. Roger told Steve Broidy at Allied Artists that he could deliver the picture in eight weeks and that if Broidy was interested he should get the advertising department busy with a campaign while Roger was shooting the picture.

Dick Miller was cast as the hero, which made him a little uncomfortable. "It was written for a typical six-foot-two leading man," Miller said. "I was a character actor. That didn't mean I couldn't do leads or that I couldn't do romantic leads but it had to be tailored for me. I was playing a young scientist going into space, a part that should have been given to William Lundigan or Richard Carlson. And I looked at Dick Devon, who's about six-foot-two, and I said, 'Jesus Christ. I gotta beat *him* up?' It was good for the character; gave it more dimension. But a lot of the stuff got lost. Some of the stuff at the beginning was namby-pamby because they didn't know where they were going with the character. It was well written but it was written fast. You know we had four arches to make all the hallways in the spaceship. They made 'em long or short but at the end you always had to make a turn. Four arches. That was the entire ship. Four arches and two lounge chairs."

Life magazine ran a spread on the rash of science fiction pictures glutting the market at the time and mentioned that something called *War of the Satellites* was in production and that its producers claimed it contained "the ultimate in scientific monsters." Allied Artists' publicity department lifted that quote and put it on their advertisements as if *Life* had made the boast.

More amusing than that was the one-column item in *Variety* that said Roger had revised the screenplay in order to take a poke at the U.S. officials whose footdragging had allowed the Russians to beat the United States in the space race. The writer of the piece felt it was an editorial stand almost without precedent in filmmaking. Roger was quoted as saying, "There is no question of lack of patriotism in knocking policy for its failure. I believe, in fact, that it is a patriotic service to point up the inertia which permits this country, with its tremendous capacity, to fall behind other countries."

The Wasp Woman. "A Beautiful Woman by Day, a Lusting Queen Wasp by Night!" 1959 B&W 73 min. PRO-DIR Roger Corman, SP Leo Gordon from a story by Kinta Zertuche, ED Carlo Lodato, DP Harry C. Newman, ART DIR Daniel Haller, MUS Fred Katz. Santa Clara/Filmgroup.

The Cast: Susan Cabot (Janice Starlin), Fred (Anthony) Eisley (Bill Lane), Barboura Morris (Mary Dennison), Michael Marks (Zinthrop), William Roerick (Arthur Cooper), Frank Gerstle (Hellman), Frank Wolff, Bruno Ve Sota.

The Story: Janice Starlin, the head of a large cosmetics firm, is worried that her fading good looks will adversely affect the sale of her products. Which makes her a prime candidate for an unorthodox scientist named Zinthrop. Zinthrop has been experimenting with wasp enzymes and is certain their royal jelly (combined with his know-how) can create a youth formula. Janice willingly becomes the doctor's guinea pig, against the advice of her coworkers, in particular Arthur Cooper who believes Zinthrop is after Janice's money.

Cooper breaks into Zinthrop's lab, searching for incriminating evidence. He is attacked by Janice who has transformed into something half-human, half-wasp. The next morning Janice appears normal except for one striking difference: she looks twenty years younger. Zinthrop's discovery is a miracle and plans to market his product are in the works. But each night Janice seeks another victim as she goes buzzing about the office. The janitor is the next to go. One of Janice's assistants, Mary Dennison, decides to do some snooping of her own. Simultaneously Zinthrop learns that his formula has a deadly side effect. A cat he's experimented on turns carnivorous and attacks him.

Zinthrop kills the cat and is on his way to warn Janice about the danger when he's hit by a car. In a daze, Zinthrop manages to tell Mary and her boyfriend Bill Lane who in turn attempt to convey the message to Janice. But

Janice has transformed into the wasp again. She attacks Zinthrop, kills his nurse, and is about to do the same to Mary when Bill intervenes. Using a chair he pushes Janice through an upper story window and she falls to her death.

Behind the Scenes: There's simply no time to dawdle on a five-day shooting schedule nor is there really the time to shoot a scene properly, especially if it's an action sequence, since action sequences usually require many different camera angles and a lot of rehearsal. For the action climax of *The Wasp Woman,* Roger Corman wanted to do it in a single take.

The scene to be shot was as follows: Fred Eisley was supposed to burst into the room where Susan Cabot, in her wasp-woman mask, was about to kill Barboura Morris. Tony and Susan were to battle with a stool, then Tony was to throw a bottle of "acid" at her. Susan would then duck out of sight just long enough for someone off stage to sprinkle some liquid smoke on her mask, then she would pop back into the scene, struggle a little more and fall backwards out of the window.

Everything went according to plan until Fred threw the bottle. Somebody had filled the thing with water. It hit Susan like a rock. For a few seconds she thought her lower teeth had been pushed through her nose. But she continued on like the trouper she was. She ducked out of camera range so the propman could douse her antennae with the liquid smoke. But he used too much and Susan crashed through the window, falling on the mattress on the other side, choking on the smoke that filled her mask. There was no mouth on the mask, just two little nostrils; nowhere for the smoke to go but in her lungs. She clawed and scratched until somebody finally caught on to the fact that she was in trouble. They poured water on her and finally she was able to tear part of the mask away, taking a piece of her skin with it.

Harry Essex had a similar experience when he directed *Octaman* in 1971. He and his crew were at Bronson Canyon and Harry thought he could film one of the action sequences in one take without rehearsing. The Octaman was supposed to leap out of a Winnebago, knock two men to the ground, scoop the leading lady into his arms and make a getaway.

Just before they were ready to roll, Harry spotted a large two by four on the ground and thought it would add an exciting touch if one of the guys hit the Octaman with it. The guy inside the costume thought it was a really bad idea but it wasn't until somebody convinced Harry that the suit might be damaged that he revised his plan. The actor would start to swing the board and the monster would knock it from his hand. And it was at that point that everything went wrong.

The actor made his lunge with the board and the monster knocked him off his feet. The board sailed into the air and landed on the actor's hand. Nobody saw it hit so when the guy started yelling everyone assumed it was part of the performance. The monster grabbed the leading lady but since he couldn't see very well got turned around and inadvertently lumbered toward the injured actor who was lying spread eagle on the ground. The monster's tentacled rubber foot landed squarely on the actor's crotch. He jerked free in pain which threw the monster off balance. The monster in turn threw the leading lady into the air and she landed with a smack against the Winnebago.

You can't win 'em all.

"Their Credo Is Violence. Their God Is Hate and They Call Themselves...
The Wild Angels. 1966 C-Scope 93 min. PRO-DIR Roger Corman, SP Charles B. Griffith, DP Richard Moore, ED Monte Hellman, ART DIR Leon Ericksen, MUS Mike Curb. American International.

The Cast: Peter Fonda (Heavenly Blues), Nancy Sinatra (Mike), Bruce Dern (Loser), Diane Ladd (Gaysh), Buck Taylor (Dear John), Lou Procopio (Joint), Coby Denton (Bull Puckey), Marc Cavell (Frankenstein), Norm Alden (Medic), Michael J. Pollard (Pigmy), Joan Shawlee (Mama Monahan), Gayle Hunnicut (Suzie), Art Baker (Thomas), Frank Maxwell (preacher), Frank Gerstle (hospital policeman), Kim Hamilton (nurse), Dick Miller (hard hat), and members of the Hell's Angels, Venice, Calif.

The Story: Heavenly Blues heads an outlaw motorcycle gang residing in the beach town of Venice, California. His friend, Loser, is angry over the loss of his bike, stolen by a rival Mexican gang. The bikers invade the desert town of Mecca, find Loser's bike and start a fight with the Mexican gang which attracts the attention of the police. Loser swipes a police motorcycle and rides off through the mountains with the cops hot on his tail. Loser is shot and stuck in a hospital from which Blues and the gang abduct him, in spite of his critical condition, knowing he'll be sent to prison the minute he recovers.

Without medical attention Loser dies and a ceremonial burial is planned in Loser's hometown. During the service, the minister pauses in his eulogy to challenge the philosophy of the bikers. Blues attempts to defend their creed but he's too inarticulate so he decides to turn the funeral into a party. Loser's corpse is propped up in a position of honor while his "old lady" is gang raped by several of his friends. Blues comes to understand the futility of their lifestyle but still leads the procession to the graveyard. A group of irate locals taunt the Angels into a fight. Approaching police sirens dispel the group, except for Blues who stays to bury his friend, realizing there's nowhere to go.

Behind the Scenes: *The Wild Angels* was shown to the Theater Owners Association during the summer of 1966 and AIP vice president Samuel Z. Arkoff remembered well the reaction: "You gotta visualize the crowd. This is after dinner. A substantially Jewish crowd. Very few kids because this was for the convention. The Christian types weren't much younger. First there was some disapproving looks, principally from the women. About half way through the picture I can see what's coming so I get up and go out to the lobby. Jim [Nicholson] follows me. Now they trickle out, two by two. By the time there was the scene in the church, which is blasphemous by most people's standards, there's a mass exodous. Some of them stop to say, 'We know it's going to make a lot of money,' which is always the kiss of death, 'but it's too strong for our theaters.' A few women who can't be restrained by their men say, 'This is a dirty picture,' and look disapprovingly as if to say, 'What kind of people are you to make this kind of picture?' You can't believe this evening. Remember, the

people who come to the convention are the owners, not the sons who run the theaters. These are the so-called legitimate people of the community. Semi-porno pictures could be running in their theaters and they wouldn't even know about it."

"X" The Man with X-Ray Eyes. **"He Can See Through Pumpkin Pies!"** 1963 C 80 min. PRO-DIR Roger Corman, EXEC PRO James H. Nicholson, Samuel Z. Arkoff, SP Robert Dillon, Ray Russell from a story by Ray Russell, DP Floyd Crosby, SPFX Butler-Glouner, Inc., ED Anthony Carras, MUS Les Baxter. Alta Vista / American International.

The Cast: Ray Milland (James Xavier), Diana Van Der Vlis (Diane Fairfax), Harold J. Stone (Sam Brant), John Hoyt (Willard Benson), Don Rickles (Crane), John Dierkes (Preacher), Lorie Summers (Party Dancer), Vicki Lee (young girl patient), Kathryn Hart (Mrs. Mart), Carol Irey (woman patient), Barboura Morris (nurse), Dick Miller (heckler).

The Story: Dr. James Xavier is obsessed with expanding the limits of human eyesight. He complains to his colleague, Sam Brant, that man is virtually blind, able to see only one-tenth of the lightwave spectrum. Sam replies, "Only the Gods see everything." Xavier responds smugly, "My dear doctor, I am closing in on the Gods." Xavier invents a solution that enables a monkey to see colors through opaque panels. But later the animal shrieks and dies. Xavier can't wait to find out what the animal saw that terrified him so. And when Diane Fairfax tells him that the foundation which has been financing his experiments is about to cut off support, Xavier uses the serum on himself.

Using his newly acquired X-ray vision, Xavier is able to see that one of his colleagues, Dr. Willard Benson, has incorrectly diagnosed one of his patients, a little girl scheduled for a heart operation. If the operation goes as scheduled the child will die but Benson thinks Xavier is talking through his hat. As Benson is about to slice the child open, Xavier cuts Benson's hand with a scalpel so that Benson will be unable to perform the operation. Xavier steps in and saves the girl but Benson's vanity prevails and Xavier is dismissed from the staff with a malpractice suit in the works. Brant tries to persuade Xavier to stop the experiment and when he can't, tries to physically restrain him from using any more of the drops. In the struggle Brant falls out of an upper story window and Xavier becomes a fugitive.

Xavier earns money as a carnival swami, Mentalo, and later a healer, ultimately concluding that his new ability is a curse. He can't sleep because for him there is no darkness. His X-ray vision isolates him to the point that his sanity is in the balance. His only hope is to discover an anecdote but to do that he must have money. He goes to Las Vegas and is accused of cheating. Chased by the police Xavier wanders into a revival meeting where the preacher assumes Xavier has come to be saved. "Saved? No. I've come to tell you what I see. There

Top: Nancy Sinatra and Roger Corman between scenes; bottom: Corman and script girl Bonnie Prendergast — behind the scenes on *The Wild Angels* (AIP, 1966).

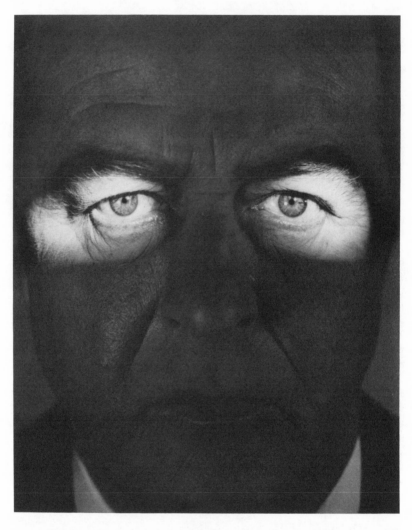

Ray Milland as the doctor who could strip souls as bare as bodies in *"X" The Man with X-Ray Eyes* (AIP, 1963).

are great darknesses . . . farther than time itself. And beyond the darkness a light that glows and changes. And in the center of the universe the Eye that sees us all," Xavier says. "You have seen sin and the devil," the preacher retorts. "But the Lord has told us what to do about it. Said Matthew in Chapter Five, 'If thine eye offend thee, pluck it out.'" Which is precisely what Xavier does.

Behind the Scenes: Rumor has it that in the original ending of this picture, after Xavier pokes his eyes out, he looks into the camera with his bloody sockets and screams, "I can still see!" Supposedly, Roger chose to freeze frame before the line because the scene was thought to be too frightening, which is like cutting a line from a comedy because it's too funny.

"I feel it was an opportunity that was slightly missed," said Roger about the film, which is an understatement to say the least. "The original idea to do a picture about a man who could see through objects was Jim Nicholson's and then the development of the basic idea was mine and Ray Russell's. I almost didn't do the picture for two reasons: one, I felt the script had not turned out as well as I had expected and two, the more I got into it the more I felt we were going to be heavily dependent on the special effects. The picture was shot in three weeks on a medium low budget and I felt we were not going to be able to photograph what Xavier could see, and that the audience would be cheated. The picture turned out reasonably well but I think, when finished, it did suffer from that. The effects just weren't there. We did the best we could. To show a man seeing through a building I photographed buildings that were in various stages of construction, on the basis he could see through the outer skin, which was a reasonable cheat, but it was still a cheat."

From the pressbook: "When a totally new human experience is depicted for the first time in a motion picture, the knowledge and skill . . . and even wits of film technical craftsmen are put to the acid test.

"Such was the challenge flung to the producers of American International's contemporary science fiction thriller, *X*. Ray Milland stars as a doctor-scientist who perfects a serum which gives him fantastic X-Ray vision.

"Core of the special effects problem of the motion picture story of *X* was to effectively depict Milland's rapidly increasing X-Ray vision from his point of view. Biggest difficulty was the climax in which the X-Ray vision gets out of control and runs wild until Milland becomes in effect blind, a crazed man with total all-seeing and all-penetrating vision in a blinding white and limitless world.

"The solution found by film editor Anthony Carras and special effects experts, Butler-Glouner, Inc., was the utilization for the first time in motion pictures of a totally new optical system — 'Spectarama' — as Milland's X-Ray vision point of view.

"'Spectarama' is an entirely new film optical process which, in effect, changes the whole point of view of the audience. Through a patented arrangement of prisms, light images are bent and color changes with the resulting distortions appearing to be impressionistic paintings in motion.

"With 'Spectarama,' we see the frightening X-Ray world of *X* with its weird sense of a strange and maddening Fourth Dimension. American International's technicians have achieved what many experts said couldn't be done — they have visually depicted a new human experience and added a new dimension to vision and to films.

"The special 'Spectarama' optical process enabled *X* special effects technicians to achieve another first — to shoot directly at the sun for amazing film footage of the blazing globe. Other unusual effects were obtained with nighttime views of the colorful lights of Las Vegas and of other familiar spots in the

West—all converted into exciting Fourth Dimension-appearing scenes of a madening X-Ray vision world.

"Other unusual special effects included shots of the insides of a goat for the operating room sequences; a specially constructed full-scale model of a human eye; a built-to-order slot machine (none are allowed by law in California), which was torn apart to reveal the inside mechanism, and a complete laboratory made of skeletal metal only.

"The result is the frightening realism of one of the most unusual and exciting science fiction films ever made, an imaginary trip into a world that may be opened to one of our scientists tomorrow or the day after, the world of Ray Milland's X."

The Young Racers. "They Treated Beautiful Women as If They Were Fast Cars . . . ROUGH!" 1963 C 82 min. PRO-DIR Roger Corman, SP R. Wright Campbell, DP Floyd Crosby, ED Ronald Sinclair, ART DIR Albert Locatelli, MUS Les Baxter. Alta Vista / American International.

The Cast: Mark Damon (Stephen Children), William Campbell (Joe Machin), Luana Anders (Henny), Robert Campbell (Robert Machin), Patrick Magee (Sir William Dragonet), Bruce McLaren (Lotus Team Manager), Milo Quesada (Italian Driver), Anthony Marsh (Announcer), Marie Versini (Sesia Machin), Beatrice Altariba (Monique), Margreta Robsahn (Lea), Christina Gregg (Daphne).

The Story: The Monte Carlo Grand Prix is won by American Joe Machin through reckless driving, which does not endear him to his fellow drivers. Joe ignores his brother's remarks about the danger of his behavior, convinced that his actions are necessary in order to win the race. Joe's brother Robert is also critical of the way Joe flaunts his extramarital exploits but Joe continues his affair with Monique, fiancée of racer-turned-writer Steve Children who arrives in Monte Carlo in time to witness an emotional scene between Monique and Joe at a sidewalk cafe.

Steve arranges to meet Joe, gets his consent to a story and follows him to Spa, Belgium, where another Grand Prix race is taking place. To get closer to his subject, Steve persuades the Lotus team captain to allow him to race along with the other drivers. Steve follows the race track circuit through Rouen and Reims in France and despite his desire for revenge grows fond of Joe. At Aintree, England, a man bitter and cynical over an affair Joe had with his wife takes relish in revealing to Joe that Monique was Steve's fiancée and that Steve plans to expose Joe for the scoundrel he is.

During the race at Aintree, Steve and Joe try to kill each other on the track. But Joe has a change of heart at the last minute and injures himself in order to avoid hitting Steve. The accident makes Joe take stock of himself and months later Steve finds him living happily with his wife Sesia, a changed man. He even asks Steve for an autographed copy of his book.

Behind the Scenes: *"The Young Racers* was a lot of fun," said Charles Griffith. "I was stranded in Israel for two years and Roger wouldn't send me the money to come back. I promised to write him a picture for free.

"I tried to make an Arab-Israeli war picture here right after *Little Shop of Horrors*. Mel Welles and I had a company. For eleven thousand we were trying to do this war picture in color out by the Salton Sea. We were picketed by the unions. They shut us down. I had some Israeli friends here who said, 'Let's finish the picture in Israel.' We had to start over again. I went off on a boat with my Volkswagen to Israel dead broke, and arrived there sort of a ward of the state. We had 29,000 feet of short-ends [unexposed rolls of left-over film, purchased for a low price with the risk they might be unuseable] that we were going to sell but when we got there it was all fogged. My lawyer didn't send me the money to leave so I was stranded. I was living on a rooftop. I had a good time there. Two years."

Roger Corman made a deal with Sunbeam to use one of their sports cars in the film but he needed somebody to drive the car from Monte Carlo to Paris so he hired Griffith to do it.

"We got wiped out in route," Griffith said, referring to his Israeli girlfriend and himself. "We got to racing a TR3 and there was a little piece of freeway in the south of France but that didn't have anything to do with the accident."

In spite of Griffith's mishap, *The Young Racers* was a very inexpensive picture. Roger was able to travel lightly because all of his equipment was packed into a specially built Volkswagen microbus.

"It occurred to me," Roger said, "that I had essentially a floating studio. Everything was in the microbus. I had to go back to America to do another film immediately afterwards but I thought I could have somebody stay and do another film. I had three assistants on the film. One was Francis Coppola. Two was Bob Towne. And the third was Menachem Golan of Cannon. Now Menachem came to me with an idea to put the microbus on a ship, send it to Israel (I'd give him a little bit of money) and he would shoot a picture for me. It sounded like an interesting idea but I'd never been to Israel and I didn't know what kind of picture I was going to get out of Israel. So Francis said, 'I'd like to make a film.' I said, 'All right, Francis. We're going to be finishing the picture at the English Grand Prix in Liverpool. Although I have faith in Menachem, it's certainly much easier to put the microbus on a ferry from Liverpool to Dublin which is just a couple of hours across the Irish channel. And you can start shooting in Ireland if you can come up with a low budget horror film in Dublin I will back you.' Which he did and that was *Dementia 13* which was his first film. Menachem is still giving interviews stating that I made a mistake and should have given the money to him."

The Roger Corman Stock Company Players

Anders, Luana (1940–)
This blue-eyed, blonde actress began her career during her high school years as cousin Bella in *The Barretts of Wimpole Street*. She was offered the lead in that play but passed it up because of the love scenes she would have had to play. She didn't want her classmates laughing at her. She enrolled in Jeff Corey's acting class, joined a little theater group, and got her first motion picture role in American International's *Reform School Girl* (1957). She's appeared in over 50 television shows including "Alcoa Presents," "Rawhide," and "Sugarfoot." On stage she was Rex Harrison's daughter in *The Fighting Cock*. She was born in Los Angeles, the only child of a Spanish mother and a Swedish father.

Her credits include: *Life Begins at 17* (1958), *The Pit and the Pendulum* (1961), *Night Tide, The Young Racers, Dementia 13* (all 1963), *The Trip* (1967), *How Sweet It Is!* (1968), *Easy Rider, That Cold Day in the Park* (both 1969), *Sex and the College Girl* (1970), *When Legends Die* (1972), *The Last Detail, The Killing Kind* (both 1973), *The Missouri Breaks* (1976), *Goin' South* (1978).

Birch, Paul (d.1964)
Born and educated in Alabama, he came to Hollywood in the late 1940s. His acting career began in low budget films and graduated to more prestigious productions but always in minor roles. He was a semiregular on television's popular "The Fugitive" as the extremely patient police captain who allowed Lt. Phillip Gerard to go chasing after Richard Kimble every week. One of his most memorable roles was the icy alien in Corman's *Not of This Earth*. He was a good actor and it's unfortunate that so little is known about him.

His credits include: *The War of the Worlds* (1953), *Five Guns West* (1955), *Apache Woman, The Day the World Ended, The Beast with 1,000,000 Eyes, The Fastest Gun Alive* (all 1956), *The Tattered Dress* (1957), *Portrait in Black* (1960), *The Man Who Shot Liberty Valance* (1962).

Bradley, Leslie
One of the most interesting, if overzealous actors in the Corman corral, Bradley had a sporadic career in motion pictures which began in the 1940s.

His credits include: *The Young Mr. Pitt* (1942), *No Orchids for Miss Blandish, The Crimson Pirate* (1952), *Kiss of Fire, Good Morning, Miss Dove* (both 1955), *Naked Paradise, Attack of the Crab Monsters* (both 1957), *Teenage Caveman* (1958).

Luana Anders looks appropriately terrified in this scene from Francis Ford Coppola's first feature, *Dementia 13* (New World, 1963).

Cabot, Susan (1927–1986)

Born Harriet Shapiro in Boston, she attended college in New York where she began acting in off–Broadway theater productions and won the New York Critics Award for her performance in *A Stone for Danny Fisher*. On television she appeared in some of the top dramatic shows: "Alcoa," "Playhouse 90," "Studio One." In the early 1950s this dark-haired, petite lady was under contract to Universal, where she played opposite the studio's top leading men, usually as Indian squaws. She had the opportunity to play a wider range of roles when she went to work for Roger Corman but she soon grew tired of working in low budget productions ("I mean, how many wasp women can you do?") and retired from acting. She married Michael Roman and they had a son, Timothy

Scott. "I couldn't walk for eight months following his birth," Miss Cabot said. "Both baby and I barely made it. The poor little fellow spent his first four months in an oxygen tent."

Twenty-three years later, Timothy Scott beat his mother to death with a metal pipe. When the police first found her body, her skull bashed in, Scott claimed the murder had been committed by someone who had broken into the house dressed like a Ninja warrior. As the truth began to unravel, Scott pleaded insanity, blaming an experimental growth hormone he'd been taking for 15 years that supposedly caused neurological problems. Had Miss Cabot's life not ended so dramatically, her passing would have no doubt gone virtually unnoticed. She was a fine actress and from all accounts a kind person.

Her credits include: *On the Isle of Samoa* (1950), *Flame of Araby*, *The Enforcer*, *Tomahawk* (all 1951), *The Battle of Apache Pass*, *Son of Ali Baba* (both 1952), *Gunsmoke* (1953), *Ride Clear of Diablo* (1954), *Sorority Girl* (1957), *Carnival Rock*, *Viking Women and the Sea Serpent*, *Machine Gun Kelly*, *Fort Massacre*, *War of the Satellites* (all 1958), *Surrender Hell!*, *The Wasp Woman* (both 1959).

Campbell, William (1926–)

Born in New Jersey, he joined the Navy when he was only 15 and did his time aboard a minesweeper in the Southwest Pacific. He enrolled at Columbia University under the G.I. Bill to study journalism, which had been his high school major, but the drama class seemed more interesting. Several summers were spent in Eastern stock companies until Campbell finally landed a part in *The Biggest Thief in Town* with Thomas Mitchell on Broadway. But it wasn't until *The Man Who Came to Dinner* that he was spotted by a talent scout who got him a part in the John Garfield film *The Breaking Point* (1950). After that he became active in both films and television. His brother Bobby wrote screenplays and often tailored parts for him.

His credits include: *Escape from Fort Bravo* (1953), *The High and the Mighty* (1953), *Man Without a Star*, *Cell 2455 Death Row* (both 1955), *Backlash*, *Running Wild*, *Love Me Tender* (all 1956), *Eighteen and Anxious* (1957), *The Naked and the Dead* (1958), *The Young Racers*, *Dementia 13* (both 1963), *The Secret Invasion*, *Hush, Hush Sweet Charlotte* (both 1964), *Blood Bath* (1966), *Dirty Mary, Crazy Larry* (1974).

Carol, Sheila

Her real name Sheila Nichols, she made her motion picture debut in 1959 and retired from acting one year later. She studied acting with Jeff Corey while earning a living as a fashion buyer, moved to New York where she landed a few parts in television, did some summer stock in New Mexico and returned to Hollywood. "My career had its highs and lows," she said. "One week I was a star, the next a waitress. Don't ask me which weeks were the highs." She decided to bow out of the business and become a horticulturist.

Her two credits: *Beast from Haunted Cave* (1959), *Ski Troop Attack* (1960).

Carbone, Antony

Born in the province of Calabria in Italy, he grew up in Syracuse, New York, and Los Angeles. He graduated from Los Angeles State College and went to New York to study drama with Harold Clurman and Eva Le Galliene. He appeared in several Broadway plays, directed a few off–Broadway plays which led to his being cast in television shows like "Studio One," "Kraft Theatre," and "The Untouchables." He's 5 foot 10, has black hair and hazel eyes and plays his parts in a casual, offhand manner.

His credits include: *A Bucket of Blood* (1959), *The Last Woman on Earth, Creature from the Haunted Sea, The Pit and the Pendulum* (all 1961), *Newman's Law* (1974).

Connors, Michael ("Touch") (1925–)

He first appeared in films in 1952 in supporting roles, then found a niche as a leading man at American International where he alternated between heroes and heavies. He coproduced *The Flesh and the Spur* (1957) for AIP and was shocked when the poster they'd designed depicted a scene not in the picture (it was ultimately added). A lot of years passed in between but Mike again tried his hand at producing, something titled *Too Scared to Scream* (1985), and discovered that he'd rather not act in the films he produced.

His biggest success came from television, first in 1958 with "Tightrope" and later as "Mannix," a role he played for eight years. At one time he studied law and ended up playing a lawyer his first time on stage. He still pops up in television movies now and then and recently has been telling me I have bad breath more often.

He's a good actor and we should be seeing him in something besides breath commercials. Real name: Kreker Ohanian from Fresno, California.

His credits include: *Sudden Fear* (1952), *The 49th Man, Sky Commando* (both 1953), *Naked Alibi* (1954), *Five Guns West, Swamp Women* (both 1955), *Oklahoma Woman, The Day the World Ended, Jaguar, Shake, Rattle and Rock* (all 1956), *Voodoo Woman* (1957), *Suicide Battalion, Live Fast, Die Young* (both 1958), *Good Neighbor Sam, Panic Button, Where Love Has Gone* (all 1964), *Harlow, Situation Hopeless But Not Serious* (both 1965), *Stagecoach* (1966), *Kiss the Girls and Make Them Die* (1967), *Cruise Missile* (1978).

Court, Hazel (1926–)

Born in Sutton Coldfield, England, she had a desire to act at a very early age but her parents didn't approve. Finally, after a number of years at school, she was sent to the Birmingham School of Drama and Arts. On her 18th birthday she signed with J. Arthur Rank and appeared in over 34 successive films as well as appearing on stage. She was in the CBS television series "Dick and the Duchess." Formerly married to actor Dermot Walsh she later married Don Taylor. Whether she likes it or not she is probably best remembered for her horror roles and was a welcome sight to a genre where the leading ladies often looked like the men.

Her credits include: *Champagne Charlie* (1944), *Dreaming* (1945), *Dear*

Hazel Court in a scene from *The Masque of the Red Death* (Alta Vista/American International, 1964).

Murderer, Meet Me at Dawn, Carnival, Gaiety George (all 1946), *Bond Street, Holiday Camp* (both 1947), *It's Not Cricket* (1948), *Forbidden* (1949), *Bond Street* (1950), *Ghost Ship* (1952), *Counterspy* (1953), *Devil Girl from Mars* (1954), *The Curse of Frankenstein* (1957), *Model for Murder* (1958), *The Man Who Could Cheat Death* (1959), *The Shakedown* (1960), *Dr. Blood's Coffin, Mary Had a Little...* (both 1961), *The Premature Burial* (1962), *The Raven* (1963), *The Masque of the Red Death* (1964).

Dalton, Abby

Her real name is Marlene Wasden; she was born in Las Vegas, Nevada, the daughter of Ray Wasden, a boxer turned lathe and plaster contractor. She grew

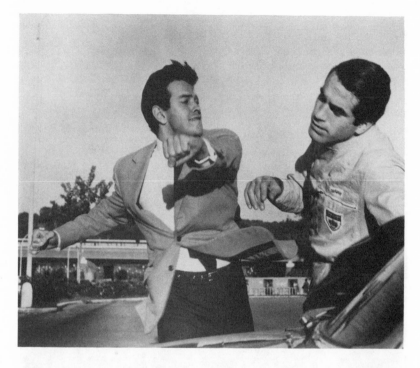

Mark Damon gives Robert Campbell a biff in the jaw in this scene from *The Young Racers* (AIP, 1963).

up in Glendale, California, and spent seven months in New York designing clothes. She returned to California to enter show business and was voted by *Cosmopolitan* magazine as one of the ten most talented newcomers. "I wasn't much of an actress," she admitted, "but boy oh boy, how I could get on that horse!" She was in a lot of television westerns and has had more success in television than movies.

She was a regular on "Hennessey," "The Joey Bishop Show," and most recently "Falcon Crest." In her teens she used to pick up extra money as a baby-sitter and one of the kids she used to take care of was Dennis Muren, who has become quite a celebrity himself doing special effects on George Lucas and Steven Spielberg films. Abby was once married to an Apache jazz musician, Joe Mondragon.

Her credits include: *Teenage Doll, Rock All Night* (both 1957), *Stakeout on Dope Street, Girls on the Loose, Cole Younger, Gunfighter, Viking Women and the Sea Serpent* (all 1958).

Damon, Mark (1935–)

Born in Chicago, his family moved to Los Angeles where he attended Fairfax High School and later UCLA. During college he tried out for the chorus of a musical and was given one line to read. He enrolled in Sandy Meisner's drama school and landed his first role in Columbia's 1955 melodrama *Inside Detroit*. After knocking around Hollywood for a while he went to Italy where he had much better luck with his career as an actor and producer. He likes to recall the day during his high school years when he was working at an amusement park and was approached by a man who told him he had "motion picture potential." The man said his brother was a theatrical agent and gave him a business card: Gummo Marx. He'd been talking to Groucho.

His credits include: *Between Heaven and Hell, Screaming Eagles* (both 1956), *Young and Dangerous* (1957), *Life Begins at 17, The Party Crashers* (both 1958), *House of Usher* (1960), *Beauty and the Beast, The Young Racers* (both 1963), *Black Sabbath* (1964), *Anzio* (1968).

Denning, Richard (1914–)

His real name Louis A. Denninger, he was born in Poughkeepsie, New York, educated at Woodbury College, and has been in movies since 1937. His athletic appearance made him a natural for beefcake roles and later he graduated to second leads. Although he was never a superstar he had an extremely active career in films and television. He married actress Evelyn Ankers and before her death they both resided in Hawaii, where Denning has been an active member of the Wailuku Union Church in Maui and honorary president of Maui's Chamber of Commerce. He was always a pleasure to watch and was generally liked by everyone he worked with. His television series include "Mr. and Mrs. North," "Michael Shayne," "The Flying Doctor," "Karen," and "Hawaii Five-O."

His credits include: *Her Jungle Love* (1938), *Million Dollar Legs* (1939), *Geronimo, Golden Gloves, North West Mounted Police* (all 1940), *Adam Had Four Sons* (1941), *Beyond the Blue Horizon, The Glass Key* (1942), *Black Beauty* (1946), *Unknown Island* (1948), *No Man of Her Own* (1950), *Hangman's Knot* (1952), *The 49th Man, The Glass Web* (both 1953), *Creature from the Black Lagoon, Target Earth, Battle of Rogue River* (all 1954), *Creature with the Atom Brain, The Magnificent Matador* (both 1955), *The Day the World Ended, Oklahoma Woman* (both 1956), *Naked Paradise, An Affair to Remember, The Black Scorpion* (all 1957), *The Lady Takes a Flyer* (1958), *Twice Told Tales* (1963).

Dern, Bruce (1936–)

Chicago born, Dern dropped out of college to pursue an acting career. He made his film debut in *Wild River* (1960). The bulk of his early film career was spent playing hillbillies and psychos, but he is one of the finest actors around (and a personal favorite of Roger Corman). It took him a while but he's finally earned a little of the recognition he deserves.

Credits include: *Marnie* (1964), *Hush, Hush Sweet Charlotte* (1965), *The Wild Angels* (1966), *The St. Valentine's Day Massacre, Waterhole #3, The Trip, The War Wagon* (all 1967), *Psych-Out, Hang 'em High* (both 1968), *They Shoot Horses, Don't They?* (1969), *Bloody Mama* (1970), *The Cowboys, Silent Running, The King of Marvin Gardens* (all 1972), *The Laughing Policeman*

Dependable Richard Denning sets out to save Lori Nelson in this scene from *The Day the World Ended* (American Releasing Corp., 1955).

(1973), *Smile, Posse* (both 1975), *Coming Home* (1978), *Middle Age Crazy* (1980).

Devon, Richard (1927–)

Born in Glendale, California, the youngest of four children, Devon's parents wanted him to be a minister but he wanted to be an actor. His job as a stable boy at the Dubrock Riding Academy in the San Fernando Valley trained him well for the hundreds of television westerns that he would ultimately appear in—"Broken Arrow," "Wyatt Earp," "Wagon Train," "Bonanza," to name just a few. He made his film debut in 1956 in a Fox film called *The Racers*. His real name is Richard Gibson Ferraiole.

His credits include: *The Undead, Blood of Dracula, Teenage Doll* (all 1957), *Viking Women and the Sea Serpent, War of the Satellites, Machine Gun Kelly* (all 1958), *The Comancheros* (1961), *Kid Galahad* (1962), *The Silencers* (1966).

Dickerson, Charles ("Beach") (1924–)

Born in Glenville, Georgia, he used to sweep out movie theaters so he could get in for free. Dickerson came to Hollywood in 1942, went to drama school, and was seen by Roger Corman at the Player's Ring in *End as a Man*. Corman signed him for a role in *Attack of the Crab Monsters*. Dickerson and actor Ed Nelson both took turns playing the title character. He produced his own movie, *Shell Shock* (1961), then retired from acting to become an architect—and ended up building Roger Corman's home.

His credits include: *Rock All Night, Attack of the Crab Monsters* (both 1957), *War of the Satellites, Teenage Caveman* (both 1958), *Creature from the Haunted Sea* (1961), *Savage Seven, The Wild Racers, Killers Three* (all 1968), *The Trip* (1967), *The Dunwich Horror* (1970), *Unholly Rollers* (1971).

Duncan, Pamela (1931–)

The brown-haired, brown-eyed actress was born in New York City, the daughter of Joseph and Lucille Duncan. Her mother took her to the 1939 World's Fair where Pamela was chosen to appear on one of the first television shows. She came to Hollywood in 1953 after appearing on live television in New York and got her first starring role in a Roger Corman film. She felt that her sexy image hurt her career. She cites as an example a role she played on "Perry Mason." She wore a negligee and got murdered during the first half of the show. "When you're a corpse," she said, "even in a sexy negligee, you have to stop acting—and I like to act."

Her credits include: *Seven Men from Now, Julie, Man from Monterey* (all 1956), *Attack of the Crab Monsters, No Place to Die, The Undead* (all 1957).

Durant, Don (1934–)

Born in Long Beach, California, his mother remarried and moved to Nevada after his father died. He did a little singing at several Vegas clubs then joined a road company. After a stint in the Army he landed his first movie role at Warner Brothers and began showing up on television in shows like "Maverick," "Gunsmoke," "Trackdown," and "Life of Riley." When he was a boy he lived on a cattle ranch and learned to ride horses which he continued to enjoy, along with other outdoor sports like hunting, fishing, skin-diving and swimming. Which made him a perfect candidate for Roger Corman's *She Gods of Shark Reef*.

His credits include: *Battle Cry, Top of the World* (both 1955), *She Gods of Shark Reef* (1958).

Peter Fonda (left) and Michael J. Pollard in a scene from *The Wild Angels* (AIP, 1966).

Fonda, Peter (1939–)

The son of actor Henry Fonda, he was born in New York City and educated at the University of Omaha. He joined the Omaha Playhouse and appeared in their production of *Harvey*, after which he went to New York and became an apprentice at the Cecilwood Theatre. A year later he was on Broadway in *Blood, Sweat and Stanley Poole*. The show ran two months.

He came to Hollywood to test for the role of John Kennedy in *PT 109* (1963), but didn't get it. Instead, Universal hired him for the lead in *Tammy*

Michael Forest was a bit of a disappointment in the muscles department as *Atlas* (Filmgroup, 1960), but his lean appearance was a metaphor of the film's budget.

and the Doctor (1963). But it wasn't until his starring role in Roger Corman's *The Wild Angels* (1966), a few years later that his career began to take shape, and reached its peak three years later with *Easy Rider* (1969), which Fonda cowrote and produced.

His films include: *The Victors* (1963), *Lilith, The Young Lovers* (both 1964), *The Trip* (1967), *Spirits of the Dead* (1968), *The Hired Hand, The Last Movie* (both 1971), *Dirty Mary, Crazy Larry* (1974), *Race with the Devil* (1975), *Futureworld, Fighting Mad* (1976), *Wanda Nevada* (1979).

Beverly Garland and Morgan Jones in *Not of This Earth* (Allied Artists, 1957).

Forest, Michael

Although born in South Dakota, he spent his early years in Seattle, where he attended the University of Washington for one year then moved to California to major in drama and English at San Jose State College. He won the best actor award at the 1954 Shakespeare Festival in San Diego, then drifted to Hollywood where he appeared in a number of stage productions at the Player's Ring. He's been seen on television in "Highway Patrol," "Tombstone Territory," and "The Rifleman."

His credits include: *Beast from Haunted Cave, Ski Troop Attack* (both 1960), *Atlas* (1961), *The Last Rebel* (1971), *Deathwatch* (1980).

Garland, Beverly (1926–)

Her real name Beverly Fessenden, she was born in Santa Cruz, California, and educated at Glendale College. Her first film role was in *D.O.A.* (1949) under the name Beverly Campbell. She made a casual remark about the picture not deserving an Academy Award and the word spread that she was an impossible actress to work with. Her career suffered a setback until 1953 when she appeared in *The Glass Web* at Universal. But the bulk of her career was in B movies.

"There was a stigma to B pictures," she remarked. "You were nothing if you were in B pictures. The only way you can be any good is to get out of B movies." But Beverly Garland was *very* good and always gave her all to any film she was in. She was seen on television in "Stump the Stars," "Decoy," "The Bing Crosby Show," "My Three Sons," and "Planet of the Apes."

Her credits include: *Bitter Creek, The Miami Story, Killer Leopard* (all 1954), *The Desperate Hours, New Orleans Uncensored, Swamp Women* (all 1955), *Gunslinger, Curucu, Beast of the Amazon, The Steel Jungle, It Conquered the World* (all 1956), *Not of This Earth, Naked Paradise, Chicago Confidential, The Joker Is Wild* (all 1957), *The Alligator People* (1959), *Stark Fear, Twice Told Tales* (both 1963), *Pretty Poison* (1968), *Where the Red Fern Grows* (1975), *Roller Boogie* (1979).

Garland, Richard (1927–1969)

Born in Mineral Wells, Texas, he first thought of an acting career after his stint in the Merchant Marine during World War II. He came to Hollywood in 1946 and just hung around the beach for a while ("I'm really lazy, you see"), finally joining the Player's Ring in 1949 and appearing in their production of *Dark of the Moon*, which got him a contract with Universal. He once described himself as "happy but lonesome" and I heard that his death in 1969 was a suicide. He seemed to be a rather wooden performer with the exception of his role in *Panic in Year Zero* (1962) in which he let a little of that loneliness peek through.

His credits include: *Cimmaron Kid* (1951), *Battle at Apache Pass, Red Ball Express, Son of Ali Baba* (all 1952), *Untamed* (1955), *Friendly Persuasion* (1956), *Attack of the Crab Monsters, The Undead* (both 1957).

Gordon, Leo V. (1922–)

Born in New York City, he's most often seen in westerns or gangster dramas as the heavy, a role he played very well. He's also a writer and in that capacity his credits include *Black Patch* (1957), *Hot Car Girl, Crybaby Killer* (both 1958), *Attack of the Giant Leeches* (1959), *The Tower of London* (1962), and *Tobruk* (1966).

Credits include: *China Venture, Hondo* (both 1953), *Riot on Cell Block 11* (1954), *Johnny Concho* (1956), *The Restless Breed, Baby Face Nelson* (both 1957), *The Intruder* (1962), *The Haunted Palace, Kings of the Sun* (both 1963), *Kitten with a Whip* (1964), *The St. Valentine's Day Massacre, Hostile Guns* (both 1967), *My Name Is Nobody* (1973).

Richard Garland and Pamela Duncan in *Attack of the Crab Monsters* (Los Altos/Allied Artists, 1957).

Hayes, Allison (1930–1977)

Of the many films in which she appeared, this chestnut-haired, hazel-eyed lady is probably best remembered as the title character of the camp classic, *Attack of the Fifty-Foot Woman* (1958). She was born in Charleston, West Virginia, of French and Irish parents, the daughter of an engineer whose job with the Navy brought her to Washington. Her 37–23–36 figure made her Washington's entry for the 1949 "Miss America" beauty pageant, which helped her secure a job with a local television station. Legend has it that a casual remark made by the wife of Supreme Court Chief Justice Earl Warren led to her first break in the movies. Mrs. Warren saw her dancing at a party and said: "My, what a beautiful girl!" Her remark was overheard by some motion picture executive who later arranged for a screen test.

"I thought she was beautiful," said Yvette Vickers, Miss Hayes' costar in *The Fifty-Foot Woman.* "There have been a few women in this town who have been really nice, really warm (not very many 'cause I seem to have a problem there) but she was." Allison had an active career in B movies and was on television in a short-lived series, "Acapulco" and later on "General Hospital."

Her credits include: *Francis Joins the WACS, Sign of the Pagan* (both 1954), *The Purple Mask, Chicago Syndicate, Count Three and Pray* (all 1955), *Gunslinger, Mohawk, The Steel Jungle* (all 1956), *The Undead, The Unearthly, Zombies of Mora Tau, The Disembodied* (all 1957), *The Hypnotic Eye* (1959), *The Crawling Hand, Who's Been Sleeping in My Bed?* (both 1963), *Tickle Me* (1965).

Haze, Jonathan (1929–)

He wanted to be in the limelight, somehow, for as long as he could remember. He started acting when he was in high school, went to New York to do summer stock, then came to California to act in films. He was born in Pittsburgh, Pennsylvania, where he got his first taste of show business by hanging around his cousin, Buddy Rich, who played drums with people like Artie Shaw and Harry James. Jonathan's father, a jeweler, would have liked him to be a jockey but boxing was the only sport Jonathan fancied and it was just for fun.

Acting seemed like the best way to make money but he never had the sort of career that he wanted. His only break from the B movies was his role in *East of Eden* (1955) as the son of Mario Siletti and 80 percent of his part ended on the cutting room floor. Jonathan still likes acting but he won't audition for parts anymore. He finds rejection too depressing. But if a friend wants him for something, he'll do it. He works mostly in commercials. His marriage to Roberta Keith ended in divorce. They share custody of their daughter Rebecca.

His credits include: *Monster from the Ocean Floor, The Fast and the Furious* (1954), *Five Guns West, Cell 2455, Death Row* (both 1955), *Apache Woman, The Day the World Ended, Swamp Women, The Bold and the Brave, Gunslinger, Oklahoma Woman, It Conquered the World* (all 1956), *Carnival Rock, Naked Paradise, Not of This Earth, Rock All Night, Bayou* (all 1957), *Viking Women and the Sea Serpent, Stakeout on Dope Street, Teenage Caveman, Ghost of the China Sea* (all 1958), *Forbidden Island* (1959), *The Little Shop of Horrors* (1960), *The Terror, "X" The Man with the X-Ray Eyes* (both 1963), *Vice Squad* (1981), *Heart Like a Wheel* (1982).

Ireland, John (1914–)

Ireland was born in Vancouver, Canada, and raised in New York. He began his career in films during the mid-40s and was nominated for his supporting role in *All the King's Men* (1949). More often the heavy than the hero, he appeared

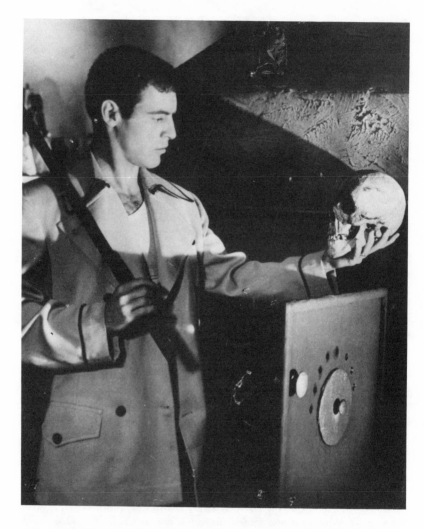

Jonathan Haze in *Not of This Earth* (Allied Artists, 1957).

in a wagon-full of westerns. For a brief period he was married to actress Joanna Dru. He recalled his experience directing Roger Corman's *The Fast and the Furious* with fondness: "I enjoyed the hustle and the spontaneity of it. I remember one scene with Dorothy Malone and myself running from one set to the other, making up dialogue as we went along. When we got to the next set I said, 'Okay. That's it.' And she said, 'Can't we rehearse?' And I said, 'We just did.'"

His credits include: *A Walk in the Sun, My Darling Clementine* (both 1946), *The Gangster* (1947), *Red River, Joan of Arc* (both 1948), *I Shot Jesse*

James, Anna Lucasta (both 1949), *Little Big Horn, The Basketball Fix, The Bushwhackers* (all 1951), *Hurricane Smith* (1952), *The 49th Man, Outlaw Territory* (both 1953), *Queen Bee* (1955), *Gunslinger* (1956), *Gunfight at the O.K. Corral* (1957), *Spartacus* (1960), *Wild in the Country* (1961), *55 Days at Peking* (1963), *The Fall of the Roman Empire* (1964), *I Saw What You Did* (1965), *The Swiss Conspiracy* (1977), *Tomorrow Never Comes* (1978).

Johnson, Russell (1924–)

He was born in Ashley, Pennsylvania, the oldest of six children; his father was a railroad detective who died when Russell was nine. His mother was unable to support the large family as it was during the Depression so the children were made wards of the state. In 1943 Johnson joined the Air Force and on the G.I. Bill enrolled in a Hollywood drama school, where he was spotted by Paul Henreid who cast him in *For Men Only* (1952). He was in two television series: "Black Saddle" and "Gilligan's Island." He appeared in dozens of movies in the 1950s, so many in fact that when I asked him about the alcoholic father that he played in *The Space Children* (1958) he jokingly replied: "Was I in that? I must have *been* drunk because I don't remember." He's one of those actors who's consistently believable.

His credits include: *It Came from Outer Space, Seminole, Column South* (all 1953), *Ma and Pa Kettle in Waikiki, Many Rivers to Cross, This Island Earth* (all 1955), *Attack of the Crab Monsters, Rock All Night* (both 1957), *The Greatest Story Ever Told* (1965), *A Distant Trumpet* (1964).

Jones-Moreland, Betsy

Born in New York, she attended private schools in Madison, New Jersey, and in Virginia. She studied drama with Betty Cashman in New York and her first Broadway role was in "The Solid Gold Cadillac." She made her motion picture debut in *The Eddie Duchin Story* in 1956. She's been in many television shows: "Studio One," "The Donna Reed Show," "Perry Mason," "Zane Grey Theater."

Her credits include: *Operation Mad Ball* (1957), *Thunder in the Sun* (1959), *Viking Women and the Sea Serpent* (1958), *Strangers When We Meet* (1960), *The Last Woman on Earth, Creature from the Haunted Sea* (both 1961), *The St. Valentine's Day Massacre* (1967).

Karloff, Boris (1887–1969)

Born William Henry Pratt in Dulwich, England, he was the youngest of eight children. He emigrated to Canada and worked as a farmhand, was attracted to the stage and joined a touring company. There were many touring companies and many parts before he made his screen debut in 1916 as an extra in *The Dumb Girl of Portici*.

Unable to support himself on the money he made, he became a truck driver and was about to give up on show biz when he was cast as the Frankenstein monster in what has become one of the classic horror films of all time. After that Karloff was typed as a bogeyman and he was one of the best in the

Betsy Jones-Moreland, in *Creature from the Haunted Sea* (Filmgroup, 1961).

business. He was always a pleasure to watch and if his performances seem a little hammy in retrospect, considering the material, the hammier the better.

His credits include: *The Deadlier Sex* (1920), *The Infidel* (1922), *Forbidden Cargo* (1925), *Old Ironsides* (1926), *Two Arabian Knights* (1927), *The Unholy Night* (1929), *The Criminal Code* (1931), *Scarface, The Old Dark House, The Mask of Fu Manchu, The Mummy* (all 1932), *The Ghoul* (1933), *The Lost Patrol, The Black Cat, The Gift of Gab* (all 1934), *The*

June Kenney in *Teenage Doll* (Allied Artists, 1957).

Bride of Frankenstein, The Black Room, The Raven (all 1935), *The Invisible Ray, The Walking Dead* (1936), *Son of Frankenstein* (1939), *Before I Hang* (1940), *The Devil Commands* (1941), *The Body Snatcher, Isle of the Dead* (both 1945), *Bedlam* (1946), *The Secret Life of Walter Mitty* (1947), *Tap Roots* (1948), *Abbott and Costello Meet Dr. Jekyll and Mr. Hyde* (1953), *Voodoo Island* (1957), *Frankenstein 1970* (1958), *The Raven, The Terror* (both 1963), *Targets* (1968).

Kenney, June

Born in Boston, Massachusetts, June was the daughter of Frederick J. Kenney, the owner of a construction business. She was active in show business before she reached her teens, appearing on radio shows in and around Boston, as well as some Warner Bros. musical shorts. When she was 11 her family moved to California. She became active in school plays and when she was 15 went on tour with a ballet company.

Kenney began popping up on television — "Loretta Young Show," "Hallmark Hall of Fame," "Trackdown" — and worked her way into motion pictures. But the 5'2" blue-eyed blonde never graduated out of the B movies. But she was cute and had a sweetness about her.

Her credits include: *Teenage Doll, Sorority Girl* (both 1957), *Attack of the Puppet People, Hot Car Girl, Viking Women and the Sea Serpent, Attack of the Puppet People, The Spider* (all 1958).

Knight, Sandra (1939–)

"Since I was 13 my one dream has been to be an actress," said Sandra back in 1958 when she got her first motion picture role in *Thunder Road*. She'd been in a little theater production of *The Moon Is Blue* when she was "discovered." Shortly after, the theater on Larchmont Avenue was torn down. She'd been discovered just in time. She married Jack Nicholson in 1962 and they appeared together in *The Terror* (1963).

Her credits include: *Frankenstein's Daughter* (1959), *The Tower of London* (1962), *Blood Bath* (1966).

Malone, Dorothy (1925–)

Born in Chicago, the daughter of a phone company auditor, she was a child model and a regular in school plays. At 18 she was signed to an RKO contract and later joined Warner Bros. In 1956 she won the Best Actress Oscar for her portrayal of a tramp in *Written on the Wind* but the parts that followed were sparse and unrewarding. Her role in television's "Peyton Place" paid the bills for four years but in 1968 she'd had enough and moved to Dallas. She's been married three times. Real name: Dorothy Eloise Maloney.

Her credits include: *The Falcon and the Co-Eds* (1943), *The Big Sleep* (1946), *The Killer That Stalked New York* (1950), *Scared Stiff* (1953), *The Fast and the Furious, Pushover, Young at Heart* (all 1954), *Five Guns West, Battle Cry, Artists and Models, Sincerely Yours* (all 1955), *Pillars of the Sky* (1956), *Quantez, Man of a Thousand Faces, Tip on a Dead Jockey* (all 1957), *Too*

Susan Cabot and Dick Miller in *War of the Satellites* (Allied Artists, 1958).

Much Too Soon (1958), *The Last Voyage* (1960), *The Last Sunset* (1961), *Beach Party* (1963), *Winter Kills* (1979).

Miller, Richard ("Dick") (1929–)

It was during a lunchbreak, while he was working as a flunky at a New York department store, that Dick Miller decided 9–5 jobs simply weren't for him. He'd finished his sandwich and was watching a flock of pigeons just to kill time when it suddenly occurred to him that if the pigeons could be free then so could he. He quit the job and came to California looking for work as a writer. Only he couldn't make any money at it, so he became an actor. He'd always toyed with the idea. Miller had taken classes at the New York Theater School of Dramatic Arts before heading west.

When one of his buddies from New York introduced him to Roger Corman, who was looking for actors, Dick figured it beat working. As a kid he'd always liked playing cowboys and Indians. Why not get paid for it? Over the years he's played a lot of different characters but he seems to score best when he's playing a streetwise, slightly pushy, no-nonsense kind of a guy. He's had a long and active career, first with Roger Corman and later with Corman's graduates.

Dick doesn't think much about writing anymore. When he's not working on a movie he's hanging around a little outdoor coffee house on Melrose near La Cienega. In the old days he used to hang out at Schwaab's. He was so much a part of the place that one morning someone took note of his absence and considered phoning the hospital to make sure Dick was okay.

His credits include: *Apache Woman, Oklahoma Woman, Gunslinger, It Conquered the World* (all 1956), *Not of This Earth, The Undead, Rock All Night, Naked Paradise, Carnival Rock, Sorority Girl* (all 1957), *War of the Satellites, I, Mobster* (both 1958), *A Bucket of Blood* (1959), *The Little Shop of Horrors* (1960), *The Premature Burial* (1962), *The Terror, "X" The Man with the X-Ray Eyes* (both 1963), *The Wild Angels* (1966), *The Trip* (1967), *Executive Action* (1973), *Candy Stripe Nurses* (1974), *Piranha* (1978), *Rock and Roll High School* (1979), *The Howling* (1981), *Gremlins, The Terminator* (both 1984), *Explorers* (1985), *Chopping Mall* (1986).

Montell, Lisa (1938–)

Born in Warsaw, Poland, she traveled with her family to New York, Florida, Lima, Peru, and finally Hollywood. She had a fire about her but obviously not enough to ignite much of a career. Real name: Irene Montwill.

Her credits include: *World Without End* (1956), *Naked Paradise* (1957), *She Gods of Shark Reef* (1958).

Morris, Barboura

After graduating from UCLA, where she majored in theater arts, she joined the Stumptown stock group in Northern California, then returned to Los Angeles to study acting with Jeff Corey, where she met Roger Corman who was taking the same class. He signed her for a role in one of his pictures in which she was billed as Barboura O'Neill. She appeared in many Corman films in roles that ranged from bit to star, depending on the budget. She was always one of my favorites. She died some time in the early 1970s. I miss her.

Her credits include: *Rock All Night, Sorority Girl, Teenage Doll* (all 1957), *Machine Gun Kelly, Viking Women and the Sea Serpent* (both 1958), *A Bucket of Blood, The Wasp Woman* (both 1959), *Atlas* (1961), *"X" The Man with the X-Ray Eyes, The Haunted Palace* (both 1963), *The St. Valentine's Day Massacre, The Trip* (both 1967), *The Dunwich Horror* (1970).

Nelson, Ed (1928–)

Born in New Orleans, he quit high school to try his hand at theatrics, was in the Navy for a year and a half (he must have quit that, too), and got a football scholarship at Tulane University. He starred in little theater productions of *Death of a Salesman* and *The Detective Story* and got his first part in a feature film when Roger Corman came to Louisiana to film *Swamp Women* (1955). He's been in dozens of television shows— "Gunsmoke," "The Fugitive," "Have Gun, Will Travel"—including his regular appearance as Dr. Rossi on "Peyton Place."

His credits include: *New Orleans Uncensored* (1955), *Attack of the Crab Monsters, Carnival Rock, Rock All Night, Invasion of the Saucer-Men, Teenage Doll* (all 1957), *The Brain Eaters, Night of the Blood Beast, Teenage Caveman, Crybaby Killer* (all 1958), *A Bucket of Blood, T-Bird Gang* (both 1959), *The Devil's Partner* (1961), *Soldier in the Rain* (1963), *Airport 1975* (1974).

Neumann, Dorothy (1912–)

Thin, wiry actress made her motion picture debut in *The Snake Pit* in 1948. Before coming to Hollywood she studied fine arts at Yale and did some little theater from 1938 to 1940, after which she went to New York and got a job writing for and acting in radio. "I don't believe in all this 'becoming the character,'" Miss Neumann once remarked. "Acting is the result of a lot of observations you've been making all your life."

Her favorite role was in *Desiree* (1954). She didn't have any lines but she thought she looked good for a change. On television she's been seen on "Gunsmoke," "Andy Griffith," "Adam 12," and "The Waltons."

Her credits include: *Sorry, Wrong Number, The Luck of the Irish* (both 1948), *The Ten Commandments* (1956), *Teenage Doll, The Undead, Carnival Rock* (all 1957), *Gigi* (1958), *The Terror* (1963), *The Greatest Story Ever Told* (1965).

Nicholson, Jack (1937–)

Nicholson was born in Neptune, New Jersey, moved to Los Angeles and went to work as an office boy in MGM's cartoon department. Then he joined the Player's Ring, where he met Roger Corman, who put him in the leading role in *The Cry Baby Killer* (1958). Nicholson thought the film would make him a star but he didn't get another acting job for nine months. He married actress Sandra Knight in 1962 but when his career finally started taking off it put a strain on the marriage and they divorced in 1969.

His off-beat portrayals are always a delight and generally if Jack Nicholson's in a movie you can anticipate the unusual. He won the Best Actor Oscar for *One Flew Over the Cuckoo's Nest* in 1975 and has been nominated many times since.

His credits include: *Too Soon to Love, The Wild Ride* (both 1960), *The Little Shop of Horrors* (1961), *The Raven, The Terror* (both 1963), *Ensign Pulver* (1964), *The St. Valentine's Day Massacre, The Trip, Hell's Angels on Wheels* (1967), *Easy Rider* (1969), *Five Easy Pieces* (1970), *Carnal Knowledge* (1971), *The Last Detail* (1973), *Chinatown* (1974), *The Missouri Breaks* (1976), *The Shining* (1979), *Terms of Endearment* (1983), *Prizzi's Honor* (1985), *Heartburn* (1986).

Debra Paget (1933-)

Real name Debralee Griffin. She was born in Denver, Colorado, to Margaret Gibson and Frank Griffin. Her sisters—Lisa Gaye and Teala Loring—are also actresses. Debra studied drama with Queenie Smith of the New York Theatre Guild and took her screen name from Lord and Lady Paget of England. At 13 she was on stage in *The Merry Wives of Windsor* and two years later was in her first film, *Cry of the City* (1948).

While she was under contract to Fox she was quite active (she was Elvis Presley's leading lady) but after she left Fox her career tapered off. She retired in 1963 and went to live in Texas. She's been married three times, first to singer David Street, then to director Budd Boetticher, and finally to Louis C. Kung, a Chinese oilman whose worth is estimated in the billions.

Her credits include: *Broken Arrow* (1950), *14 Hours, Bird of Paradise* (both 1951), *Les Miserables, Stars and Stripes Forever* (both 1952), *Prince Valiant, Demetrius and the Gladiators, Princess of the Nile* (all 1954), *The Ten Commandments, Love Me Tender* (both 1956), *Omar Khayyam, The River's Edge* (both 1957), *From the Earth to the Moon* (1958), *Journey to the Lost City* (1959), *Why Must I Die?* (1960), *The Most Dangerous Man Alive* (1961), *Tales of Terror* (1962), *The Haunted Palace* (1963).

Price, Vincent (1911-)

Art collector, author, and gourmet cook, Price became Roger Corman's number one leading man in the 1960s. Born in St. Louis Missouri, the son of a wealthy candy manufacturer, Vincent was given a tour of Europe's art museums as a high school graduation present and it obviously made quite an impression on him. After graduation from Yale, he got a master's degree in fine arts at the University of London and made his stage debut in 1935. He was an established stage actor when Universal signed him to a contract in 1938.

Later, at Fox, Price appeared in a number of films but never really clicked until, in 1953, he appeared as the mad villain of Warner Brothers' *House of Wax*. It took a while but eventually he became the King of the Grand Guignol, a title he held for 15 years. His performances were often "over the top" but always fun. He pops up in commercials still and always brings a smile to my lips.

His credits include: *The Private Lives of Elizabeth and Essex, The Tower of London* (both 1939), *The Invisible Man Returns, The House of the Seven Gables* (both 1940), *The Song of Bernadette (1943), Laura* (1944), *The Keys of the Kingdom, Leave Her to Heaven* (both 1945), *Dragonwyck* (1946), *The Three Musketeers* (1948), *Champagne for Caesar, The Baron of Arizona* (both 1950), *Adventures of Captain Fabian* (1951), *Casanova's Big Night, The Mad Magician* (both 1954), *The Ten Commandments* (1956), *The Story of Mankind* (1957), *The Fly* (1958), *House on Haunted Hill, The Bat, The Tingler* (all 1959), *House of Usher* (1960), *The Pit and the Pendulum, Master of the World* (both 1961), *Confessions of an Opium Eater, Tower of London* (both 1962), *The Raven, Diary of a Madman, Twice Told Tales, Comedy of Terrors* (all 1963), *The Haunted Palace, The Masque of the Red Death, The Tomb of Ligeia* (all

Don Post Studios made the rubber head of Peter Lorre that Vincent Price is holding in this studio shot from *Tales of Terror* (Alta Vista / American International, 1962).

1964), *Dr. Goldfoot and the Bikini Machine* (1965), *The Conqueror Worm* (1968), *The Abominable Dr. Phibes* (1971), *Theatre of Blood* (1973).

Shayne, Robert (1910–)

This stocky character actor has more or less retired from films to run his investment financial service. He was born in Yonkers, New York, and was educated at Boston and Chicago universities. Before embarking on an acting career he was a newspaper reporter and is probably best remembered as Inspector Henderson on television's "Superman." Real name: Robert Shaen Dawe.

His credits include: *Keep 'Em Rolling*, *The Shepherd of the Hills* (both

Bruno Ve Sota and unidentified actress in *Rock All Night* (American Releasing Corp., 1957).

1934), *Mr. Skeffington* (1941), *Rhapsody in Blue, San Antonio* (both 1945), *Behind the Mask, The Face of Marble* (both 1946), *Backlash, I Cover the Big Town, The Spirit of West Point, The Swordsman* (all 1947), *Best Man Wins, The Strange Mrs. Crane, Loaded Pistols* (all 1948), *Forgotten Women, Law of the Barbary Coast, The Threat* (all 1949), *The Neanderthal Man* (1953), *The Giant Claw* (1957), *I, Mobster, War of the Satellites, Teenage Caveman* (all 1958), *Valley of the Redwoods* (1961).

Ve Sota, Bruno (1921–1976)

This heavy-set character actor began his career in 1946 with *The Passion Play,* which he produced and directed, reportedly the first dramatic hour-long television show. He directed a bizarre experimental film, *Dementia* (1955), parts of which can be seen in *The Blob* (1958) under the title *Daughter of Horror*. For 13 years he played the bartender on television's "Bonanza," and died of a heart attack in 1976.

His credits include: *The Wild One, The Last Time I Saw Paris* (both 1954), *Kismet, Jupiter's Darling* (both 1955), *Gunslinger, Oklahoma Woman* (both 1956), *Rock All Night, The Undead, Carnival Rock* (all 1957), *War of the Satellites* (1958), *A Bucket of Blood, Attack of the Giant Leeches, The Wasp Woman* (all 1959), *Night Tide* (1963).

Vickers, Yvette (1936–)

Born in Kansas City, Missouri, the daughter of Mr. and Mrs. Charles Vedder, she grew up in Malibu, California; Paradise Cove was her sandbox. "I'm one of those people, you know, that everybody hates because I had a happy childhood," she says. "I was one of those kids who used to get the neighbors together in the garage and dress up and put on shows. I always performed." At UCLA she majored in theater arts and was doing a play at the Player's Ring when she got her first break in commercials.

Her first film was in *Short Cut to Hell,* directed by James Cagney in 1957. "After the film came out I was at a party, walking from one room to the other, and I heard somebody say, 'Yvette Vickers is here.' And this other person said, 'She's got nothing to worry about. She's set for life. Cagney's keeping her.'" It hurt her feelings. She was active in television—"Dragnet," "The Bob Cummings Show," "Switch"—and in 1959 was the July *Playboy* Playmate, photographed by veteran filmmaker Russ Meyer. "He came out in his Marine outfit and his boots and his cameras. He never made a pass. Never said an offensive word. Nothing. He was a perfect gentleman." Yvette was married to musician Don Prell.

Her credits include: *Sunset Boulevard* (1950), *The Sad Sack* (1957), *Reform School Girl* (1957), *The Saga of Hemp Brown, I, Mobster, Attack of the 50ft Woman, Juvenile Jungle* (all 1958), *Attack of the Giant Leeches* (1959), *Pressure Point* (1962), *Hud* (1963), *What's the Matter with Helen?* (1971), *Vigilante Force* (1978).

Welles, Mel (1924–)

Welles attended Penn State, Columbia, and the University of West Virginia, obtaining a Ph.D. in psychology. After working in the field for a year he decided psychology was "full of it" and turned to the arts. "I didn't really think I wanted to put the effort or the time into being a musical virtuoso of any kind," Welles said. "Besides, I had a reputation for having a tin ear. Being a starving artist painting pictures didn't appeal to me and because of my intellectual prowess I thought writing would be a good place for me to go." He wrote stories for *Argosy* and *True* magazines but gradually drifted into the theater.

"I always looked older than I was so I always played character roles right from the beginning." He went into production so he could hire himself as a director. Most of the films he directed were made abroad. Lately, he's been

Mel Welles played Sir Bop, a hip-talking promoter in *Rock All Night* (American Releasing Corp., 1957). To help the audience interpret what he was saying, Welles wrote "The Hiptionary."

earning a living doing voice-overs for commercials and cartoons. He was born in New York City.

His credits include: *Appointment in Honduras*, *Gun Fury* (both 1953), *The Silver Chalice*, *Abbott and Costello Meet the Mummy* (both 1955), *Attack of the Crab Monsters*, *Designing Woman*, *Rock All Night*, *The Undead* (all 1957), *High School Confidential*, *Tip on a Dead Jockey*, *The Brothers Karamazov* (all 1958), *The Little Shop of Horrors* (1961), *The Red Sheik*, *The Reluctant Saint* (both 1962), *The Christine Keeler Affair* (1964), *The She-Beast* (1966), *Smokey Bites the Dust* (1981), *Dr. Hekyll and Mr. Hype* (1980), *Chopping Mall* (1986).

Wolff, Frank (1929–1971)

His real name Frank Hermann, he was born in San Francisco of German parents, majored in dramatic arts at Stanford University, served in the Navy, then went to New York and worked with the American Wing in Off-Broadway productions. In Elia Kazan's *America, America* (1963) he was second-billed in the role of Vartan Damadian. One of his first roles was in Roger Corman's *I, Mobster* in 1958. In America his acting career was rather uneventful but when he went to Italy he did quite well. His personal life must have been quite another matter for in 1971 he was found dead in his apartment, his throat slashed with a razor, a successful suicide.

His credits include: *I, Mobster* (1958), *The Wild and the Innocent, Beast from Haunted Cave* (both 1959), *Ski Troop Attack* (1960), *Atlas* (1961), *The Four Days of Naples* (1963), *Judith, A Stranger in Town* (both 1966), *Villa Rides* (1968), *God Forgives—I Don't, Once Upon a Time in the West* (both 1969), *The Lickerish Quartet* (1970), *When Women Lost Their Tails* (1971).

Woronov, Mary (1923–)

Her career in show business began in New York in the mid–1960s, when she appeared in some of Andy Warhol's experimental films. She landed major roles in a couple of low budget shockers, one of them directed by Oliver Stone who has recently made quite a name for himself. Mary, however, is still a prisoner of low budget pictures, often teamed with actor-director Paul Bartell.

Her films include: *Silent Night, Bloody Night* (1973), *Seizure* (1974), *Death Race 2000, Cover Girl Models* (both 1975), *Cannonball, Hollywood Boulevard* (both 1976), *Jackson County Jail* (1977), *Deathsport* (1978), *Rock and Roll High School, The Lady in Red* (both 1979), *Heartbeeps* (1981), *Eating Raoul, Silent Rage, Angel from H.E.A.T.* (all 1982), *Hellhole* (1985), *Chopping Mall* (1986).

Films Produced by
Roger Corman

Included here are films on which Roger Corman was listed as either producer or executive producer. These do not include films which were credited as a "Roger Corman Production," or listed as "Roger Corman Presents," or films on which Roger Corman functioned as a silent partner.

Attack of the Giant Leeches. 1959 B&W. American International. DIR Bernard L. Kowalski, PRO Gene Corman, EXEC PRO Roger Corman, SP Leo Gordon, DP John M. Nickolaus, Jr., ART DIR Dan Haller, MUS Alexander Laszlo.
   The Cast: Ken Clark (Steve Benton), Yvette Vickers (Liz Walker), Jan Shepard (Nan Greyson), Michael Emmet (Cal Moulton), Tyler McVey (Doc Greyson).

Avalanche. 1979 C 91 min. New World. DIR Corey Allen, PRO Roger Corman, EXEC PRO Paul Rapp, SP Claude Pola, Corey Allen, STO Frances Doel, DP Pierre-William Glenn, ED Stuart Schoolnik, Larry Bock, ART DIR Phillip Thomas, MUS William Kraft.
   The Cast: Rock Hudson (David Shelby), Mia Farrow (Caroline Bruce), Robert Forster (Nick Throne), Jeanette Nolan (Florence Shelby), Rick Moses (Bruce Scott).

Battle Beyond the Stars. 1980 C 102 min. New World. DIR Jimmy Murakami, PRO Ed Carlin, EXEC PRO Roger Corman, SP John Sayles, STO John Sayles, Anne Dyer, DP Daniel Lacambre, SPFX Chuck Comisky, MUS James Horner.
   The Cast: Richard Thomas (Shad), Robert Vaughn (Gelt), John Saxon (Sador), George Peppard (Cowboy), Darlanne Fluegel (Nanelia).

Big Bad Mama. 1974 C 83 min. New World. DIR Steve Carver, PRO Roger Corman, SP William Norton, Frances Doel, DP Bruce Logan, ED Tina Hirsch, ART DIR Peter Jamison, SPFX Roger George, MUS David Grisman.
   The Cast: Angie Dickinson (Wilma McClatchie), William Shatner (William J. Baxter), Tom Skerritt (Fred Diller), Susan Sennet (Billy Jean McClatchie), Robbie Lee (Polly McClatchie).

MEN, MONEY and MOONSHINE
WHEN IT COMES TO VICE, MAMA KNOWS BEST!

HOT LEAD
HOT CARS
HOT DAMN!

ANGIE DICKINSON
is
BIG BAD MAMA

WILLIAM SHATNER · TOM SKERRITT · SUSAN SENNETT · ROBBIE LEE [R] RESTRICTED

WRITTEN BY
WILLIAM NORTON & FRANCES DOEL

DIRECTED BY
STEVE CARVER

PRODUCED BY
ROGER CORMAN

A NEW WORLD PICTURE · METROCOLOR

Boxcar Bertha. 1972 C 92 min. American International. DIR Martin Scorsese, PRO Roger Corman, SP Joyce H. and John W. Corrington, DP John Stephens, MUS Gib Guilbeau, Thad Maxwell.

The Cast: Barbara Hershey (Bertha), David Carradine (Bill Shelby), Barry Primus (Rake Brown), Bernie Casey (Von Morton), John Carradine (H. Buckram Sartoris).

The Cry Baby Killer. 1958 B&W 62 min. Allied Artists. DIR Jus Addis, PRO David Kramarsky, David March, EXEC PRO Roger Corman, SP Leo Gordon, Melvin Levy, MUS Gerald Fried.

The Cast: Harry Lauter, Jack Nicholson, Carolyn Mitchell, Brett Halsey, Lynn Cartwright.

Death Race 2000. 1975 C 80 min. New World. DIR Paul Bartel, PRO Roger Corman, SP Robert Thom, Charles Griffith, DP Tak Fujimoto, ED Tina Hirsch, ART DIR Robinson Royce, B.B. Neel, SPFX Richard MacLean, MUS Paul Chihara.

The Cast: David Carradine (Frankenstein), Simone Griffeth (Annie), Sylvester Stallone (Machine Gun Joe Viterbo), Mary Woronov (Mathilda the Hun), Roberta Collins (Nero the Hero).

Dementia 13. 1963 B&W 81 min. Filmgroup/American International. DIR-SP Francis Ford Coppola, PRO Roger Corman, DP Charles Hannawalt, ART DIR Albert Locatelli, ED Stewart O'Brien, MUS Ronald Stein.

The Cast: William Campbell (Richard Holoran), Luana Anders (Louise Haloran), Bart Patton (Billy Haloran), Mary Mitchel (Kane), Patrick McGee (Justin Caleb).

De Sade. 1969 C 120 min. American International. DIR Cy Endfield (and Roger Corman, uncredited), PRO Samuel Z. Arkoff, James H. Nicholson, EXEC PRO Artur Brauner, Louis M. Heyward, SP Richard Matheson, DP Heinz Pehlke, ED Max Benedict, ART DIR Jurgen Keibach, MUS Billy Strange.

The Cast: Keir Dullea (Marquis de Sade), Senta Berger (Anne de Montreuil), Lili Palmer (Mme. de Montreuil), Anna Massey (Renee de Montreuil), Sonja Ziemann (La Beauvoisin).

Deathsport. 1978 C 82 min. New World. DIR Henry Suso, Allan Arkush, PRO Roger Corman, SP Henry Suso, Donald Stewart, STO Frances Doel, DP Gary Graver, ED Larry Bock, SPFX Jack Rabin, ART DIR Sharon Compton, MUS Andrew Stein.

The Cast: David Carradine (Kaz Oshay), Claudia Jennings (Deneer), Richard Lynch (Ankar Moor), William Smithers (Doctor Karl), Will Walker (Marcus Karl).

Big Bad Mama (New World, 1974) is more famous for Angie Dickinson's nude scene than anything else.

The Dunwich Horror. 1970 C 90 min. American International. DIR Daniel Haller, PRO James H. Nicholson, Samuel Z. Arkoff, EXEC PRO Roger Corman, SP Curtis Lee Hanson, Henry Rosenbaum, Ronald Silkosky, STO H.P. Lovecraft, DP Richard C. Glouner, MUS Les Baxter.

The Cast: Sandra Dee (Nancy), Dean Stockwell (Wilbur), Ed Begley (Armitage), Lloyd Bockner (Cory), Donna Baccala (Elizabeth).

Eat My Dust. 1976 C 90 min. New World. DIR-SP Charles Griffith, PRO Roger Corman, DP Eric Saarinen, ED Tina Hirsh, ART DIR Peter Jamison, MUS David Grisman.

The Cast: Ron Howard (Hoover), Christopher Norris (Darlene), Warren Kemmerling, Dave Madden, Robert Broyles.

Fighting Mad. 1976 C 90 min. 20th Century–Fox. DIR-SP Jonathan Demme, PRO Roger Corman, DP Michael Watkins, ED Anthony Margo, MUS Bruce Landhorne.

The Cast: Peter Fonda (Tom), Lynn Lowry (Lorene), John Douchette (Jeff), Philip Carey (Pierce), Scott Glen (Charlie).

Forbidden World. 1983 C 86 min. New World. DIR Allan Holzman, PRO Roger Corman, SP Tim Curnen, STO Jim Wynorski, R.J. Robertson, DP Tim Suhstedt, ED Allan Helzman, ART DIR Joe Garrity, Wayne Springfield, MUS Susan Justin.

The Cast: Jesse Vint (Mike), June Chadwick (Dr. Glaser), Dawn Dunlap (Tracy), Linden Chiles (Dr. Hauser), Fox Harris (Dr. Tinburgen).

Galaxy of Terror. 1982 C 80 min. New World. DIR Bruce Clark, PRO Roger Corman, SP Marc Siegler, Bruce Clark, DP Jacques Haitkin, ED Robert J. Kizer, Larry Bock, Barry Zetlin, MUS Barry Schrader.

The Cast: Edward Albert, Erin Moran, Ray Walston, Bernard Behrens, Zalman King.

Grand Theft Auto. 1977 C 85 min. New World. DIR Ron Howard, PRO Jon Davison, EXEC PRO Roger Corman, SP Rance and Ron Howard, DP Gary Graver, ED Joe Dante, ART DIR Keith Michl, SPFX Roger George.

The Cast: Ron Howard (Sam Freeman), Nancy Morgan (Paula Powers), Marion Ross (Vivian Hedgeworth), Pete Isacksen (Sparky), Barry Cahill (Bigby Powers).

Highway Dragnet. 1954 B&W 71 min. Allied Artists. DIR Nathan Juran, PRO William F. Broidy, Jack Jungmeyer, Jr., SP Herb Meadow, Jerome Odlum, STO U.S. Anderson, Roger Corman, MUS Edward J. King.

The Cast: Richard Conte (Jim), Joan Bennet (Mrs. Cummings), Wanda Henrix (Susan), Reed Hadley (White Eagle), Mary Beth Hughes (Terry).

Hot Car Girl. 1958 B&W 71 min. Allied Artists. DIR Bernard L. Kowalski, PRO Gene Corman, EXEC PRO Roger Corman, SP Leo Gordon, MUS Cal Tjader.

The Cast: Richard Bakalyan (Duke), June Kenney (Peg), John Brinkley (Fred), Robert Knapp, Jana Lund (Janice).

I Escaped from Devil's Island. 1973 C 87 min. United Artists. DIR William Witney, PRO Roger and Gene Corman, SP Richard L. Adams, DP Rosalio Solano, ED Alan Collins, Tom Walls, Barbara Pokras, ART DIR Robert Silva, MUS Les Baxter.

The Cast: Jim Brown (Le Brus), Christopher George (Davert), Rick Ely (Jojo), Richard Rust (Zamorra).

Jackson County Jail. 1976 C 89 min. New World. DIR Michael Miller, PRO Jeff Begun, EXEC PRO Roger Corman, SP Donald Stewart, DP Bruce Logan, ED Caroline Ferriol, ART DIR Michael McCloskey, MUS Loren Newkirk.

The Cast: Yvette Mimieux (Dinah Hunter), Tommy Lee Jones (Coley Blake), Robert Carradine (Bobby Ray), Frederic Cook (Hobie), Severn Darden (Sheriff Dempsey).

Love Letters. 1983 C 98 min. New World. DIR-SP Amy Jones, PRO Roger Corman, EXEC PRO Mel Pearl, Don Levin, DP Alec Hirschfeld, ED Wendy Green, ART DIR Jeannine Oppewall, MUS Ralph Jones.

The Cast: Jamie Lee Curtis (Anna), James Keach (Oliver), Amy Madigan (Wendy), Bud Cort (Danny), Matt Clark (Winter).

Monster from the Ocean Floor. 1954 B&W 64 min. Lippert. DIR Wyott Ordung, PRO Roger Corman, SP William Danch, DP Floyd Crosby, ART DIR Ben Hayne, ED Ed Samson, MUS Andre Brumer.

The Cast: Anne Kimbell (Julie Blair), Stuart Wade (Steve Dunning), Dick Pinner (Dr. Baldwin), Jack (Jonathan) Hayes (Joe), Wyott Ordung (Pablo).

Moving Violation. 1976 C 91 min. 20th Century–Fox. DIR Charles S. Dubin, PRO Julie Corman, EXEC PRO Roger Corman, SP David R. Osterhout, William Norton, DP Charles Correll, ED Richard Sprague, Howard Terrell, ART DIR Sherman Loudermilk, MUS Don Peake.

The Cast: Stephen McHattie (Eddie), Kay Lenz (Cam), Eddie Albert (Alex), Lonny Chapman (Sheriff), Will Geer (Rockfield).

Night of the Blood Beast. 1958 B&W 65 min. American International. DIR Bernard L. Kowalski, PRO Gene Corman, EXEC PRO Roger Corman, SP Martin Varno, STO Gene Corman, DP John Nicholaus, Jr., ART DIR Dan Haller, MUS Alexander Laszlo.

The Cast: Michael Emmet (John Corcoran), Angela Greene (Julie Benson), John Baer (Steve Dunlap), Ed Nelson (Dave Randall), Tyler McVey (Alex Wyman).

Piranha. 1976 C 92 min. New World. DIR Joe Dante, PRO Jon Davison, SP John Sayles, STO Richard Robinson, John Sayles, EXEC PRO Roger Corman, Jeff Schechtman, DP Jamie Anderson, ART DIR Mill Mellin, Kerry Mellin, MUS Pino Donaggio.

The Cast: Bradford Dillman (Paul), Heater Menzies (Maggie), Kevin McCarthy (Joak), Keenan Wynn (Jack), Dick Miller (Buck).

Rock and Roll High School. 1979 C 93 min. New World. DIR Allan Arkush, PRO Michael Finnell, EXEC PRO Roger Corman, SP Richard Whitley, Russ Dvonch, Joseph McBride, STO Allan Arkush, Joe Dante, DP Dean Cundey, ED Larry Bock, Gail Werbin, ART DIR Marie Kordus, MUS The Ramones.

The Cast: P.J. Soles (Riff), Vincent Van Patten (Tom), Clint Howard (Eaglebauer), Dey Young (Kate), Mary Woronov (Miss Togar).

Saint Jack. 1979 C 112 min. New World. DIR Peter Bogdanovich, PRO Roger Corman, EXEC PRO Hugh M. Hefner, Edward L. Rissien, SP Howard Sackler, Paul Theroux, Peter Bogdanovich from the novel by Paul Theroux, DP Robby Muller, ED William Carruth, ART DIR David Ng.

The Cast: Ben Gazzara (Jack Flowers), Denholm Elliot (William Leigh), James Villiers (Frogget), Joss Ackland (Yardley), Rodney Bewes (Smale).

Space Raiders. 1983 C 85 min. New World. DIR-SP Howard R. Cohen, PRO Roger Corman, DP Alex Hirschfeld, ED Robert Kizer, ART DIR Wayne Springfield.

The Cast: Vincent Edwards (Hawk), David Mendenhall (Peter), Drew Snyder (Aldebaran), Patsy Pease (Amanda), Luca Bercovici (Ace).

Target: Harry. 1969 C 85 min. ABC Pictures. DIR Henry Neill (Roger Corman), PRO Roger Corman, EXEC PRO Gene Corman, SP Bob Barbash, DP Patrice Pouget, ED Monte Hellman, ART DIR Sharon Compton, MUS Les Baxter.

The Cast: Vic Morrow (Harry), Suzanne Pleshette (Diane), Victor Buono (Mosul), Cesar Romero (Duval), Stanley Holloway (Jason).

Thunder and Lightning. 1977 C 95 min. 20th Century–Fox. DIR Corey Allen, PRO Roger Corman, SP William Hjortsberg, ED Anthony Redman, DP James Pergola, MUS Andy Stein.

The Cast: David Carradine (Harley), Kate Jackson (Nancy Sue), Roger C. Carmel (Ralph, Jr.), Sterling Holloway (Hobe), Ed Barth (Rudi).

Index

Page references in boldface indicate a photograph.